1

Compact
ACTUAL iBT Reading & Listening Book 1

Publisher Chung Kyudo
Editors Lee Dongho, Cho Sangik
Authors Darakwon TOEFL Research Team
Proofreader Michael A. Putlack
Designers Zo Hwayoun, Park Sunyoung

First published in May 2011
By Darakwon, Inc.
Darakwon Bldg., 211, Munbal-ro, Paju-si, Gyeonggi-do 10881
Republic of Korea
Tel: 82-2-736-2031 (Ext. 250)
Fax: 82-2-732-2037

Copyright © 2011 Darakwon, Inc.

All rights reserved. No part of this publication may be reproduced, stored in a retrieval system, or transmitted in any form or by any means, electronic, mechanical, photocopying or otherwise, without the prior consent of the copyright owner. Refund after purchase is possible only according to the company regulations. Contact the above telephone number for any inquiries. Consumer damages caused by loss, damage, etc. can be compensated according to the consumer dispute resolution standards announced by the Korea Fair Trade Commission. An incorrectly collated book will be exchanged.

ISBN 978-89-277-0582-6 18740
       978-89-277-0581-9 18740 (set)

www.darakwon.co.kr

Components Main Book / Answer Book
15 14 13 12 11 10 9   23 24 25 26 27

Contents

- Introduction — 6
- Actual Test **01** — 8
- Actual Test **02** — 20
- Actual Test **03** — 32
- Actual Test **04** — 44
- Actual Test **05** — 56
- Actual Test **06** — 68
- Actual Test **07** — 80
- Actual Test **08** — 92
- Actual Test **09** — 104
- Actual Test **10** — 116

Introduction

One of the most important standardized tests students of the English language may ever take is the TOEFL® iBT. Because getting a high score on the test is so crucial, it is important to prepare for the test as much as possible prior to taking it.

That is the purpose of *Compact Actual iBT Reading & Listening* series. This book focuses on two of the four sections on the TOEFL® iBT: the Reading and Listening sections. These are arguably the two most difficult parts of the TOEFL® iBT. In both the Reading and the Listening sections, test takers will face passages and lectures that cover a wide variety of topics. These include subjects in the arts, social sciences, physical sciences, and life sciences. For that reason, a familiarity with many of these topics is crucial. So is having an extensive vocabulary that includes knowledge of specialized words in each of the fields. Fortunately, *Compact Actual iBT Reading & Listening* provides exactly what students need. The Reading passages and Listening lectures cover many of the very topics that often appear on the TOEFL® iBT. In addition, the Listening conversations do the same: They cover topics that frequently appear on the TOEFL® iBT, which can only serve to assist test takers when they sit for the actual test.

Compact Actual iBT Reading & Listening has been designed to be used both in the classroom and by test takers working on an individual basis. Each compact test consists of one Reading passage, one Listening conversation, and one Listening lecture. All three of them are the standard length of actual TOEFL® iBT passages, conversations, and lectures. In addition, they all have the same number of questions and the same types of questions that are found on the actual test. By using this book, test takers will be more prepared for the test when they actually take it.

This book, however, is merely a tool. Both students and teachers must make use of this tool in the best possible manner so that test takers may do as well as possible when they take the TOEFL® iBT.

About This Book

Compact Actual iBT Reading & Listening consists of ten units. Each unit consists of one compact test. A single compact test contains one Reading passage, one Listening conversation, and one Listening lecture. The passage, conversation, and lecture are followed by questions. These questions are of the same type and number that are found on the TOEFL® iBT.

In addition, the subjects of the passages in the Reading section are those that have all appeared on recent TOEFL® iBT tests. As many topics on the TOEFL® iBT Reading section tend to repeat, this can be a great benefit to test takers. By familiarizing themselves with the topics, subject matter, and vocabulary used in the passages in the Reading section of each compact test, test takers can be more confident when they take the Reading section of the TOEFL® iBT.

The same is true of the conversation and lectures in the Listening section. The Listening conversations contain situations that have appeared on recent TOEFL® iBT tests while the Listening lectures are all on topics that have occurred recently as well. By familiarizing themselves with the topics, subject matter, situations, and vocabulary used in the conversations and lectures, test takers can be more confident when they take the Listening section of the TOEFL® iBT.

Reading Section

The Reading section of each compact test consists of one full-length Reading passage followed by either thirteen or fourteen questions. Each passage covers a field that commonly occurs on the TOEFL® iBT. This includes fields such as history, archaeology, biology, and art.

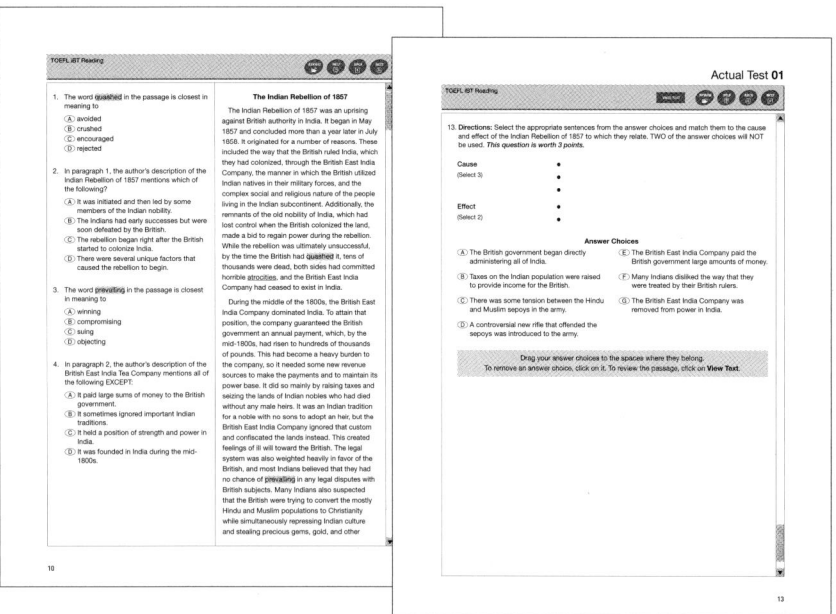

Listening Section

The Listening section of each compact test consists of one full-length Listening conversation followed by five questions and one full-length Listening lecture followed by six questions. Each conversation concerns either an office hours situation or a service situation whereas each lecture covers a topic that commonly occurs on the TOEFL® iBT. These topics are in the following four categories: arts, life sciences, physical sciences, and social sciences.

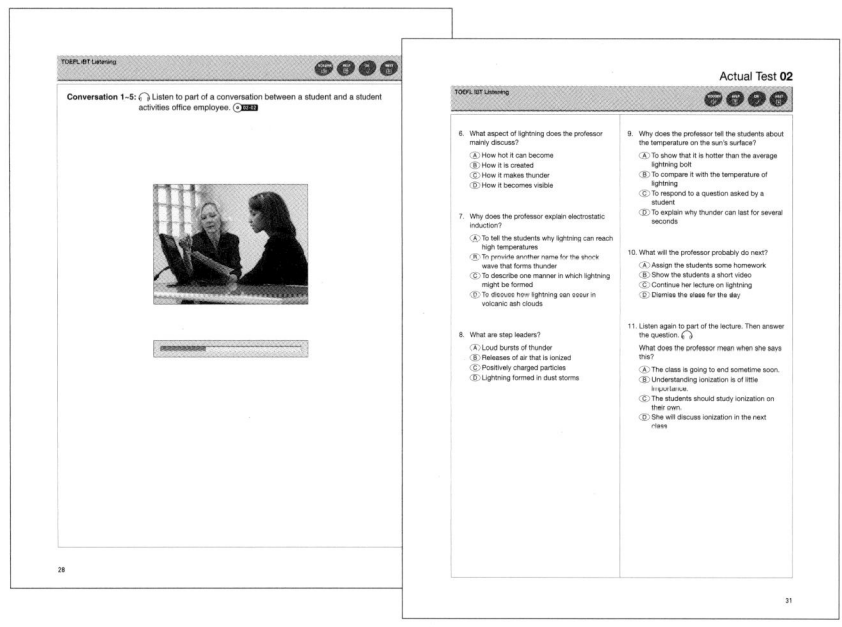

Actual Test
01

Reading
Section Directions

This section measures your ability to understand academic passages in English.

In this part, you will read 1 passage and answer reading comprehension questions about the passage. Most questions are worth one point, but the last question is worth more than one point. The directions indicate how many points you may receive.

Some passages include a word or phrase that is underlined in blue. Click on the word or phrase to see a definition or an explanation.

When you want to move on to the next question, click on **Next**. You may skip questions and go back to them later. If you want to return to previous questions, click on **Back**. You can click on **Review** at any time and the review screen will show you which questions you have answered and which you have not answered. From this review screen, you may go directly to any question you have already seen in the Reading section.

You may now begin the Reading section. You will read 1 reading passage. You will have **20 minutes** to read the passage and answer the questions.

Click on **Continue** to go on.

1. The word quashed in the passage is closest in meaning to
   - Ⓐ avoided
   - Ⓑ crushed
   - Ⓒ encouraged
   - Ⓓ rejected

2. In paragraph 1, the author's description of the Indian Rebellion of 1857 mentions which of the following?
   - Ⓐ It was initiated and then led by some members of the Indian nobility.
   - Ⓑ The Indians had early successes but were soon defeated by the British.
   - Ⓒ The rebellion began right after the British started to colonize India.
   - Ⓓ There were several unique factors that caused the rebellion to begin.

3. The word prevailing in the passage is closest in meaning to
   - Ⓐ winning
   - Ⓑ compromising
   - Ⓒ suing
   - Ⓓ objecting

4. In paragraph 2, the author's description of the British East India Company mentions all of the following EXCEPT:
   - Ⓐ It paid large sums of money to the British government.
   - Ⓑ It sometimes ignored important Indian traditions.
   - Ⓒ It held a position of strength and power in India.
   - Ⓓ It was founded in India during the mid-1800s.

The Indian Rebellion of 1857

The Indian Rebellion of 1857 was an uprising against British authority in India. It began in May 1857 and concluded more than a year later in July 1858. It originated for a number of reasons. These included the way that the British ruled India, which they had colonized, through the British East India Company, the manner in which the British utilized Indian natives in their military forces, and the complex social and religious nature of the people living in the Indian subcontinent. Additionally, the remnants of the old nobility of India, which had lost control when the British colonized the land, made a bid to regain power during the rebellion. While the rebellion was ultimately unsuccessful, by the time the British had quashed it, tens of thousands were dead, both sides had committed horrible atrocities, and the British East India Company had ceased to exist in India.

During the middle of the 1800s, the British East India Company dominated India. To attain that position, the company guaranteed the British government an annual payment, which, by the mid-1800s, had risen to hundreds of thousands of pounds. This had become a heavy burden to the company, so it needed some new revenue sources to make the payments and to maintain its power base. It did so mainly by raising taxes and seizing the lands of Indian nobles who had died without any male heirs. It was an Indian tradition for a noble with no sons to adopt an heir, but the British East India Company ignored that custom and confiscated the lands instead. This created feelings of ill will toward the British. The legal system was also weighted heavily in favor of the British, and most Indians believed that they had no chance of prevailing in any legal disputes with British subjects. Many Indians also suspected that the British were trying to convert the mostly Hindu and Muslim populations to Christianity while simultaneously repressing Indian culture and stealing precious gems, gold, and other

5. According to paragraph 2, the British East India Company was able to increase its land holdings in India because

 Ⓐ many rich Indians donated parcels of land to the company
 Ⓑ it appropriated land whenever some Indians died with no heirs
 Ⓒ some Indians left the company much of their land when they died
 Ⓓ it purchased land from some landowners who needed cash

6. The author discusses sepoys in paragraph 3 in order to

 Ⓐ compare their abilities with those of British soldiers
 Ⓑ mention how many of them were in the Indian army
 Ⓒ describe their role in the Indian Rebellion of 1857
 Ⓓ emphasize the religious nature of many soldiers

7. In paragraph 4, which of the following is true of the new muzzle-loading rifles?

 Ⓐ They were designed to allow the weapons to be loaded in an easy manner.
 Ⓑ They used grease from animals to let the bullets be loaded more quickly.
 Ⓒ The bullets were loaded first, and then the gunpowder was added.
 Ⓓ The weapons were highly desired by the majority of the sepoys.

8. The word retaliated in the passage is closest in meaning to

 Ⓐ recompensed
 Ⓑ reversed
 Ⓒ repudiated
 Ⓓ reciprocated

commodities from the land.

To some extent, many of these accusations were factual in nature. Religion was a key issue and, ultimately, was the catalyst for the rebellion by Indian military forces. In India, there were 200,000 native troops supported and led by 40,000 British soldiers, all of whom were under operational control of the British East India Company. ■ The native troops, called "sepoys," were a combination of Hindus and Muslims and were virtually all recruited from the higher castes of society. ■ The stationing of soldiers from two religious groups in the same units caused some tension. ■ Other problems, such as low pay and slow promotions, were further causes of unhappiness among the sepoys. ■ These factors all came to a head when trouble started from an unexpected source in the spring of 1857.

That year, the British issued the sepoys new muzzle-loading rifles. The bullets and gunpowder for the rifles were wrapped in paper, which formed a cartridge. The top of the cartridge had to be bitten off to be opened. Then, the gunpowder was poured into the muzzle of the rifle, and the bullet was subsequently rammed into the muzzle to hold the powder inside until the weapon was fired. The paper and bullet were greased to enable the easy ramming of the bullet. However, a rumor that the British utilized animal fat to grease the cartridges spread. The touching of pig fat was taboo to the Muslim sepoys while the touching of cow fat was forbidden to the Hindu sepoys.

In the spring of 1857, a series of incidents concerning these cartridges led to the open rebellion of the sepoys against British troops at Meerut on May 10, 1857. From there, the rebellion swiftly spread, and most of northern India was soon revolting against British rule. British soldiers and civilians were besieged, captured, and, in some cases, massacred. The British retaliated in kind. It took a year of hard fighting, but the rebellion was crushed. The British government

9. The word it in the passage refers to
   - Ⓐ a year of hard fighting
   - Ⓑ the British government
   - Ⓒ the blame for the rebellion
   - Ⓓ the British East India Company

10. In paragraph 5, the author implies that British soldiers
    - Ⓐ could not bring all of the regions of India under control
    - Ⓑ were as violent as the Indians during the rebellion
    - Ⓒ maintained peace in India for more than a century
    - Ⓓ ignored orders from their superiors to massacre Indians

11. According to paragraph 5, why did the British East India Company stop operating in India?
    - Ⓐ It lost too many men during the fighting to continue operating.
    - Ⓑ The British thought it had been the main cause of the rebellion.
    - Ⓒ It went bankrupt during the rebellion and could not recover financially.
    - Ⓓ The British crown decided to take over the company for itself.

12. Look at the four squares [■] that indicate where the following sentence could be added to the passage.

    After all, Muslims and Hindus frequently did not get along well with one another.

    Where would the sentence best fit?

    Click on a square [■] to add the sentence to the passage.

placed most of the blame for the rebellion on the British East India Company, so it was disbanded, and the British crown—through civilian administrators—took over the direct ruling of India. Still, the underlying causes of the rebellion did not entirely vanish. Nearly a century later, the Indian people would again turn against their British masters and, that time, would succeed in getting the British to leave their country.

Glossary
atrocity: an act of violence, often against a civilian
taboo: not allowed; not permitted
massacre: to kill a large number of people

13. **Directions:** Select the appropriate sentences from the answer choices and match them to the cause and effect of the Indian Rebellion of 1857 to which they relate. TWO of the answer choices will NOT be used. *This question is worth 3 points.*

Cause
(Select 3)

-
-
-

Effect
(Select 2)

-
-

Answer Choices

(A) The British government began directly administering all of India.

(B) Taxes on the Indian population were raised to provide income for the British.

(C) There was some tension between the Hindu and Muslim sepoys in the army.

(D) A controversial new rifle that offended the sepoys was introduced to the army.

(E) The British East India Company paid the British government large amounts of money.

(F) Many Indians disliked the way that they were treated by their British rulers.

(G) The British East India Company was removed from power in India.

Drag your answer choices to the spaces where they belong.
To remove an answer choice, click on it. To review the passage, click on **View Text**.

TOEFL iBT Listening

Listening
Section Directions

This section measures your ability to understand conversations and lectures in English.

In this part, you will listen to 1 conversation and 1 lecture. You will hear the conversation or lecture only **one** time. After the conversation or lecture, you will answer some questions about it. The questions typically ask about the main idea and supporting details. Some questions ask about a speaker's purpose or attitude. Answer the questions based on what is stated or implied by the speakers.

You may take notes while you listen. You may use your notes to help you answer the questions. Your notes will **not** be scored.

If you need to change the volume while you listen, click on the **Volume** icon at the top of the screen.

In some questions, you will see this icon: 🎧 This means that you will hear, but not see, part of the question.

Some of the questions have special directions. These directions appear in a gray box on the screen.

Most questions are worth one point. If a question is worth more than one point, it will have special directions that indicate how many points you can receive.

You must answer each question. After you answer, click on **Next**. Then click on **OK** to confirm your answer and go on to the next question. After you click on **OK**, you cannot return to previous questions.

A clock at the top of the screen will show you how much time is remaining. The clock will not count down while you are listening. The clock will count down only while you are answering the questions.

Now you may begin the Listening section.

Conversation 1~5: Listen to part of a conversation between a student and a professor.

Actual Test 01

TOEFL iBT Listening

1. Why does the student visit the professor?
   - Ⓐ To ask when the class will have a guest lecturer
   - Ⓑ To find out where to hear an audio recording
   - Ⓒ To talk about a class that he failed to attend
   - Ⓓ To get the class notes for a recent lecture

2. Why does the professor mention Terrance Witherspoon?
   - Ⓐ To name one of the most important people in music therapy
   - Ⓑ To tell the student who gave a lecture in the class
   - Ⓒ To invite the student to enroll in his upcoming class
   - Ⓓ To encourage the student to listen to his lectures

3. What can be inferred about the student?
   - Ⓐ He is discouraged by his recent record of class attendance.
   - Ⓑ He is excited to get to hear the lecture that he missed.
   - Ⓒ He wishes the professor had told him about the assignment.
   - Ⓓ He will watch the video recording as soon as possible.

4. What will the professor probably do next?
   - Ⓐ Go to her next class
   - Ⓑ Let the student borrow the audiotape
   - Ⓒ Give the student the class notes
   - Ⓓ Pay a visit to the library

5. Listen again to part of the conversation. Then answer the question.

   What can be inferred from the student's response to the professor?
   - Ⓐ The professor gives the students handouts in most of her classes.
   - Ⓑ The student is disappointed that the teacher has no handouts for him.
   - Ⓒ The student thinks the topic of the day's class is somewhat strange.
   - Ⓓ The professor expects the students to study her handouts for their tests.

Lecture 6~11: Listen to part of a lecture in a zoology class.

Actual Test 01

TOEFL iBT Listening

6. What is the main topic of the lecture?
   - Ⓐ The types of birds that have feathers
   - Ⓑ How birds use their feathers to fly
   - Ⓒ The uses of various kinds of feathers
   - Ⓓ The importance of color in birds' feathers

7. How does the professor organize the information about vaned feathers that she presents to the class?
   - Ⓐ By comparing the feathers on various species of birds
   - Ⓑ By referring to a journal article that she recently read
   - Ⓒ By answering questions the students had previously asked
   - Ⓓ By showing slides of feathers and discussing their purposes

8. Based on the information in the lecture, indicate whether the statements refer to remiges or rectrices.

   Click in the correct box for each statement.

	Remiges	Rectrices
Ⓐ Enable birds to steer while they are flying		
Ⓑ Include the longest feathers birds have		
Ⓒ Help birds slow down and land safely		
Ⓓ Let birds move themselves forward		

9. According to the professor, what is molting?
   - Ⓐ The period when birds lose some of their feathers
   - Ⓑ The camouflage effect provided by birds' feathers
   - Ⓒ The ability of birds to take off and land successfully
   - Ⓓ The waterproof nature of birds' feathers

10. Listen again to part of the lecture. Then answer the question.

    What does the professor imply when she says this?
    - Ⓐ Down feathers mostly cover birds' wings.
    - Ⓑ Down feathers help keep birds warm.
    - Ⓒ Down feathers are useful for flight.
    - Ⓓ Down feathers are larger than vaned feathers.

11. Listen again to part of the lecture. Then answer the question.

    Why does the professor say this?
    - Ⓐ To provide the students with a definition of a term
    - Ⓑ To answer her own question about how birds fly
    - Ⓒ To explain the major uses of birds' wings
    - Ⓓ To note the importance of flying to most birds

Actual Test
02

TOEFL iBT Reading

Reading
Section Directions

This section measures your ability to understand academic passages in English.

In this part, you will read 1 passage and answer reading comprehension questions about the passage. Most questions are worth one point, but the last question is worth more than one point. The directions indicate how many points you may receive.

Some passages include a word or phrase that is underlined in blue. Click on the word or phrase to see a definition or an explanation.

When you want to move on to the next question, click on **Next**. You may skip questions and go back to them later. If you want to return to previous questions, click on **Back**. You can click on **Review** at any time and the review screen will show you which questions you have answered and which you have not answered. From this review screen, you may go directly to any question you have already seen in the Reading section.

You may now begin the Reading section. You will read 1 reading passage. You will have **20 minutes** to read the passage and answer the questions.

Click on **Continue** to go on.

TOEFL iBT Reading

The Development of the Computer

Computers are as ubiquitous as televisions and telephones nowadays, and the most modern ones are not only portable but can also provide their users with a wealth of information and entertainment from virtually anywhere on the planet. This was not the case for the first computers, which were massive machines with little computing power. The origins of the modern computer lie several decades in the past, yet they are not so obscure that they cannot be determined. What began first as programmable machines transformed later into room-sized computers designed to make calculations for the military and then into the early personal computers developed in the 1970s. From those humble beginnings, the modern computer has seen numerous advances.

In the middle of the nineteenth century, Charles Babbage of Britain developed several ideas for programmable machines that could perform calculations based upon cards that had holes punched in them. Despite never successfully completing any of the devices he designed, Babbage is frequently referred to as "the father of the modern computer" because of his pioneering ideas and work. Unlike Babbage, one man who was able to make the technology work was Herman Hollerith, an American. He took the idea of punch cards and developed machines that could calculate information from these cards. Hollerith later formed the company that came to be called International Business Machines, or IBM. Additionally, in the late 1930s, British mathematician Alan Turing announced his theory of a Turing machine, which, while not a working, practical computing machine, foresaw many of the functions for which computers are used in the present.

Like many other fields of technology, computers received a boost during the 1940s when World War II was being fought. In 1941, German

1. The word obscure in the passage is closest in meaning to
   Ⓐ obtuse
   Ⓑ regarded
   Ⓒ unclear
   Ⓓ dismissed

2. Which of the sentences below best expresses the essential information in the highlighted sentence in the passage? *Incorrect* answer choices change the meaning in important ways or leave out essential information.
   Ⓐ Babbage came up with many ideas about computers that other people were able to turn into successful devices.
   Ⓑ After Babbage managed to create a machine that actually worked, he was called "the father of the modern computer."
   Ⓒ People recognize Babbage for his contributions to the modern computer even though he never made a working machine.
   Ⓓ The work that Babbage did managed to get him recognized as one of the leaders in computer technology.

3. The word foresaw in the passage is closest in meaning to
   Ⓐ anticipated
   Ⓑ guessed
   Ⓒ guaranteed
   Ⓓ produced

4. According to paragraph 2, Charles Babbage is called "the father of the modern computer" because
   Ⓐ he was the first person to design any kind of programmable machine
   Ⓑ it was his ideas that enabled other people to create modern computers
   Ⓒ he built the first machine that could be considered a type of computer
   Ⓓ the company that he founded went on to make many types of computers

22

5. According to paragraph 2, which of the following is NOT true of Herman Hollerith?

   Ⓐ He worked together with Charles Babbage on some early computers.
   Ⓑ He established the company known as International Business Machines.
   Ⓒ Some of the work he did concerned machines that used punch cards.
   Ⓓ He built some machines that were able to make calculations.

6. In paragraph 3, why does the author mention Konrad Zuse?

   Ⓐ To note his engineering contributions during World War II
   Ⓑ To focus on his ideas concerning Alan Turing's theories
   Ⓒ To criticize his work for Germany's guided missile program
   Ⓓ To state that the first modern computer was made by him

7. The word These in the passage refers to

   Ⓐ The Allied powers
   Ⓑ British code breakers
   Ⓒ Bombes
   Ⓓ German codes

8. Which of the following can be inferred from paragraph 3 about Konrad Zuse?

   Ⓐ He moved to the West after World War II to continue working on computers.
   Ⓑ Some of his work was integral to the American atomic bomb project.
   Ⓒ The work he did during World War II was done to oppose the Allied powers.
   Ⓓ Even though he worked for Germany, he was morally against the war.

engineer Konrad Zuse built the first of several machines that relied on Alan Turing's theories. These machines are widely considered the first modern computers. Zuse worked in Germany during World War II, so most of his work, including using computers to program guided missiles, concerned military matters. Meanwhile, the Allied powers also worked on computers during the war. They used them on two vital projects: to make calculations for the American Manhattan Project, which was developing atomic weapons, and to break the secret codes utilized by the Germans and Japanese to communicate with their armed forces. Thanks to computers, the time needed to solve complex problems for both projects decreased, which definitely helped end the war more quickly and in favor of the Allied powers. For instance, British code breakers, led by men such as Alan Turing, built what they called "bombes" to break German codes. These were enormous machines that used vacuum tubes to make tens of thousands of calculations in a very short period of time. The Americans also built another huge vacuum tube computer to make calculations for their atomic bombs.

The major problems with these early computers were their large sizes and reliance on vacuum tubes, which constantly broke down and had to be replaced. But, in the 1950s, transistors began to replace the vacuum tube. This development allowed for smaller and more reliable computers. For the next twenty years, computers continually became smaller yet more powerful. It was the development of the microprocessor chip that was the primary impetus for the creation of the modern personal computer. Intel invented the first microprocessor in the late 1960s, and it went on sale in 1971. This small, but powerful, device enabled computers to shrink in size. Although they were originally expensive, the costs of microprocessor chips soon declined, and thus the modern personal computer revolution began.

TOEFL iBT Reading

9. In paragraph 3, the author's description of the use of computers during World War II mentions which of the following?

    (A) Computers were used to make communications between the Allied powers easier.
    (B) Computers were crucial in enabling the Allied powers to emerge victorious in the war.
    (C) Several computers were utilized by scientists on the American Manhattan Project.
    (D) Some computers were used to design bombs with more effective guidance systems.

10. The word impetus in the passage is closest in meaning to

    (A) concept
    (B) invention
    (C) force
    (D) notion

11. The word they in the passage refers to

    (A) transistors
    (B) computers
    (C) the costs
    (D) microprocessor chips

12. According to paragraph 4, how did transistors change modern computers?

    (A) They enabled the prices of modern computers to decline.
    (B) They combined with the microprocessor chip to make faster computers.
    (C) They decreased the amount of power that computers required.
    (D) They permitted people to create computers that were smaller than before.

There is much disagreement on what was actually the first personal computer. During the 1970s, many computer companies developed machines that had some—but not all—aspects of modern personal computers. The Xerox PARC Research Center in California made the first personal computer with a screen, keyboard, mouse, and hard drive in 1973. This was the Xerox Alto, which is also notable for being the first personal computer with a graphical user interface. This interface served as the basis for later versions of operating systems such as Microsoft's Windows. By the mid-1980s, personal computers were being found in offices, schools, and homes. With the explosion of the Internet in the 1990s, owning and using personal computers became regular activities for millions of people around the world.

Glossary
humble: modest; simple
vacuum tube: a tube with almost no air or gas in it and which is often used for electronics
shrink: to become smaller

13. Why does the author mention the Xerox Alto?

   Ⓐ To declare that some people consider it to be the first personal computer
   Ⓑ To relate its importance in the development of the Windows operating system
   Ⓒ To describe the various innovative technical features that it contained
   Ⓓ To emphasize the fact that it was made by the Xerox PARC Research Center

14. **Directions:** An introductory sentence for a brief summary of the passage is provided below. Complete the summary by selecting the THREE answer choices that express the most important ideas of the passage. Some sentences do not belong because they express ideas that are not presented in the passage or are minor ideas in the passage. *This question is worth 2 points.*

   There were several developments that led to the creation of the modern computer.

   -
   -
   -

   Answer Choices

   Ⓐ The Turing machine was the creation of Alan Turing, who also did important work during World War II.

   Ⓑ Charles Babbage was never able to construct a machine that would actually work properly.

   Ⓒ Early machines that relied upon punch cards to make calculations were some of the first computers.

   Ⓓ Inventions such as the transistor and microprocessor chip let computers become much smaller in size.

   Ⓔ It is generally agreed by people that the Xerox Alto was the first real personal computer ever made.

   Ⓕ During World War II, computers became more developed as people worked on various war projects.

   Drag your answer choices to the spaces where they belong.
   To remove an answer choice, click on it. To review the passage, click on **View Text**.

Listening
Section Directions

This section measures your ability to understand conversations and lectures in English.

In this part, you will listen to 1 conversation and 1 lecture. You will hear the conversation or lecture only **one** time. After the conversation or lecture, you will answer some questions about it. The questions typically ask about the main idea and supporting details. Some questions ask about a speaker's purpose or attitude. Answer the questions based on what is stated or implied by the speakers.

You may take notes while you listen. You may use your notes to help you answer the questions. Your notes will **not** be scored.

If you need to change the volume while you listen, click on the **Volume** icon at the top of the screen.

In some questions, you will see this icon: 🎧 This means that you will hear, but not see, part of the question.

Some of the questions have special directions. These directions appear in a gray box on the screen.

Most questions are worth one point. If a question is worth more than one point, it will have special directions that indicate how many points you can receive.

You must answer each question. After you answer, click on **Next**. Then click on **OK** to confirm your answer and go on to the next question. After you click on **OK**, you cannot return to previous questions.

A clock at the top of the screen will show you how much time is remaining. The clock will not count down while you are listening. The clock will count down only while you are answering the questions.

Now you may begin the Listening section.

TOEFL iBT Listening

Conversation 1~5: Listen to part of a conversation between a student and a student activities office employee.

Actual Test 02

TOEFL iBT Listening

1. What are the speakers mainly discussing?
   - Ⓐ How to join one of the school's existing film clubs
   - Ⓑ The student's interest in running for president of a club
   - Ⓒ Where the film clubs on campus screen their movies
   - Ⓓ The student's desire to start a new club on campus

2. According to the student, what kinds of movies will her club show?
   - Ⓐ Black and white movies
   - Ⓑ Science fiction movies
   - Ⓒ Modern movies
   - Ⓓ Blockbuster movies

3. What is the employee's attitude toward the student?
   - Ⓐ She feels that the student's idea for a club is insufficient.
   - Ⓑ She praises the student for her thoroughness.
   - Ⓒ She is uncaring about the student's idea for a club.
   - Ⓓ She compliments the student for signing up early.

4. Listen again to part of the conversation. Then answer the question.

   What is the purpose of the woman's response?
   - Ⓐ To show her enthusiasm for the student's project
   - Ⓑ To express doubt that the student's idea will work
   - Ⓒ To encourage the student to form a book club
   - Ⓓ To state that the student has an original idea

5. Listen again to part of the conversation. Then answer the question.

   What does the woman imply when she says this?
   - Ⓐ Doing paperwork is crucial to starting a new club.
   - Ⓑ The student's application will likely be accepted.
   - Ⓒ She has no interest in filling out papers for the student.
   - Ⓓ She wants her meeting with the student to end soon.

Lecture 6~11: Listen to part of a lecture in a meteorology class.

Actual Test 02

TOEFL iBT Listening

6. What aspect of lightning does the professor mainly discuss?
   - Ⓐ How hot it can become
   - Ⓑ How it is created
   - Ⓒ How it makes thunder
   - Ⓓ How it becomes visible

7. Why does the professor explain electrostatic induction?
   - Ⓐ To tell the students why lightning can reach high temperatures
   - Ⓑ To provide another name for the shock wave that forms thunder
   - Ⓒ To describe one manner in which lightning might be formed
   - Ⓓ To discuss how lightning can occur in volcanic ash clouds

8. What are step leaders?
   - Ⓐ Loud bursts of thunder
   - Ⓑ Releases of air that is ionized
   - Ⓒ Positively charged particles
   - Ⓓ Lightning formed in dust storms

9. Why does the professor tell the students about the temperature on the sun's surface?
   - Ⓐ To show that it is hotter than the average lightning bolt
   - Ⓑ To compare it with the temperature of lightning
   - Ⓒ To respond to a question asked by a student
   - Ⓓ To explain why thunder can last for several seconds

10. What will the professor probably do next?
    - Ⓐ Assign the students some homework
    - Ⓑ Show the students a short video
    - Ⓒ Continue her lecture on lightning
    - Ⓓ Dismiss the class for the day

11. Listen again to part of the lecture. Then answer the question.

    What does the professor mean when she says this?
    - Ⓐ The class is going to end sometime soon.
    - Ⓑ Understanding ionization is of little importance.
    - Ⓒ The students should study ionization on their own.
    - Ⓓ She will discuss ionization in the next class.

Actual Test
03

Reading
Section Directions

This section measures your ability to understand academic passages in English.

In this part, you will read 1 passage and answer reading comprehension questions about the passage. Most questions are worth one point, but the last question is worth more than one point. The directions indicate how many points you may receive.

Some passages include a word or phrase that is underlined in blue. Click on the word or phrase to see a definition or an explanation.

When you want to move on to the next question, click on **Next**. You may skip questions and go back to them later. If you want to return to previous questions, click on **Back**. You can click on **Review** at any time and the review screen will show you which questions you have answered and which you have not answered. From this review screen, you may go directly to any question you have already seen in the Reading section.

You may now begin the Reading section. You will read 1 reading passage. You will have **20 minutes** to read the passage and answer the questions.

Click on **Continue** to go on.

TOEFL iBT Reading

1. The word divulge in the passage is closest in meaning to
   - (A) reveal
   - (B) consider
   - (C) partake
   - (D) arrange

2. In paragraph 1, the author's description of dating methods mentions all of the following EXCEPT:
   - (A) Humans have learned a lot about the past by using various dating methods.
   - (B) They are sometimes not completely effective with objects that are very old.
   - (C) Carbon-14 dating is a more effective method than potassium-argon dating.
   - (D) Scientists examine the physical makeup of an object to learn how old it is.

3. The word they in the passage refers to
   - (A) plants, animals, and humans
   - (B) the carbon-14 isotopes
   - (C) scientists
   - (D) 5,730 years

4. According to paragraph 2, which of the following is true of carbon-14?
   - (A) It is more common than any other isotope of carbon.
   - (B) It is found in plants that are eaten by various life forms.
   - (C) Humans are more likely to have it in them than are plants.
   - (D) It takes almost 6,000 years for it to disappear completely.

5. The word fluctuations in the passage is closest in meaning to
   - (A) disturbances
   - (B) continuations
   - (C) distributions
   - (D) variations

Dating Historical Objects

When an object is extremely old, it is frequently difficult to determine precisely when it was made. In some cases, certain clues, such as writing or other markings on the object as well as the style and the materials it was made from, may divulge information that can provide its age. However, these methods are not always able to ascertain the ages of large numbers of old objects. As a result, experts have developed various tests, including carbon-14 dating and potassium-argon dating, to examine the chemical compositions of objects to establish their ages. While both dating methods are limited in some ways, they have still permitted researchers to expand mankind's knowledge of the past.

Carbon has three main isotopes: carbon-12, carbon-13, and carbon-14. The first two isotopes are stable, but carbon-14 eventually decays and, over time, transforms into nitrogen-14. Carbon-14 is created when cosmic rays strike the upper atmosphere and carbon and oxygen combine to form carbon dioxide. This is absorbed by plants, which, in turn, are consumed by animals and humans. When plants, animals, and humans die, the carbon-14 isotopes in them begin to decay at a fixed rate. Since scientists know that the half-life of carbon-14 is 5,730 years, they can compare the rate of decay of the carbon-14 in an object to the level of stable carbon-12 in the atmosphere, which enables them to estimate the age of a particular object.

Nevertheless, carbon-14 dating has some limitations. For instance, it can only be used on objects that are organic in nature, such as wood, charcoal, shells from marine life forms, animal and human bones, and peat. Another problem with this dating method is that an historical record of how much carbon-14 and carbon-12 were in the atmosphere does not exist. Changes in cosmic ray intensity and Earth's volcanic activity

6. The word erroneous in the passage is closest in meaning to
   (A) disturbed
   (B) intermediate
   (C) precise
   (D) flawed

7. Which of the sentences below best expresses the essential information in the highlighted sentence in the passage? *Incorrect* answer choices change the meaning in important ways or leave out essential information.
   (A) These factors make this dating method effective for a period of time spanning forty years.
   (B) It took scientists forty years to discover how to use the dating method more accurately.
   (C) The dating method is most commonly used on objects that are less than forty years old.
   (D) There are many factors involved in determining the exact age of something from the past.

8. According to paragraph 3, carbon-14 dating is limited because
   (A) scientists are well aware of many of the Earth's environmental factors
   (B) cosmic rays sometimes affected volcanic activity on the Earth
   (C) the testing method is effective only on objects that are organic
   (D) there is not enough carbon in many parts of the Earth's atmosphere

9. The author discusses potassium-argon dating in paragraph 4 in order to
   (A) prove that it is more effective than carbon-14 dating
   (B) explain how it can be used to date past volcanic activity
   (C) describe a dating method used on extremely old objects
   (D) go into detail on the procedures involved in that testing method

could have caused fluctuations in the amount of carbon in the atmosphere in the past, thereby making accurate determinations of dates difficult to attain. Additionally, different species of plants absorb carbon-14 at varying rates, which can make carbon-14 dating on the plants, in addition to the animals and humans that consumed them, inaccurate. Environmental factors in the area where an object is found can also play a role in the accuracy of testing. Areas with a great deal of volcanic activity in particular can cause carbon-14 dating methods to be erroneous due to the high amount of carbon found near such regions. All of these factors result in dating that is not precise to a specific year but which can be dated accurately to a forty-year period.

Another limitation of carbon-14 dating is that it is useful only for objects less than 60,000 years old on account of the almost complete decay of carbon-14 in anything older than that. This makes it virtually impossible to date truly ancient items. Because of that, researchers rely upon another method: potassium-argon dating. This dating method is useful for determining the ages of rocks that are more than 100,000 years old and are volcanic in origin. It tests volcanic rocks because, when molten rocks reach a certain temperature, any argon gas found within them is released. Later, when the molten lava rapidly cools and hardens after being ejected by a volcano, the rocks become impermeable to argon. Therefore, no new argon from the atmosphere can enter the rocks. Most rocks also contain traces of potassium-40, which eventually decays and becomes argon-40. Since researchers know the half-life of the potassium-40 isotope and because no new argon entered the rock after it cooled, by comparing the amount of potassium-40 to argon-40 in the rock, scientists can get a rough estimate of the rock's age.

Potassium-argon dating is not as accurate as carbon-14 dating, yet it is still a useful tool.

TOEFL iBT Reading

10. The word impermeable in the passage is closest in meaning to
    Ⓐ filled
    Ⓑ resistant
    Ⓒ comparable
    Ⓓ exposed

11. In paragraph 4, which of the following can be inferred about potassium-argon dating?
    Ⓐ It requires more complex laboratory equipment than the carbon-14 dating method.
    Ⓑ The sizes of the items that it is able effectively to test must be fairly small.
    Ⓒ It is only successful when the rocks that are being tested are in a molten state.
    Ⓓ It cannot be used on objects that may be dated with the carbon-14 dating method.

12. In paragraph 5, the author's description of potassium-argon dating mentions which of the following?
    Ⓐ It can be used to test the remains of various animals.
    Ⓑ Objects that are billions of years old can be dated with it.
    Ⓒ A large number of scientists prefer it to carbon-14 dating.
    Ⓓ Scientists can use it for all kinds of different rocks.

By dating the rocks located in the layers of the Earth in which objects such as human and animal remains are found, researchers can make close estimates of the ages of the rocks and, by extension, the ages of other objects. The primary limitation of potassium-argon dating is that it can only date objects found in regions that have a history of volcanic activity. Still, with potassium-argon dating, rocks can be dated to more than four billion years of age, which is almost as old as the Earth itself.

Glossary
composition: the makeup of something
isotope: a form of an element that has a different number of neutrons than normal
decay: to decompose; to change in form

13. **Directions:** Select the appropriate statements from the answer choices and match them to the dating method to which they relate. TWO of the answer choices will NOT be used. *This question is worth 3 points.*

Carbon-14 Dating Method
(Select 3)
-
-
-

Potassium-Argon Dating Method
(Select 2)
-
-

Answer Choices

(A) Is used by scientists to test how old the Earth actually is

(B) Can be used on items that once contained living matter

(C) Is the less accurate of the two dating methods

(D) Provides results that are accurate to a time covering forty years

(E) Can only date objects between 60,000 and 100,000 years old

(F) May be affected by cosmic rays that strike the Earth

(G) Is used on rocks of a volcanic origin

Drag your answer choices to the spaces where they belong.
To remove an answer choice, click on it. To review the passage, click on **View Text**.

Listening
Section Directions

This section measures your ability to understand conversations and lectures in English.

In this part, you will listen to 1 conversation and 1 lecture. You will hear the conversation or lecture only **one** time. After the conversation or lecture, you will answer some questions about it. The questions typically ask about the main idea and supporting details. Some questions ask about a speaker's purpose or attitude. Answer the questions based on what is stated or implied by the speakers.

You may take notes while you listen. You may use your notes to help you answer the questions. Your notes will **not** be scored.

If you need to change the volume while you listen, click on the **Volume** icon at the top of the screen.

In some questions, you will see this icon: 🎧 This means that you will hear, but not see, part of the question.

Some of the questions have special directions. These directions appear in a gray box on the screen.

Most questions are worth one point. If a question is worth more than one point, it will have special directions that indicate how many points you can receive.

You must answer each question. After you answer, click on **Next**. Then click on **OK** to confirm your answer and go on to the next question. After you click on **OK**, you cannot return to previous questions.

A clock at the top of the screen will show you how much time is remaining. The clock will not count down while you are listening. The clock will count down only while you are answering the questions.

Now you may begin the Listening section.

Conversation 1~5: Listen to part of a conversation between a student and a professor.

Actual Test 03

TOEFL iBT Listening

1. Why did the professor ask to see the student?
   - Ⓐ To point out a mistake on her transcript
   - Ⓑ To inquire about a class she intends to take
   - Ⓒ To request that the student transfer to another school
   - Ⓓ To encourage the student to take a different class

2. What are the speakers mainly discussing?
   - Ⓐ The way a student can get a transfer credit approved
   - Ⓑ The student's interest in a microeconomics class
   - Ⓒ The student's desire to attend Western University
   - Ⓓ A grade of the student's that was recorded incorrectly

3. What does the professor tell the student that she needs to do?

   Click on 2 answers.
   - Ⓐ Fill out a form in the Economics Department
   - Ⓑ Submit her transcript to the professor
   - Ⓒ Provide a copy of her transcript to a secretary
   - Ⓓ Give a description of the course to a committee of professors

4. What will the student probably do next?
   - Ⓐ Visit the Economics Department
   - Ⓑ Return to her friends in the library
   - Ⓒ Make a trip to her dormitory
   - Ⓓ Photocopy her Western University transcript

5. Listen again to part of the conversation. Then answer the question.

   What does the professor imply when he says this?
   - Ⓐ The microeconomics class has more than one prerequisite.
   - Ⓑ The university made an error on the student's transcript.
   - Ⓒ The student should reconsider majoring in Economics.
   - Ⓓ The student catalog may contain some incorrect information.

Lecture 6~11: 🎧 Listen to part of a lecture in a literature class.

Actual Test 03

TOEFL iBT Listening

6. What is the lecture mainly about?
   - Ⓐ The most famous stories of Alexander Pushkin
   - Ⓑ The life and influence of Alexander Pushkin
   - Ⓒ The types of works that Alexander Pushkin composed
   - Ⓓ The influence of Alexander Pushkin on the Russian language

7. Why does the professor discuss Pushkin's wife Natalya?
   - Ⓐ To mention the reason why Pushkin was exiled
   - Ⓑ To focus on Natalya's influence on Pushkin's writing
   - Ⓒ To explain why Pushkin's marriage was not a happy one
   - Ⓓ To talk about the events that led to Pushkin's death

8. Why does the professor explain the importance of French in Russian education?
   - Ⓐ To stress how influential it was that Pushkin wrote in Russian
   - Ⓑ To mention how unusual it was for Pushkin to speak Russian fluently
   - Ⓒ To name some works of French literature influential in Russia
   - Ⓓ To praise Pushkin for breaking tradition and not writing in French

9. According to the professor, how did Pushkin influence Russian writers who came after him?

   Click on 2 answers.
   - Ⓐ He wrote works that were similar to those of William Shakespeare.
   - Ⓑ His stories contained characters that were distinctly Russian.
   - Ⓒ He created new words that helped establish modern written Russian.
   - Ⓓ He actively encouraged Russians to write in Russian rather than in French.

10. Listen again to part of the lecture. Then answer the question.

    What does the professor mean when he says this?
    - Ⓐ Pushkin was a leading force in some Russian revolutionary groups.
    - Ⓑ There were few radical movements during Pushkin's lifetime.
    - Ⓒ Pushkin did not become an active member of any radical groups.
    - Ⓓ It took years to convince Pushkin to join some revolutionary movements.

11. Listen again to part of the lecture. Then answer the question.

    What does the professor imply when he says this?
    - Ⓐ He enjoys reading Pushkin's works more than any other writer's.
    - Ⓑ He believes that Pushkin was the greatest writer in Russian.
    - Ⓒ He learned Russian just to be able to read Pushkin's writing.
    - Ⓓ He feels that people should only read Pushkin in the original language.

Actual Test 04

TOEFL iBT Reading

Reading
Section Directions

This section measures your ability to understand academic passages in English.

In this part, you will read 1 passage and answer reading comprehension questions about the passage. Most questions are worth one point, but the last question is worth more than one point. The directions indicate how many points you may receive.

Some passages include a word or phrase that is underlined in blue. Click on the word or phrase to see a definition or an explanation.

When you want to move on to the next question, click on **Next**. You may skip questions and go back to them later. If you want to return to previous questions, click on **Back**. You can click on **Review** at any time and the review screen will show you which questions you have answered and which you have not answered. From this review screen, you may go directly to any question you have already seen in the Reading section.

You may now begin the Reading section. You will read 1 reading passage. You will have **20 minutes** to read the passage and answer the questions.

Click on **Continue** to go on.

The Woolly Mammoth

The woolly mammoth was a gargantuan land mammal that dwelled in various northern regions for tens of thousands of years. The elephant-like species is currently extinct; however, the manner and place in which the woolly mammoth died has made it one of the best known and studied of all extinct animals. The reason is that many woolly mammoths died in frozen muddy riverbanks and lakebeds, where their remains were well preserved. Thousands of years later, humans discovered the remains of many animals in the frozen tundra of northern Siberia in Russia and other places. After being carefully exhumed and then transported to research facilities, they have provided scientists with valuable insight into the species and its environment.

In appearance, the woolly mammoth greatly resembled the modern-day elephant as it was comparable in size with the elephant and, with a few exceptions, had a similar body shape. Concerning these exceptions, the woolly mammoth had much smaller ears than the modern-day elephant, yet its tusks were significantly larger and had a pronounced curvature. Its body was also covered with thick, shaggy hair that helped keep it warm in the cold environments where it made its home and which could grow up to one meter in length. Woolly mammoths ate vegetation, mostly the short grass that grew on the tundra. It is believed that they used their enormous tusks to move layers of snow so that they could reach the grass growing underneath it. Like elephants, woolly mammoths almost certainly traveled in herds and had a social structure they adhered to.

It is generally accepted that woolly mammoths and other elephant species evolved from a common ancestor millions of years in the past. Approximately four million years ago, the branch that became woolly mammoths broke off from the North African elephant and migrated north where,

---

1. The word **exhumed** in the passage is closest in meaning to
   Ⓐ transplanted
   Ⓑ detected
   Ⓒ unearthed
   Ⓓ reconstructed

2. The word **they** in the passage refers to
   Ⓐ the remains of many animals
   Ⓑ Russia and other places
   Ⓒ research facilities
   Ⓓ scientists

3. According to paragraph 1, which of the following is NOT true of the woolly mammoth?
   Ⓐ Its home environment was in cold northern locations.
   Ⓑ It frequently made its homes alongside riverbanks.
   Ⓒ Scientists have been able to learn much about it.
   Ⓓ No members of the species are presently alive.

4. The word **pronounced** in the passage is closest in meaning to
   Ⓐ unique
   Ⓑ marked
   Ⓒ exquisite
   Ⓓ random

5. According to paragraph 2, how did woolly mammoths look different from modern-day elephants?
   Ⓐ They had tusks that were longer than elephants.
   Ⓑ Their ears were larger than those of elephants.
   Ⓒ They tended to be smaller in size than elephants.
   Ⓓ They had much less hair on their bodies than elephants.

6. Which of the sentences below best expresses the essential information in the highlighted sentence in the passage? *Incorrect* answer choices change the meaning in important ways or leave out essential information.

    (A) Earth endured many ice ages for hundreds of thousands of years, and that was the time period when the woolly mammoth dominated Earth's surface.
    (B) Many woolly mammoths were able to survive during the ice ages that caused much of the planet to be covered in snow for thousands of years.
    (C) Since the woolly mammoth was able to handle living in cold weather, it had more advantages over other animals during Earth's numerous ice ages.
    (D) Some animals, such as the woolly mammoth, became more prominent when Earth underwent thousands of years of severe ice ages.

7. Which of the following can be inferred from paragraph 3 about the North African elephant?

    (A) It was able to adapt to cold environments like the woolly mammoth.
    (B) More is known about it than about the woolly mammoth.
    (C) It once lived in northern places such as Siberia and Alaska.
    (D) It has been a distinct species of animal for millions of years.

8. Why does the author mention Wrangel Island?

    (A) It was a well-known breeding ground for the woolly mammoth.
    (B) Some remains of woolly mammoths have been found there.
    (C) It is one of the largest islands in the Arctic Ocean.
    (D) That was where the last of the woolly mammoths died.

over time, it adapted to the frigid climate. Woolly mammoths lived primarily in Europe and Asia as well as across much of the land in modern-day Alaska, Canada, and the northern United States. In their fully evolved form, woolly mammoths first appeared around 400,000 B.C and then thrived from that time until the last one died around 1700 B.C. For a few hundred thousand years, the northern part of Earth experienced a series of ice ages that gave the woolly mammoth a distinct advantage over other species because of its ability to survive in extremely cold temperatures.

It was around the end of the last major ice age when humans first appeared in woolly mammoths' territories. The shrinking of the ice fields and the pressure from growing numbers of human hunters steadily pushed the woolly mammoths into smaller regions. Between 40,000 and 14,000 B.C., enormous numbers of woolly mammoths died; they were either killed by hunters or succumbed to death by starvation due to limited food supplies. Eventually, only a few were left alive on various islands in the Arctic Ocean. The last one is believed to have died on Wrangel Island sometime around 1700 B.C. When some woolly mammoths died, they fell into rivers or lake beds, where their bodies were covered up. This prevented scavengers from consuming their remains, and the cold and mud combined to preserve their organic matter for thousands of years.

Legends of huge hairy beasts existed in many northern cultures long after woolly mammoths became extinct. In Siberia, hunters and trappers sometimes found tusks and bones on the ground or just beneath its surface. ■ They sold them to traders, who were particularly interested in the ivory tusks. ■ By the eighteenth century, stories of these fossilized animals had reached the ears of European scientists. ■ At first, they believed the remains were those of elephants that had lived in the north during an age when

TOEFL iBT Reading

9. The word consuming in the passage is closest in meaning to

    Ⓐ despoiling
    Ⓑ degrading
    Ⓒ devouring
    Ⓓ devolving

10. According to paragraph 4, one reason that the woolly mammoth went extinct was that

    Ⓐ the weather that most mammoths preferred began to change
    Ⓑ many of them were hunted and killed in large numbers
    Ⓒ various diseases killed thousands of the mammoths
    Ⓓ humans intentionally starved most of them to death

11. According to paragraph 5, the tusks and bones of many woolly mammoths

    Ⓐ were made of ivory, which was quite valuable
    Ⓑ were sold to people who extracted some DNA
    Ⓒ were only found lying about the ground
    Ⓓ were discovered by hunters in parts of Siberia

12. According to paragraph 5, why have some individuals extracted woolly mammoth DNA?

    Ⓐ To conduct research on the animals' genetic makeup
    Ⓑ To attempt to produce a woolly mammoth clone
    Ⓒ To inject some of the DNA into a full-grown elephant
    Ⓓ To compare the DNA with that of modern elephants

the Earth had been warmer. ■ But when some Siberians began finding fully intact woolly mammoths with their skin, hair, bones, and internal organs all preserved, experts realized that these animals were an entirely new species rather than elephants. Interestingly, a few modern-day researchers are not satisfied with studying only the remains of these animals. Some have extracted woolly mammoth DNA from various well-preserved specimens in the hope of being able to clone a woolly mammoth by impregnating a female elephant. It is their desire that, after breeding several generations of hybrid woolly mammoth-elephants, they can create a species of animals as close to a genuine woolly mammoth as possible.

Glossary
gargantuan: extremely large; huge
tundra: a flat, treeless plain found in arctic areas
shaggy: having long and rough hair

13. Look at the four squares [■] that indicate where the following sentence could be added to the passage.

The large sizes of the tusks made them particularly valuable.

Where would the sentence best fit?

Click on a square [■] to add the sentence to the passage.

14. **Directions:** An introductory sentence for a brief summary of the passage is provided below. Complete the summary by selecting the THREE answer choices that express the most important ideas of the passage. Some sentences do not belong because they express ideas that are not presented in the passage or are minor ideas in the passage. *This question is worth 2 points.*

While the woolly mammoth is no longer alive today, its unique body enabled it to thrive in the frigid environment in which it lived.

-
-
-

Answer Choices

(A) The remains of some woolly mammoths have been found in highly preserved states, so scientists have extensively studied them.

(B) Some scientists are considering the feasibility of cloning woolly mammoths to recreate the species.

(C) Mammoths' physical features, such as their hair and tusks, facilitated their living in places with cold temperatures.

(D) Because they adapted so well during the various ice ages, woolly mammoths lived in many northern areas.

(E) The woolly mammoth went extinct due to a number of factors, but the appearance of man was a major reason.

(F) For thousands of years, some cultures had stories and legends about enormous elephant-like creatures that were probably woolly mammoths.

Drag your answer choices to the spaces where they belong.
To remove an answer choice, click on it. To review the passage, click on **View Text**.

Listening
Section Directions

This section measures your ability to understand conversations and lectures in English.

In this part, you will listen to 1 conversation and 1 lecture. You will hear the conversation or lecture only **one** time. After the conversation or lecture, you will answer some questions about it. The questions typically ask about the main idea and supporting details. Some questions ask about a speaker's purpose or attitude. Answer the questions based on what is stated or implied by the speakers.

You may take notes while you listen. You may use your notes to help you answer the questions. Your notes will **not** be scored.

If you need to change the volume while you listen, click on the **Volume** icon at the top of the screen.

In some questions, you will see this icon: 🎧 This means that you will hear, but not see, part of the question.

Some of the questions have special directions. These directions appear in a gray box on the screen.

Most questions are worth one point. If a question is worth more than one point, it will have special directions that indicate how many points you can receive.

You must answer each question. After you answer, click on **Next**. Then click on **OK** to confirm your answer and go on to the next question. After you click on **OK**, you cannot return to previous questions.

A clock at the top of the screen will show you how much time is remaining. The clock will not count down while you are listening. The clock will count down only while you are answering the questions.

Now you may begin the Listening section.

TOEFL iBT Listening

Conversation 1~5: Listen to part of a conversation between a student and a librarian.

Actual Test 04

TOEFL iBT Listening

1. Why does the student visit the librarian?
   - Ⓐ To inquire about checking out a book
   - Ⓑ To show him a problem with a book
   - Ⓒ To have him photocopy a page from a book
   - Ⓓ To get him to find out where a book is

2. Why does the student ask the librarian to look inside her book?
   - Ⓐ To prove that she has already checked out the book
   - Ⓑ To have him confirm a reference in the book
   - Ⓒ To let him see that parts of the book are unreadable
   - Ⓓ To show him that the book is missing a page

3. What will the student probably do next?
   - Ⓐ Check out another book that she needs
   - Ⓑ Give the librarian her personal information
   - Ⓒ Contact someone at a library in New York City
   - Ⓓ Send an email to the librarian

4. Listen again to part of the conversation. Then answer the question.

   What does the student mean when she says this?
   - Ⓐ She wants the librarian to be patient and to listen to her.
   - Ⓑ She has no interest at all in speaking with Wayne.
   - Ⓒ Her problem is one that a reference librarian can solve.
   - Ⓓ The librarian can likely solve her problem very quickly.

5. Listen again to part of the conversation. Then answer the question.

   What does the student imply when she says this?
   - Ⓐ The librarian is doing a good job of solving her problem.
   - Ⓑ The school's library has an insufficient book collection.
   - Ⓒ She cannot visit any of the places the librarian mentions.
   - Ⓓ Her school is located somewhere close to California.

Lecture 6~11: Listen to part of a lecture in a physiology class.

Actual Test 04

TOEFL iBT Listening

6. According to the professor, when does systolic blood pressure get measured?
   - Ⓐ When the heart is contracting
   - Ⓑ When the heart is relaxing
   - Ⓒ When the heart is under stress
   - Ⓓ When the heart is stimulated

7. What aspect of high blood pressure does the professor mainly discuss?
   - Ⓐ The best ways for people to avoid getting it
   - Ⓑ Some of the negative effects it has on people
   - Ⓒ The importance of testing for it on a regular basis
   - Ⓓ Why doctors sometimes get incorrect readings

8. Why does the professor mention lipids?
   - Ⓐ To note that they are particles of cholesterol
   - Ⓑ To state that they are the leading cause of hypertension
   - Ⓒ To claim that they can lower a person's blood pressure
   - Ⓓ To say that they often block arteries in the body

9. What is hypotension?
   - Ⓐ A hormonal problem in the body
   - Ⓑ Low blood pressure
   - Ⓒ Another name for Addison's disease
   - Ⓓ Severe dizziness

10. Based on the information in the lecture, indicate whether the statements refer to high blood pressure or low blood pressure.

    Click in the correct box for each statement.

	High Blood Pressure	Low Blood Pressure
Ⓐ Is the less common of the two conditions		
Ⓑ Is frequently caused by hormonal problems		
Ⓒ Can be treated by various medicines		
Ⓓ May happen because of a person's lifestyle		

11. Listen again to part of the lecture. Then answer the question.

    What does the professor imply when he says this?
    - Ⓐ Most people fail to take good enough care of their kidneys.
    - Ⓑ Although the kidneys are little known, they are important to people's health.
    - Ⓒ The kidneys are involved in the circulation of the blood in the body.
    - Ⓓ There are some arteries that go straight from the heart to the kidneys.

Actual Test
05

TOEFL iBT Reading

Reading
Section Directions

This section measures your ability to understand academic passages in English.

In this part, you will read 1 passage and answer reading comprehension questions about the passage. Most questions are worth one point, but the last question is worth more than one point. The directions indicate how many points you may receive.

Some passages include a word or phrase that is underlined in blue. Click on the word or phrase to see a definition or an explanation.

When you want to move on to the next question, click on **Next**. You may skip questions and go back to them later. If you want to return to previous questions, click on **Back**. You can click on **Review** at any time and the review screen will show you which questions you have answered and which you have not answered. From this review screen, you may go directly to any question you have already seen in the Reading section.

You may now begin the Reading section. You will read 1 reading passage. You will have **20 minutes** to read the passage and answer the questions.

Click on **Continue** to go on.

TOEFL iBT Reading

1. The word convey in the passage is closest in meaning to
   - A consider
   - B distract
   - C respect
   - D express

2. According to paragraph 1, the initial use of montage was to
   - A pass on background information in a swift manner
   - B give some sort of intellectual message to the viewers
   - C show the audience how time was passing in the movie
   - D avoid using dialogue when showing various scenes

3. In paragraph 2, why does the author mention Sergei Eisenstein?
   - A To discuss his pioneering work on the use of montage
   - B To compare his usage of montage with that of other directors
   - C To describe some of the scenes in which he used montages
   - D To mention his five basic methods for the use of montage

4. The word interspersed in the passage is closest in meaning to
   - A distributed
   - B combined
   - C interrupted
   - D considered

Montage

A film montage portrays a rapid sequence of events by using short snippets of film that often have limited or no dialogue but which are accompanied by music. The purpose of a montage is to portray the passing of events over time. These frequently pertain to the main character of the story but may also simply show the occurring of certain events that serve as background to the story. In addition, while montages were first intended to convey intellectual messages to the viewing audience, for the most part, they are used in a different manner by modern filmmakers.

Montages were first utilized in Soviet films in the 1920s, most particularly by director Sergei Eisenstein. He believed that a montage was a way to show the collision of images that would transmit messages of an intellectual nature to the audience. For example, in one of his films, a group of striking workers is attacked by the police. Images of this event are interspersed with clips showing the killing of a bull. Eisenstein intended for the message to be that the workers were being treated no better than animals in a slaughterhouse. He formulated a theory on montage that included five basic methods—all of which he employed in his works—for producing them.

While Eisenstein is viewed as one of the intellectual giants of the cinema, his notions about montage did not translate well to mainstream movie production in other nations. This was particularly true of the Hollywood movies being produced in the United States. When adapted by Hollywood directors, montages became methods of showing the passage of time and events. Montages were primarily included as acts of continuity rather than as exercises intended to make the audience think. By the 1930s, montages had become common in Hollywood movies. One type of montage utilized a rapidly spinning

5. The author's description of Sergei Eisenstein mentions all of the following EXCEPT:

   Ⓐ He came up with several methods on how to use montages.
   Ⓑ He directed some of his films during the 1920s.
   Ⓒ He was the first person ever to use a montage in a film.
   Ⓓ His montages were meant to send messages to his audiences.

6. Which of the sentences below best expresses the essential information in the highlighted sentence in the passage? *Incorrect* answer choices change the meaning in important ways or leave out essential information.

   Ⓐ Eisenstein felt that, as a noted intellectual, his ideas on montage should be utilized by directors making all kinds of films.
   Ⓑ Movie directors making films in other countries often used montages in a variety of different ways.
   Ⓒ Despite being a noted cinematic intellectual, the montages that Eisenstein used were not effective in movies in other places.
   Ⓓ Eisenstein is widely regarded by historians of the cinema as one of the most intellectual of all movie directors.

7. The word plot in the passage is closest in meaning to

   Ⓐ story
   Ⓑ character
   Ⓒ theme
   Ⓓ paragraph

newspaper that suddenly stopped as the camera focused on the headline. In many cases, there was a rapid sequence of newspapers, all of which provided headlines concerning events that had happened and which provided crucial information that the audience needed to understand the plot. Another type frequently utilized was the travel montage. The characters' journey was portrayed by showing multiple images of them engaging in various activities in different places. There was typically a map in the background showing the characters' progress as they moved from place to place.

Another standard use of montages in Hollywood films was to build tension toward the climactic moment. A rapid sequence of shots between different characters and the showing of various aspects of a single scene were used to build tension. With the right music—and the right events—a filmmaker could create a powerful moment. Arguably the greatest example of this type of montage is the final gun duel between the three lead characters in Sergio Leone's 1966 film *The Good, the Bad, and the Ugly*. The haunting music and the quick flashes between the characters' eyes, guns, and hands increase the tension until it explodes in one of the best climaxes in movie history.

Presently, montages are utilized in virtually all film genres in a number of ways. They are often included in the beginning title and end title sequences. Montages are used with especially powerful effects in many sports movies. For instance, they frequently show training sequences as an athlete prepares for a big event. In the 1976 film *Rocky*, a montage is used to show the underdog boxer Rocky Balboa as he trains for his upcoming fight against the champion Apollo Creed. Prior to the start of the montage, Rocky was shown as being out of shape and was barely even able to ascend a flight of stairs. But, during the montage, he heroically transforms himself

8. In paragraph 3, the author of the passage implies that Hollywood movies

   (A) came to rely primarily on montages to tell their stories
   (B) were complimented by critics for the montages they used
   (C) were employed in all Hollywood movies in the 1930s
   (D) utilized montages in ways that Eisenstein never did

9. According to paragraph 3, which of the following is true of montages in Hollywood movies?

   (A) The montage of a spinning newspaper was adapted from Eisenstein's movies.
   (B) They were used to tell the majority of the plot to some audiences.
   (C) They were frequently used at the ends of movies during the credits.
   (D) They were mostly used to show various events that were occurring.

10. The author's description of *The Good, the Bad, and the Ugly* mentions which of the following?

    (A) It contained the first use of montage by a mainstream Hollywood movie.
    (B) The climactic scene in the movie has an effective use of montage.
    (C) It was a movie about the American West directed by Sergio Leone.
    (D) The montage it used was what made it a world-famous movie.

11. The word uplifting in the passage is closest in meaning to

    (A) fast-paced
    (B) orchestral
    (C) inspiring
    (D) dramatic

into a fit fighting machine. The entire sequence is done with practically no dialogue but has uplifting music. It indicates to the audience that Rocky is a match for Apollo and that he has a chance of winning the title bout. Ultimately, Rocky loses, yet without the montage, the audience would have found it difficult to believe that Rocky would even have been able to last one round with the champion.

Glossary

snippet: a clip; a fragment; a short piece, often of a film
haunting: memorable; poignant
underdog: a person or team that is not expected to win in a competition such as a sporting event

12. The word It in the passage refers to
    - Ⓐ The montage
    - Ⓑ A fit fighting machine
    - Ⓒ The entire sequence
    - Ⓓ Uplifting music

13. According to paragraph 5, in the movie *Rocky*, the montage used was successful because
    - Ⓐ it made the rest of the movie more believable to the audience
    - Ⓑ it had music that inspired many members of the audience
    - Ⓒ it showed the entire fight between Rocky Balboa and Apollo Creed
    - Ⓓ it was placed at the beginning of the movie and ended quickly

14. **Directions:** An introductory sentence for a brief summary of the passage is provided below. Complete the summary by selecting the THREE answer choices that express the most important ideas of the passage. Some sentences do not belong because they express ideas that are not presented in the passage or are minor ideas in the passage. *This question is worth 2 points.*

    Montages are used to show the passing of events in a swift manner, but the message they are intended to convey to the audience changes depending on the director.

    - •
    - •
    - •

    Answer Choices

    - Ⓐ In the movie *Rocky*, a montage is used to show Rocky Balboa training for his fight against Apollo Creed.
    - Ⓑ A large number of movies in the sports genre make use of montages to show training sequences.
    - Ⓒ Hollywood movies typically utilized montages to provide background information integral to the plot.
    - Ⓓ Some directors use montages to increase the tension in a movie, which can create an effective climax.
    - Ⓔ Sergio Leone created perhaps the best montage in all filmdom during a gunfight in his movie *The Good, the Bad, and the Ugly*.
    - Ⓕ Sergei Eisenstein used montages in his movies to send intellectual messages to the audiences.

    Drag your answer choices to the spaces where they belong.
    To remove an answer choice, click on it. To review the passage, click on **View Text**.

Listening
Section Directions

This section measures your ability to understand conversations and lectures in English.

In this part, you will listen to 1 conversation and 1 lecture. You will hear the conversation or lecture only **one** time. After the conversation or lecture, you will answer some questions about it. The questions typically ask about the main idea and supporting details. Some questions ask about a speaker's purpose or attitude. Answer the questions based on what is stated or implied by the speakers.

You may take notes while you listen. You may use your notes to help you answer the questions. Your notes will **not** be scored.

If you need to change the volume while you listen, click on the **Volume** icon at the top of the screen.

In some questions, you will see this icon: 🎧 This means that you will hear, but not see, part of the question.

Some of the questions have special directions. These directions appear in a gray box on the screen.

Most questions are worth one point. If a question is worth more than one point, it will have special directions that indicate how many points you can receive.

You must answer each question. After you answer, click on **Next**. Then click on **OK** to confirm your answer and go on to the next question. After you click on **OK**, you cannot return to previous questions.

A clock at the top of the screen will show you how much time is remaining. The clock will not count down while you are listening. The clock will count down only while you are answering the questions.

Now you may begin the Listening section.

TOEFL iBT Listening

Conversation 1~5: Listen to part of a conversation between a student and a professor.

05-02

Actual Test 05

TOEFL iBT Listening

1. What are the speakers mainly discussing?
   - (A) The greatest authors of the nineteenth century
   - (B) A paper that the student recently submitted
   - (C) A lecture that the professor gave in a previous class
   - (D) An upcoming assignment that the student must do

2. What can be inferred about the student?
   - (A) She is getting a good grade in the professor's class.
   - (B) She studied with the professor in a previous semester.
   - (C) She is considering dropping the professor's class.
   - (D) She is conscientious about doing her schoolwork.

3. What does the professor recommend that the student read?

   Click on 2 answers.
   - (A) *Harry Potter*
   - (B) *The Chronicles of Narnia*
   - (C) *Alice in Wonderland*
   - (D) *The Princess and the Goblin*

4. Why does the professor tell the student about George MacDonald?
   - (A) To encourage the student to consider doing her paper on him
   - (B) To compare the importance of his works to those of Lewis Carroll
   - (C) To point out that he lived and wrote during the nineteenth century
   - (D) To remind the student that they talked about him in that day's class

5. What does the professor imply about C.S. Lewis?
   - (A) He trained together with George MacDonald.
   - (B) He wrote a large number of modern fairy tales.
   - (C) He was familiar with George MacDonald's works.
   - (D) His books are important to present-day scholars.

Lecture 6~11: Listen to part of a lecture in a biology class.

Actual Test 05

TOEFL iBT Listening

6. What is the lecture mainly about?
   - Ⓐ The characteristics of caecilians
   - Ⓑ The life cycle of a frog
   - Ⓒ Some various species of amphibians
   - Ⓓ The three main groups of amphibians

7. According to the professor, where do some frogs lay their eggs?
   - Ⓐ In rivers
   - Ⓑ In oceans
   - Ⓒ In lakes
   - Ⓓ In streams

8. How does the professor organize the information about frogs that she presents to the class?
   - Ⓐ By covering each stage of a frog's life in detail
   - Ⓑ By encouraging the students to ask her questions
   - Ⓒ By focusing on where the majority of frogs live
   - Ⓓ By going over a handout that she gave to the class

9. Based on the information in the lecture, indicate whether the statements refer to a frog's tadpole stage or its metamorphic stage.

   Click in the correct box for each statement.

	Tadpole Stage	Metamorphic Stage
Ⓐ The tail gets absorbed by the body.		
Ⓑ The frog exclusively uses gills to breathe.		
Ⓒ The position of the eyes changes.		
Ⓓ The hind and front legs develop.		

10. Why does the professor tell the students about how some amphibians are different from one another?
    - Ⓐ To name some species of amphibians that are unique
    - Ⓑ To compare and contrast caecilians, newts, and frogs
    - Ⓒ To make them realize that not all amphibians are identical
    - Ⓓ To explain how some amphibians breathe through their skin

11. Listen again to part of the lecture. Then answer the question.

    What can be inferred about the professor when she says this?
    - Ⓐ She is not interested in talking about caecilians.
    - Ⓑ She expects the students to know certain facts.
    - Ⓒ She wants the student to answer his own question.
    - Ⓓ She is surprised by the student's response.

Actual Test 06

TOEFL iBT Reading

Reading
Section Directions

This section measures your ability to understand academic passages in English.

In this part, you will read 1 passage and answer reading comprehension questions about the passage. Most questions are worth one point, but the last question is worth more than one point. The directions indicate how many points you may receive.

Some passages include a word or phrase that is underlined in blue. Click on the word or phrase to see a definition or an explanation.

When you want to move on to the next question, click on **Next**. You may skip questions and go back to them later. If you want to return to previous questions, click on **Back**. You can click on **Review** at any time and the review screen will show you which questions you have answered and which you have not answered. From this review screen, you may go directly to any question you have already seen in the Reading section.

You may now begin the Reading section. You will read 1 reading passage. You will have **20 minutes** to read the passage and answer the questions.

Click on **Continue** to go on.

Fatal Familial Insomnia

Despite having conducted years of research, experts do not know exactly why sleep is necessary for humans. What they do know, however, is that without adequate sleep, a person will eventually die. This is evident in the extremely rare disease known as fatal familial insomnia. Sufferers of this disease initially cannot nap, then cannot sleep throughout the night, and are finally unable to sleep at all. There are four major stages of this disease, and the majority of those who have it die within six months of entering its final stage. As yet, no individual has survived more than three years after contracting the disease. While doctors and scientists are certain they know its causes, they have still failed to find a cure for it.

Fatal familial insomnia is a genetic disease that gets passed on from one generation to the next and has been discovered in approximately forty families worldwide. Children have a fifty percent chance of developing the disease if one parent has the mutated gene for fatal familial insomnia. Most victims begin to see signs of the disease in their fifties although it can appear in some people when they are as young as thirty and as old as sixty.

Researchers have identified four distinct stages in the disease once it fully manifests itself in a person. In the first stage, which lasts around four months, the victim begins experiencing a mild form of insomnia as well as paranoia, panic attacks, and increased suffering from various phobias. The second stage lasts for five months and sees the onset of severe insomnia along with hallucinations and increasing panic attacks. The third stage lasts for only three months and marks the beginning of total insomnia. Its most obvious new symptom is rapid weight loss. The final stage sees the sufferer experience complete dementia and an inability to respond to any outside stimulus, including, eventually, being

---

1. The word **adequate** in the passage is closest in meaning to
   Ⓐ constant
   Ⓑ apparent
   Ⓒ intermittent
   Ⓓ sufficient

2. The word **it** in the passage refers to
   Ⓐ the night
   Ⓑ this disease
   Ⓒ the majority
   Ⓓ its final stage

3. According to paragraph 2, which of the following is true of fatal familial insomnia?
   Ⓐ There is a fifty percent chance of it affecting a person.
   Ⓑ Around forty people worldwide have gotten the disease.
   Ⓒ Children inherit the gene for it from their parents.
   Ⓓ Most people with it begin to suffer in their sixties.

4. The word **phobias** in the passage is closest in meaning to
   Ⓐ fears
   Ⓑ injuries
   Ⓒ symptoms
   Ⓓ spasms

5. The author's description of the symptoms of the first stage of fatal familial insomnia mentions all of the following EXCEPT:
   Ⓐ The person is sometimes unable to get any sleep.
   Ⓑ The sufferer is affected by certain phobias.
   Ⓒ The individual begins to see things that are not real.
   Ⓓ The victim is liable suddenly to start to panic.

6. The author's description of the final stage of fatal familial insomnia mentions which of the following?
   - (A) It can result in a person looking much older than he or she is in reality.
   - (B) A person may endure the final stages of the disease for three years.
   - (C) The weight that the person previously lost is put back on during this stage.
   - (D) An individual loses all of his or her senses but remains able to speak.

7. The author discusses the thalamus in paragraph 4 in order to
   - (A) describe its role in sending messages from the brain to the entire body
   - (B) mention that scientists have found out why plaque may build up in it
   - (C) explain how it might be responsible for causing fatal familial insomnia
   - (D) stress that it is the key to preventing the transmission of fatal familial insomnia

8. The phrase interferes with in the passage is closest in meaning to
   - (A) bans
   - (B) revokes
   - (C) impedes
   - (D) assaults

9. According to paragraph 4, some scientists study plaque in the thalamus because
   - (A) they want to explore its relationship with the entire brain
   - (B) they think that the gene for fatal familial insomnia is found in it
   - (C) they know that the plaque helps shut down all of the brain's functions
   - (D) they believe that it may be preventing people from sleeping

unable to speak. This stage can last for up to half a year and always ends in death. Some secondary symptoms are increased perspiration, heart rate, and blood pressure and the appearance of rapid aging in a relatively short period of time.

The thalamus, a part of the brain, has been identified as the key to understanding fatal familial insomnia. Researchers have discovered that in people with the disease, malformed proteins attack the thalamus, which damages it. Plaque begins building up in the thalamus, causing it to shut down. In some way not yet fully understood, this protein plaque buildup interferes with the person's ability to sleep. It may, however, be related to the fact that the thalamus is a message center that passes signals from the brain to the rest of the body. Scientists believe that, after many hours of constant activity, the thalamus becomes less efficient at transmitting messages, so it enters a stage in which it induces sleep. The buildup of protein plaque, though, may prevent the thalamus from entering this stage and thereby keep the sufferer from falling asleep.

One unfortunate aspect of fatal familial insomnia is that it does not appear in most people until later in their lives, usually after they have already had children. Therefore, carriers of the gene for the disease often unwittingly pass it on to their progeny. Nevertheless, not everyone gets the gene and the disease. One case study done on an Italian family with the mutated gene present determined that out of 228 relatives spanning six generations, twenty-nine people had the mutated gene and the disease. Additionally, there are now tests that can determine the presence of the mutated gene in the body. This may pose a dilemma for people who test positive for it: They may have to determine whether or not to have babies since their children would have a chance of inheriting the gene.

Testing for the mutated gene at an early age may be the only hope that potential carriers have

10. The word progeny in the passage is closest in meaning to
    A acquaintances
    B descendants
    C genes
    D ancestors

11. Which of the following can be inferred from paragraph 5 about fatal familial insomnia?
    A It typically only affects people who are of Italian descent.
    B Only a small number of potential victims inherit the gene for it.
    C Scientists are close to developing a cure for the mutated gene that causes it.
    D Children who get the disease from their parents come to resent them.

12. The word eradicated in the passage is closest in meaning to
    A understood
    B eliminated
    C healed
    D transplanted

13. In paragraph 6, the author of the passage implies that gene replacement therapy
    A has successfully cured individuals with fatal familial insomnia
    B is a relatively new yet inexpensive type of medical treatment
    C should lead to a cure for fatal familial insomnia within a decade
    D may be an effective treatment for a number of genetic diseases

for receiving some form of treatment. At present, researchers are developing gene replacement therapy. Some of them hope to be able to replace mutated genes in people with genetic diseases such as fatal familial insomnia. If the treatment is effective, then the disease may eventually be eradicated from the bodies of those who have it. Then, in the future, those people and their children will not have to worry about getting a good night's sleep.

Glossary
hallucination: a sensation in which a person sees something that does not actually exist
malformed: deformed; misshapen
dilemma: a serious problem; a quandary

14. **Directions:** An introductory sentence for a brief summary of the passage is provided below. Complete the summary by selecting the THREE answer choices that express the most important ideas of the passage. Some sentences do not belong because they express ideas that are not presented in the passage or are minor ideas in the passage *This question is worth 2 points.*

Fatal familial insomnia is an extremely rare, yet deadly, genetic disease that causes its sufferers to be unable to sleep.

-
-
-

Answer Choices

(A) While most people suffer from fatal familial insomnia in their fifties, others get the disease when they are much younger.

(B) The disease has four stages, all of which become progressively worse until the victim eventually dies.

(C) Scientists are trying to find a way to cure fatal familial insomnia by using gene replacement therapy.

(D) A person suffering from this disease is unable to sleep, and this is what ultimately brings about death.

(E) The thalamus is the part of the brain that sends instructions to the rest of the body concerning how to act.

(F) The gene for fatal familial insomnia has been found in a very small number of families all around the world.

Drag your answer choices to the spaces where they belong.
To remove an answer choice, click on it. To review the passage, click on **View Text**.

Listening
Section Directions

This section measures your ability to understand conversations and lectures in English.

In this part, you will listen to 1 conversation and 1 lecture. You will hear the conversation or lecture only **one** time. After the conversation or lecture, you will answer some questions about it. The questions typically ask about the main idea and supporting details. Some questions ask about a speaker's purpose or attitude. Answer the questions based on what is stated or implied by the speakers.

You may take notes while you listen. You may use your notes to help you answer the questions. Your notes will **not** be scored.

If you need to change the volume while you listen, click on the **Volume** icon at the top of the screen.

In some questions, you will see this icon: 🎧 This means that you will hear, but not see, part of the question.

Some of the questions have special directions. These directions appear in a gray box on the screen.

Most questions are worth one point. If a question is worth more than one point, it will have special directions that indicate how many points you can receive.

You must answer each question. After you answer, click on **Next**. Then click on **OK** to confirm your answer and go on to the next question. After you click on **OK**, you cannot return to previous questions.

A clock at the top of the screen will show you how much time is remaining. The clock will not count down while you are listening. The clock will count down only while you are answering the questions.

Now you may begin the Listening section.

TOEFL iBT Listening

Conversation 1~5: Listen to part of a conversation between a student and a university museum employee.

Actual Test 06

TOEFL iBT Listening

1. Why does the woman ask the student to talk about his job duties?
   - Ⓐ To try to get him to relax
   - Ⓑ To correct an error he made
   - Ⓒ To answer his question
   - Ⓓ To compare his duties with hers

2. What are the student's job duties?
   Click on 2 answers.
   - Ⓐ To give tours to museum visitors
   - Ⓑ To answer questions visitors ask him
   - Ⓒ To monitor the security cameras
   - Ⓓ To watch over the museum's visitors

3. What can be inferred about the exhibits at the museum?
   - Ⓐ Some of them are displayed for brief periods of time.
   - Ⓑ The museum does not own everything that is on display.
   - Ⓒ The ones related to archaeology are all from the local area.
   - Ⓓ The most expensive items on display are the statues.

4. Why does the student talk about the Native American artifacts at the museum?
   - Ⓐ To compare them with the works by Picasso
   - Ⓑ To note which gallery they are located in
   - Ⓒ To say that there was little about them in the brochures
   - Ⓓ To comment that he does not know much about them

5. Listen again to part of the conversation. Then answer the question.

   What can be inferred about the student when he says this?
   - Ⓐ He is considering quitting his job.
   - Ⓑ He thinks the woman is a good boss.
   - Ⓒ He feels nervous about his new job.
   - Ⓓ He is eager to start working.

Lecture 6~11: Listen to part of a lecture in a history class.

Actual Test 06

TOEFL iBT Listening

6. According to the professor, how did Spain become weak by the 1800s?
   - Ⓐ It lost most of its colonies to other European powers.
   - Ⓑ The Spanish king was assassinated by the French.
   - Ⓒ The country could not find enough gold to pay its debts.
   - Ⓓ It lost many battles in Europe and in other places.

7. Why does the professor discuss Gran Colombia?
   - Ⓐ To discuss an objective that Bolivar never successfully attained
   - Ⓑ To describe Bolivar's activities after Venezuela became independent
   - Ⓒ To show how violent Bolivar could be when people opposed him
   - Ⓓ To explain the reason why South Americans consider Bolivar a hero

8. What does the professor imply about Gran Colombia?
   - Ⓐ It failed as a state in the same year that Bolivar died.
   - Ⓑ It resisted several attacks by Spanish soldiers.
   - Ⓒ It remained united for a period lasting several decades.
   - Ⓓ It held elections for leaders in various parts of the country.

9. Put the following events of the revolution in Venezuela in the order in which they occurred.

   Click in the correct box for each statement.

Event	Order
Ⓐ Bolivar's forces captured Caracas.	
Ⓑ Venezuelan rebels declared their independence from Spain.	
Ⓒ Bolivar was exiled and had to leave Venezuela.	
Ⓓ 10,000 Spanish troops were sent to Venezuela.	

10. Listen again to part of the lecture. Then answer the question.

    What does the professor mean when he says this?
    - Ⓐ Many Spaniards approved of Napoleon's brother's right to rule.
    - Ⓑ Napoleon desired to become the king of Spain one day.
    - Ⓒ Some Spanish colonists rejected Napoleon's brother as king.
    - Ⓓ Some Spaniards became colonists rather than remain in Spain.

11. Listen again to part of the lecture. Then answer the question.

    What does the professor imply when he says this?
    - Ⓐ Bolivar was deposed by some rebels at one point.
    - Ⓑ Bolivar used violence against some of the other rebels.
    - Ⓒ Bolivar excelled at coming up with battle strategies.
    - Ⓓ Bolivar always led his soldiers when they went into battle.

Actual Test 07

TOEFL iBT Reading

Reading
Section Directions

This section measures your ability to understand academic passages in English.

In this part, you will read 1 passage and answer reading comprehension questions about the passage. Most questions are worth one point, but the last question is worth more than one point. The directions indicate how many points you may receive.

Some passages include a word or phrase that is underlined in blue. Click on the word or phrase to see a definition or an explanation.

When you want to move on to the next question, click on **Next**. You may skip questions and go back to them later. If you want to return to previous questions, click on **Back**. You can click on **Review** at any time and the review screen will show you which questions you have answered and which you have not answered. From this review screen, you may go directly to any question you have already seen in the Reading section.

You may now begin the Reading section. You will read 1 reading passage. You will have **20 minutes** to read the passage and answer the questions.

Click on **Continue** to go on.

1. According to paragraph 1, the balance of nature has been upset in parts of the western United States in that
   - (A) the forest fires that occur there happen much more regularly than before
   - (B) there are more intense forest fires there now than there were in past years
   - (C) many of the forest fires that break out there may burn for several months at a time
   - (D) entire regions have been devastated by numerous long-lasting forest fires

2. The word extinguish in the passage is closest in meaning to
   - (A) ignite
   - (B) quench
   - (C) reduce
   - (D) thwart

3. Why does the author mention World War II?
   - (A) To claim that most forest fires were ignored during that period of time
   - (B) To indicate when firefighting techniques improved in the United States
   - (C) To state that more forest fires broke out then than during other times
   - (D) To comment that forest fires were never major problems until the war

Controlling Wildfires

Fire is one of nature's ways of controlling growth in forests while it simultaneously ensures that certain trees reach maturity without being destroyed by the heat and flames. ■ Yet human activity has destroyed this balance in some regions of the western United States. ■ Due to a number of factors, this has led to a situation in which present-day forest fires are of greater intensity and duration than those that occurred decades ago. ■ As a result, it is expected that, over the long term, there will be more frequent and intense fires covering large areas of land. ■

An example of this phenomenon can be seen in the forests of the Bitterroot Mountains, which are located in Montana, a state in the western United States. During the early part of the twentieth century, the services dedicated to fighting forest fires made it their objective to extinguish all fires as soon as they broke out. This, however, was difficult to accomplish until after World War II ended in 1945. The reason for this was that, after the war, the road network improved, which let firefighters get to fires more easily, and surplus warplanes were utilized as water bombers. After a few years, the goal of stopping fires almost as soon as they started was attained. There were no problems for several decades. Then, suddenly, in the 1980s, the fires that broke out in the Bitterroot Mountains became more frequent and burned with such intensity while spreading so rapidly that some of them simply could not be put out until enough rain fell on them. This trend continued into the 1990s as well as the first decade of the twenty-first century.

The theory most commonly accepted by forest fire experts was that, by extinguishing every forest fire so quickly in previous decades, humans had upset the balance of nature in Montana's forests. In the past, most forest fires were caused by lightning and burned a region of forest approximately every decade. The forests

Actual Test 07

TOEFL iBT Reading

4. Which of the sentences below best expresses the essential information in the highlighted sentence in the passage? *Incorrect* answer choices change the meaning in important ways or leave out essential information.

   (A) Some of the strongest, most frequent, and most rapidly spreading forest fires in the world broke out in the Bitterroot Mountains in the 1980s.
   (B) Firefighters learned that sometimes it was impossible to put out fast-burning fires in the Bitterroot Mountains until rain began to fall on the flames.
   (C) The forest fires in the Bitterroot Mountains in the 1980s happened quite often and were unable to be extinguished except by rain because they were so powerful.
   (D) Because of a number of reasons, fires in the Bitterroot Mountains in the 1980s were fast-burning and intense and happened with increasing frequency.

5. The word they in the passage refers to

   (A) most places
   (B) every ten years
   (C) the fir trees and other smaller trees
   (D) great heights

6. The word germinated in the passage is closest in meaning to

   (A) sprouted
   (B) planted
   (C) flowered
   (D) nourished

7. The word bulwark in the passage is closest in meaning to

   (A) reaction
   (B) extinguisher
   (C) objective
   (D) barricade

in Montana were a combination of low-rising fir trees, which burned easily, and large, tall pine trees, which had thick bark and were extremely fire resistant. Since most places averaged one fire every ten years, there was not enough time for the fir trees and other smaller trees to grow to great heights. Instead, they burned and died, but many of their seeds were buried underground, subsequently germinated, and began growing again until the next cycle of fire came along. Meanwhile, the pine trees grew tall and strong and provided a bulwark against forest fires; their resistance to fire helped keep the fires from spreading. Yet this changed when humans began quenching the fires. Humans' actions enabled the fir trees to grow to great heights, and they soon grew rather densely alongside the pine trees.

Because of that, when forest fires broke out in the Montana forests in the 1980s, the flames climbed higher and higher into the branches of the tall fir trees. Flames were suddenly able to reach the crowns of both the firs and the pines. These fires burned so powerfully that sometimes flames leapt hundreds of meters to other trees. In some instances, virtual firestorms resulted, which caused the flames to spread so quickly that they were impossible to stop without rainfall, nature's fire extinguisher.

Another factor that contributed to the intensity of the forest fires was the actions of logging companies. These companies cut down the biggest and best pine trees, which left the forests bereft of the one tree that was highly resistant to fire. Additionally, the loggers usually chopped off the branches of the trees they cut down and left them on the forest floor. These branches acted as kindling and enabled the rapid spread of fires caused by lightning.

Because these fires were so strong, many homeowners living in Montana forests saw their houses go up in flames. Furthermore, valuable stands of timber were also destroyed.

8. According to paragraph 3, which of the following is true of the forests of Montana?

   Ⓐ Only one species comprised the majority of the trees that grew in them.
   Ⓑ Forest fires in parts of the forests tended to happen about every ten years.
   Ⓒ The pine trees in the forests burned much more easily than the fir trees.
   Ⓓ Authorities tried to put out all of the forest fires in them to preserve tree growth.

9. In paragraph 4, the author implies that forest fires in Montana in the 1980s

   Ⓐ were unable to be stopped by firefighters
   Ⓑ caused a great amount of property damage
   Ⓒ burned entire forests completely to the ground
   Ⓓ killed large numbers of forest animals

10. The word bereft in the passage is closest in meaning to

    Ⓐ deprived
    Ⓑ considerate
    Ⓒ aware
    Ⓓ full

11. According to paragraph 5, logging companies affected forest fires because

    Ⓐ some loggers working for them accidentally started a few fires
    Ⓑ they cleared much of the undergrowth that prohibited the spread of fires
    Ⓒ they did not cut down fir trees, so the fires could spread more quickly
    Ⓓ many of the trees that they cut down had been able to resist fires

Both individuals and logging companies have complained to the government and encouraged it to alter its policies. Yet government plans to allow some small controlled fires to help restore the balance of nature have met with bitter opposition by some. Whatever happens in the future, one thing is for sure: There will still be forest fires. The question that remains to be answered is with how much intensity they will burn.

Glossary

surplus: extra; left over
quench: to put out; to stop
kindling: material, such as small pieces of wood, that are used to start fires

12. According to paragraph 6, which of the following is NOT true of the results of the intense forest fires in Montana?

   (A) People have urged the government to do something about the fires.
   (B) The homes of many individuals have been consumed by the flames.
   (C) Logging companies have lost millions of dollars in potential revenue.
   (D) Some individuals have spoken out against the use of controlled fires.

13. Look at the four squares [■] that indicate where the following sentence could be added to the passage.

   This is true in places other than the U.S. as well.

   Where would the sentence best fit?

   Click on a square [■] to add the sentence to the passage.

14. **Directions:** An introductory sentence for a brief summary of the passage is provided below. Complete the summary by selecting the THREE answer choices that express the most important ideas of the passage. Some sentences do not belong because they express ideas that are not presented in the passage or are minor ideas in the passage. *This question is worth 2 points.*

Due to the previous policy of quickly extinguishing forest fires, the fires that burn in Montana today are more intense and spread more rapidly than they did before.

-
-
-

Answer Choices

(A) Nowadays, forest fires are so widespread and powerful than often only falling rain can stop them from spreading.

(B) There are many people who believe that the government should employ controlled burns to decrease the number of dangerous forest fires.

(C) Since fir trees suddenly began to grow higher, when forest fires started, this caused more parts of the forest to burn.

(D) It was after World War II ended that putting out forest fires became an easier chore for firefighters to accomplish.

(E) Logging companies have begun to lobby the government to change its policies on how to handle forest fires.

(F) By putting out forest fires quickly, the balance of nature was upset, which has caused recent fires to be more severe.

Drag your answer choices to the spaces where they belong.
To remove an answer choice, click on it. To review the passage, click on **View Text**.

TOEFL iBT Listening

Listening
Section Directions

This section measures your ability to understand conversations and lectures in English.

In this part, you will listen to 1 conversation and 1 lecture. You will hear the conversation or lecture only **one** time. After the conversation or lecture, you will answer some questions about it. The questions typically ask about the main idea and supporting details. Some questions ask about a speaker's purpose or attitude. Answer the questions based on what is stated or implied by the speakers.

You may take notes while you listen. You may use your notes to help you answer the questions. Your notes will **not** be scored.

If you need to change the volume while you listen, click on the **Volume** icon at the top of the screen.

In some questions, you will see this icon: 🎧 This means that you will hear, but not see, part of the question.

Some of the questions have special directions. These directions appear in a gray box on the screen.

Most questions are worth one point. If a question is worth more than one point, it will have special directions that indicate how many points you can receive.

You must answer each question. After you answer, click on **Next**. Then click on **OK** to confirm your answer and go on to the next question. After you click on **OK**, you cannot return to previous questions.

A clock at the top of the screen will show you how much time is remaining. The clock will not count down while you are listening. The clock will count down only while you are answering the questions.

Now you may begin the Listening section.

TOEFL iBT Listening

Conversation 1~5: Listen to part of a conversation between a student and a professor.

Actual Test 07

TOEFL iBT Listening

1. Why did the teacher ask to see the student?
   - Ⓐ To talk about some research that she did
   - Ⓑ To present her with a job offer
   - Ⓒ To ask about her ongoing work
   - Ⓓ To discuss her class schedule

2. What does the student imply about the seminar she is taking?
   - Ⓐ It lasts the longest of all of her classes.
   - Ⓑ It is being taught by the professor.
   - Ⓒ She is not learning very much in it.
   - Ⓓ It can get somewhat boring at times.

3. What is the professor currently doing her research on?
   - Ⓐ Whales
   - Ⓑ Porpoises
   - Ⓒ Dolphins
   - Ⓓ Sharks

4. What is the professor's opinion of the student?
   - Ⓐ She thinks that the student needs to work harder.
   - Ⓑ She doubts the student's excellent reputation.
   - Ⓒ She believes that the student does outstanding work.
   - Ⓓ She feels that the student should attend graduate school.

5. Listen again to part of the conversation. Then answer the question.

   Why does the student say this?
   - Ⓐ To take the opportunity to decline the professor's job offer
   - Ⓑ To give her congratulations to the professor
   - Ⓒ To avoid answering the question the professor asked her
   - Ⓓ To imply that she knows what the professor will ask her

Lecture 6~11: Listen to part of a lecture in an art history class.

Art History

6. What is the main topic of the lecture?
   - Ⓐ The importance of *Birds of America* in art
   - Ⓑ The life and work of John James Audubon
   - Ⓒ John James Audubon's interest in birds
   - Ⓓ The process by which *Birds of America* was published

7. According to the professor, how did Audubon get close views of the birds he drew?
   - Ⓐ He took photographs of many birds.
   - Ⓑ He hired people to stuff some birds for him.
   - Ⓒ He relied on his memory of how the birds looked.
   - Ⓓ He shot the birds and used them as models.

8. Why does the professor mention engraved copper plates?
   - Ⓐ To explain the method that let *Birds of America* be printed
   - Ⓑ To tell the students why Audubon needed an English publisher
   - Ⓒ To describe a new process invented for publishing illustrations
   - Ⓓ To state why Audubon's book was so expensive for buyers

9. What will the professor probably do next?
   - Ⓐ Show some pictures from *Birds of America*
   - Ⓑ Continue to discuss Audubon's illustrations
   - Ⓒ Let the students take a break from class
   - Ⓓ Ask a student to turn off the classroom lights

10. Listen again to part of the lecture. Then answer the question.

    What does the professor imply when she says this?
    - Ⓐ Audubon did not use a camera to take pictures of birds.
    - Ⓑ Audubon knew more about birds than anyone else in his time.
    - Ⓒ Audubon drew pictures that were almost as good as those of other artists.
    - Ⓓ Her favorite illustrator of animals is Audubon.

11. Listen again to part of the lecture. Then answer the question.

    What can be inferred about the professor when she says this?
    - Ⓐ She feels that taxidermists do important work.
    - Ⓑ She dislikes even looking at any kind of dead animals.
    - Ⓒ She believes some students do not know what a taxidermist is.
    - Ⓓ She thinks that taxidermy is an unnecessary profession today.

Actual Test 08

Reading
Section Directions

This section measures your ability to understand academic passages in English.

In this part, you will read 1 passage and answer reading comprehension questions about the passage. Most questions are worth one point, but the last question is worth more than one point. The directions indicate how many points you may receive.

Some passages include a word or phrase that is underlined in blue. Click on the word or phrase to see a definition or an explanation.

When you want to move on to the next question, click on **Next**. You may skip questions and go back to them later. If you want to return to previous questions, click on **Back**. You can click on **Review** at any time and the review screen will show you which questions you have answered and which you have not answered. From this review screen, you may go directly to any question you have already seen in the Reading section.

You may now begin the Reading section. You will read 1 reading passage. You will have **20 minutes** to read the passage and answer the questions.

Click on **Continue** to go on.

Pulsars and Quasars

Two of the most unique phenomena in the universe are pulsars and quasars. Yet despite the similarities in their names and the fact that they are both rare and poorly understood, pulsars and quasars have only a few characteristics in common. Pulsars are dead stars that emit radio waves while quasars, which are created by the actions of a black hole at the center of a galaxy, are the brightest objects in the universe. Additionally, the two are different in how they are created, the amount of light and radio waves they emit, and the distances from Earth they are.

In 1967, two astronomers happened to discover pulsars completely by chance. As they were observing the night sky, they noticed a source of radio waves coming at regular intervals of once a second. Soon afterward, astronomers began to discover more of these pulsating radio wave sources, so they were aptly named pulsars. Approximately 300 pulsars have been discovered since then. A pulsar is created when a star dies in a massive supernova explosion. When this occurs, a compacted core—called a neutron star— is left behind. A neutron star has an enormous magnetic field, which gives off large amounts of electromagnetic radiation, including radio waves. If the poles of the neutron star are aligned toward Earth, every time it rotates, its radio waves can be detected on Earth. Astronomers call this the lighthouse effect because the radiation emitted by a neutron star resembles a lighthouse and its rotating beacon of light.

A quasar, on the other hand, is a compact region that surrounds the black hole at the center of a galaxy. Quasars are the brightest objects in the universe, yet, notwithstanding their brightness, they are too distant from Earth to be observed by all but the most powerful telescopes. In fact, quasars are so bright that the galaxies they are located in cannot be seen due to their glares. There is a reason for their extreme

1. According to paragraph 1, which of the following is NOT true of pulsars?
   Ⓐ They are typically found by astronomers at the center of a galaxy.
   Ⓑ They do not occur very frequently anywhere in the universe.
   Ⓒ They are dissimilar from quasars in a variety of different ways.
   Ⓓ Scientists still do not know a great deal of information about them.

2. The word aligned in the passage is closest in meaning to
   Ⓐ moving
   Ⓑ perpendicular
   Ⓒ transposed
   Ⓓ lined up

3. Why does the author mention a lighthouse?
   Ⓐ To explain the method scientists use to find pulsars
   Ⓑ To prove that pulsars emit both light and radiation
   Ⓒ To compare how it and a pulsar behave similarly
   Ⓓ To explain exactly what causes pulsars to form

4. In paragraph 2, the author implies that pulsars
   Ⓐ can cause a star to explode in an enormous detonation
   Ⓑ are more common in nearby galaxies than in distant ones
   Ⓒ can send harmful radiation to solar systems throughout the galaxy
   Ⓓ were not actively being sought when they were discovered

5. According to paragraph 2, a pulsar is created because
   - Ⓐ a supernova causes a star located near it to explode
   - Ⓑ a neutron star is formed after a star violently erupts
   - Ⓒ a star that has expended its hydrogen begins releasing radio waves
   - Ⓓ the radiation from a dying star is suddenly released

6. The word it in the passage refers to
   - Ⓐ the energy
   - Ⓑ a black hole
   - Ⓒ an accretion disc
   - Ⓓ the material

7. The word luminous in the passage is closest in meaning to
   - Ⓐ large
   - Ⓑ radiant
   - Ⓒ powerful
   - Ⓓ radioactive

8. The author uses the Milky Way Galaxy as an example of
   - Ⓐ a galaxy with a super-massive central black hole
   - Ⓑ the galaxy in which the planet Earth is found
   - Ⓒ a galaxy that lacks a quasar in its center
   - Ⓓ the only galaxy known to support life forms

9. According to paragraph 4, which of the following is true of quasars?
   - Ⓐ They were created soon after the Big Bang took place.
   - Ⓑ They may be located within 300 light years of Earth.
   - Ⓒ They are sometimes responsible for pulsars that form.
   - Ⓓ They were the cause of the Big Bang that created the universe.

brightness. Because nothing—not even light—can escape from a black hole, it is theorized that the energy emitted by the material drawn into a black hole forms an accretion disc around it before the material enters the black hole. ■ Since the black hole at the center of a galaxy is believed to be of tremendous size, the accretion disc gives off massive amounts of energy, including radio and light waves, which makes it incredibly luminous. ■ There is an ongoing debate about whether or not quasars are stars; however, today, most astronomers generally accept that they are merely masses of matter that radiate light and surround the central black holes in galaxies. ■ Moreover, not every galaxy has a quasar because the material near the central black hole does not give off enough electromagnetic energy. ■ For instance, neither the Milky Way Galaxy, in which Earth's sun is found, nor the Andromeda Galaxy, a relatively close galaxy, has a quasar.

Pulsars and quasars further differ with respect to their ages. It is believed that quasars were formed soon after the Big Bang, which likely created the universe billions of years ago. Pulsars, however, may be created at any time. Quasars are also extremely distant from Earth—some are more than ten billion light years away—and are quickly moving away from Earth. As for the closest known pulsar to Earth, it is around 280 light years away.

One of the similarities between pulsars and quasars is that they can be detected in the same manner. Astronomers initially employed radio telescopes to find both since they emit radio waves; however, because of the bright light given off by quasars, an examination of the red shift in distant galaxies also shows if a quasar is present or not. The red shift is a product of the Doppler effect of light waves in which the color red is more prominent in the light waves. A greater amount of red light waves indicates that an object is moving away from Earth. The brightness of an object can also be determined by examining its

TOEFL iBT Reading

10. The word prominent in the passage is closest in meaning to

   (A) restricted
   (B) industrious
   (C) innovative
   (D) noticeable

11. According to paragraph 5, how can astronomers detect quasars?

   (A) They look for a red shift in the light waves of distant galaxies.
   (B) They focus on the Doppler shift in the light waves of various stars.
   (C) They search for radio waves that are given off by pulsars.
   (D) They use telescopes based on Earth to examine radio waves.

12. Look at the four squares [■] that indicate where the following sentence could be added to the passage.

   This also means that the quasar, since it surrounds the black hole, is huge.

   Where would the sentence best fit?

   Click on a square [■] to add the sentence to the passage.

red shift. Until the last few decades though, it was impossible actually to see any quasars. Only after large telescopes on Earth and the Hubble Space Telescope, which is in Earth orbit, were made have scientists been able to observe quasars in distant galaxies.

Glossary
pulsating: beating; throbbing
accretion disc: a disc-shaped structure that is formed of various materials and rotates a central body, such as a star or black hole
Big Bang: the event hypothesized to have occurred at the beginning of the universe

13. **Directions:** Select the appropriate statements from the answer choices and match them to the phenomenon to which they relate. TWO of the answer choices will NOT be used. *This question is worth 3 points.*

Pulsar
(Select 2)
-
-

Quasar
(Select 3)
-
-
-

Answer Choices

(A) Is located billions of light years away from Earth

(B) Is impossible to see except by special telescopes

(C) Is most prominent in the Andromeda Galaxy

(D) Forms around a black hole in the center of a galaxy

(E) Is rapidly moving closer to Earth's solar system

(F) Can be created when a supernova makes a neutron star

(G) Is one located fewer than 300 light years away from Earth

Drag your answer choices to the spaces where they belong.
To remove an answer choice, click on it. To review the passage, click on **View Text**.

TOEFL iBT Listening

Listening
Section Directions

This section measures your ability to understand conversations and lectures in English.

In this part, you will listen to 1 conversation and 1 lecture. You will hear the conversation or lecture only **one** time. After the conversation or lecture, you will answer some questions about it. The questions typically ask about the main idea and supporting details. Some questions ask about a speaker's purpose or attitude. Answer the questions based on what is stated or implied by the speakers.

You may take notes while you listen. You may use your notes to help you answer the questions. Your notes will **not** be scored.

If you need to change the volume while you listen, click on the **Volume** icon at the top of the screen.

In some questions, you will see this icon: 🎧 This means that you will hear, but not see, part of the question.

Some of the questions have special directions. These directions appear in a gray box on the screen.

Most questions are worth one point. If a question is worth more than one point, it will have special directions that indicate how many points you can receive.

You must answer each question. After you answer, click on **Next**. Then click on **OK** to confirm your answer and go on to the next question. After you click on **OK**, you cannot return to previous questions.

A clock at the top of the screen will show you how much time is remaining. The clock will not count down while you are listening. The clock will count down only while you are answering the questions.

Now you may begin the Listening section.

TOEFL iBT Listening

Conversation 1~5: Listen to part of a conversation between a student and a theater employee. 08-02

Actual Test 08

TOEFL iBT Listening

1. Why did the theater employee ask to speak with the student?
   - Ⓐ To complain about the price of one of Juliet's outfits
   - Ⓑ To discuss the costumes for an upcoming performance
   - Ⓒ To get some suggestions from the students
   - Ⓓ To encourage the student to increase the budget

2. What does the theater employee imply about Sandra?
   - Ⓐ She needs to improve her acting skills.
   - Ⓑ She cannot fit into her clothes.
   - Ⓒ She will not attend tomorrow's rehearsal.
   - Ⓓ She is playing the role of Juliet.

3. What can be inferred about the student?
   - Ⓐ He is the director of the play.
   - Ⓑ He works for the theater employee.
   - Ⓒ He will be acting the part of Romeo.
   - Ⓓ He is currently a sophomore.

4. According to the theater employee, what problems do they currently have?

   Click on 2 answers.
   - Ⓐ The students performing a Christopher Marlowe play took their costumes.
   - Ⓑ They need to adjust the sizes of some of the outfits the performers will wear.
   - Ⓒ They cannot find any of the fake swords that some of the actors need.
   - Ⓓ They have to get some outfits for Juliet to wear for some of her scenes.

5. Listen again to part of the conversation. Then answer the question.

   Why does the theater employee say this?
   - Ⓐ To warn the student
   - Ⓑ To attempt to make a joke
   - Ⓒ To give the student a choice
   - Ⓓ To make a comparison

Lecture 6~11: Listen to part of a lecture in a geology class.

Actual Test 08

TOEFL iBT Listening

6. What aspect of rift valleys does the professor mainly discuss?

   A Their sizes
   B Their relationship with volcanoes
   C Their formation
   D Their ages

7. According to the professor, how are rift valleys formed?

   A By the actions of tectonic forces
   B By erupting volcanoes
   C By forces in the planet's core
   D By the movements of Earth's oceans

8. Which of the following places are associated with rift valleys?

   Click on 2 answers.

   A Lake Baikal
   B The Pacific Ocean
   C Lake Erie
   D The Red Sea

9. What does the professor imply about the Mid-Atlantic Ridge?

   A It stretches all the way from North America to Europe.
   B Geologists are attempting to map its underwater rift valleys.
   C The plates that formed it are moving away from one another.
   D It has a large number of active undersea volcanoes.

10. Why does the professor mention Iceland?

    A To stress its proximity to North America and Europe
    B To explain its connection with volcanoes and rift valleys
    C To state that it has more active volcanoes than anywhere else
    D To encourage the students to find its location in the Mid-Atlantic Ridge

11. Listen again to part of the lecture. Then answer the question.

    Why does the professor say this?

    A To correct a student who misspoke
    B To identify a specific place in Africa
    C To point out something on a photograph
    D To clarify a statement he just made

Actual Test 09

TOEFL iBT Reading

Reading
Section Directions

This section measures your ability to understand academic passages in English.

In this part, you will read 1 passage and answer reading comprehension questions about the passage. Most questions are worth one point, but the last question is worth more than one point. The directions indicate how many points you may receive.

Some passages include a word or phrase that is underlined in blue. Click on the word or phrase to see a definition or an explanation.

When you want to move on to the next question, click on **Next**. You may skip questions and go back to them later. If you want to return to previous questions, click on **Back**. You can click on **Review** at any time and the review screen will show you which questions you have answered and which you have not answered. From this review screen, you may go directly to any question you have already seen in the Reading section.

You may now begin the Reading section. You will read 1 reading passage. You will have **20 minutes** to read the passage and answer the questions.

Click on **Continue** to go on.

TOEFL iBT Reading

1. The word pacifying in the passage is closest in meaning to
   - (A) assuaging
   - (B) amusing
   - (C) employing
   - (D) apprehending

2. According to paragraph 1, which of the following is true of the Roman people?
   - (A) As soon as the Roman Republic began, they were bribed with bread and circuses.
   - (B) They felt that the best leaders of Rome offered them the most entertainment.
   - (C) As time passed, fewer of them bothered to get involved in the world of politics.
   - (D) They enjoyed watching politicians and emperors compete against one another.

3. The word He in the passage refers to
   - (A) Juvenal
   - (B) Nero
   - (C) Caligula
   - (D) Domitian

4. In paragraph 2, which of the following can be inferred about the Roman people?
   - (A) Most of them read the works of Juvenal and other writers of the republic.
   - (B) Civic duty appealed to them more during the republic than during the empire.
   - (C) They preferred the reigns of Nero and Caligula to that of Domitian.
   - (D) They lost interest in military affairs after receiving food and entertainment.

The Roman Bread and Circus

Rome was the capital of the Roman Empire, so the people living in it wielded a tremendous amount of influence. During both the Roman Republic and the Roman Empire, politicians and emperors were cognizant of the loyalties of Rome's people and tried to maintain the favor of the populace to ensure stability and peace. For many years, this loyalty was willingly given by the people to Rome's best politicians, be they leaders of the republic or emperors. Nonetheless, over time, fewer citizens got involved in political discourse, and the process itself became corrupted. In order to achieve popular support, both politicians and emperors began staging extravagant forms of entertainment such as circuses and games. Additionally, the denizens of Rome were offered free food—mostly grain and oil—which was imported to keep them fed and complacent. These attempts at pacifying the people of Rome came to be known as "bread and circuses."

One notable feature of Rome was that it was a highly literate society which produced numerous outstanding orators, rhetoricians, and poets. Among the greatest was the poet Juvenal, who was born around 55 A.D. and died in 130 A.D. Sometime around 100 A.D., while writing a satirical work, Juvenal coined the phrase *panem et circenses*, which translates as "bread and circuses." Juvenal lived in the first century of the Roman Empire, during which time such emperors as Nero and Caligula had reigned with disastrous consequences and emperors such as Domitian had been highly corrupt. He also noted that the citizens of Rome seemed to have lost their sense of civic responsibility. During the Roman Republic, the citizens had exerted a powerful influence in determining who held the high offices in Rome. However, in the first century B.C., men such as Julius Caesar corrupted the republic and abandoned this process. They appealed to the

5. The author's description of Juvenal mentions all of the following EXCEPT:
   Ⓐ His feelings on the Roman people themselves
   Ⓑ The title of the satirical work that he wrote
   Ⓒ A famous phrase of his that described Roman life
   Ⓓ The period of Roman rule during which he lived

6. The word essential in the passage is closest in meaning to
   Ⓐ desired
   Ⓑ critical
   Ⓒ binding
   Ⓓ apparent

7. The word persecuted in the passage is closest in meaning to
   Ⓐ mistreated
   Ⓑ executed
   Ⓒ enslaved
   Ⓓ exiled

8. According to paragraph 3, which of the following is NOT true of the entertainment that the Romans staged in arenas?
   Ⓐ It often pitted humans in various situations against wild animals.
   Ⓑ It did not always involve fighting and was sometimes not violent at all.
   Ⓒ It occasionally required large numbers of people to fight one another.
   Ⓓ It featured people involved in athletic competitions such as running.

people's more basic desires—their urges to have full bellies and to be entertained. By providing free food and entertainment, men such as Julius Caesar were able to rule more easily as dictators.

The bread that was provided consisted both of grain, mostly corn, and cooking oil. Most of the grain came from North Africa, particularly from the fertile fields of Egypt. Control of the fields, the shipping ports, and the storage facilities near Rome was therefore essential to sustaining political control. Regarding the games, there were various types of entertainment that were held in huge arenas such as the Coliseum. Battles between gladiators were the most common events. Sometimes, hundreds of gladiators faced off against one another in mortal combat while other events featured gladiators fighting wild animals, including lions and tigers. The Coliseum was even occasionally flooded with water so that mock naval battles could be staged. Additionally, during the period when the Roman Empire persecuted Christians, unarmed believers were thrown to animals to be torn apart in front of thousands of cheering spectators. Not all of the games were so violent though; chariot races were an extremely popular form of entertainment as were displays of music, jugglers, exotic animals, and acrobats that were similar to modern circuses.

Feeding thousands of people and staging violent games was expensive, and few politicians could afford it. Those who did win favor with the people, such as Julius Caesar, frequently drove themselves to bankruptcy. Caligula bankrupted the entire empire because of the flamboyant displays he commonly held. Yet when it came either to winning votes or to currying the favor of the people, these men had no choice if they wanted to remain in power. This was especially true during the final centuries of the empire, when emperors rarely reigned for more than a few years. Ultimately, it did not matter how much

9. In paragraph 3, the author implies that some gladiators

   Ⓐ were able to win their freedom and no longer be slaves
   Ⓑ revolted against Rome and led some slave rebellions
   Ⓒ were killed in some of the battles that they fought in arenas
   Ⓓ were Christians who were treated poorly by the Romans

10. In paragraph 4, why does the author mention Julius Caesar?

    Ⓐ To describe his financial situation as a result of holding games
    Ⓑ To compare the way that he ruled Rome to that of Caligula
    Ⓒ To note that he was concerned about keeping the Romans satisfied
    Ⓓ To blame him partially for the eventual downfall of the Roman Empire

11. The word flamboyant in the passage is closest in meaning to

    Ⓐ exclusive
    Ⓑ violent
    Ⓒ showy
    Ⓓ extended

12. According to paragraph 4, the Roman Empire came to an end because

    Ⓐ the expenditures on bread and circuses bankrupted the state
    Ⓑ barbarians invaded the Roman Empire and then defeated it
    Ⓒ there was a lack of continuity due to too many emperors ruling
    Ⓓ men like Caligula made the empire a morally corrupt place

free food and entertainment were lavished upon the people. With barbarian hordes at the gates of Rome, all the bread and circuses in the world could not save the empire, and it was vanquished by invading tribes in 476.

Still, bread and circuses did not cease to exist following the downfall of Rome. Even today, politicians everywhere strive to appease the people they rule, and there is no easier way to ensure this than to keep their citizens well fed and entertained. As gladiatorial combat no longer takes place, politicians instead resort to offers of free education and health care as well as other measures to maintain the complacency of their people.

Glossary
rhetorician: a person skilled in the art of rhetoric; a public speaker
gladiator: a slave in Roman times who fought in arenas for the enjoyment of others
lavish: to bestow upon; to spend a great deal of money on a person or group

13. In paragraph 5, the author's description of modern-day politicians mentions which of the following?

   Ⓐ Their methods of keeping their people happy are based upon Roman ideas.
   Ⓑ They are unable to rule in the same manner that Roman politicians once did.
   Ⓒ They sometimes turn to violence in order to keep their people complacent.
   Ⓓ Their desires to maintain law and order in their lands are understandable.

14. **Directions:** An introductory sentence for a brief summary of the passage is provided below. Complete the summary by selecting the THREE answer choices that express the most important ideas of the passage. Some sentences do not belong because they express ideas that are not presented in the passage or are minor ideas in the passage. *This question is worth 2 points.*

   In order to ensure that the Roman people were complacent, various leaders of the Roman Republic and the Roman Empire resorted to pleasing them with food and entertainment.

   -
   -
   -

   Answer Choices

   Ⓐ There were numerous kinds of battles and other forms of amusement that were put on in the Roman Coliseum.

   Ⓑ By amusing the people, Rome's politicians and emperors were able to stop them from revolting against their rule.

   Ⓒ The people of Rome were given both free food, including grain and oil, and entertainment of various natures.

   Ⓓ Emperors such as Nero, Caligula, and Domitian were forced to bestow gifts upon the people due to the poor manner in which they ruled.

   Ⓔ The lessons of Roman bread and circuses have been learned by modern politicians, who offer them to their constituents.

   Ⓕ Satirists like Juvenal harshly criticized the people of Rome for being so easily bribed by the leaders of Rome.

Listening
Section Directions

This section measures your ability to understand conversations and lectures in English.

In this part, you will listen to 1 conversation and 1 lecture. You will hear the conversation or lecture only **one** time. After the conversation or lecture, you will answer some questions about it. The questions typically ask about the main idea and supporting details. Some questions ask about a speaker's purpose or attitude. Answer the questions based on what is stated or implied by the speakers.

You may take notes while you listen. You may use your notes to help you answer the questions. Your notes will **not** be scored.

If you need to change the volume while you listen, click on the **Volume** icon at the top of the screen.

In some questions, you will see this icon: 🎧 This means that you will hear, but not see, part of the question.

Some of the questions have special directions. These directions appear in a gray box on the screen.

Most questions are worth one point. If a question is worth more than one point, it will have special directions that indicate how many points you can receive.

You must answer each question. After you answer, click on **Next**. Then click on **OK** to confirm your answer and go on to the next question. After you click on **OK**, you cannot return to previous questions.

A clock at the top of the screen will show you how much time is remaining. The clock will not count down while you are listening. The clock will count down only while you are answering the questions.

Now you may begin the Listening section.

Conversation 1~5: Listen to part of a conversation between a student and a professor.

Actual Test 09

TOEFL iBT Listening

1. Why does the student visit the professor?
   - Ⓐ To ask him about a course that he needs to take
   - Ⓑ To find out how to apply for an academic scholarship
   - Ⓒ To go over his course of study with the professor
   - Ⓓ To tell the professor about his plans for the next semester

2. What does the student say about the program that he has been accepted to?
   - Ⓐ It is going to last for five months.
   - Ⓑ All of his tuition will be paid for.
   - Ⓒ He must speak fluent French for it.
   - Ⓓ He must leave the country in one month.

3. Why does the professor mention the Modern English Literature course?
   - Ⓐ To ask the student how his grades are in that class
   - Ⓑ To encourage the student to take it during the current semester
   - Ⓒ To remind the student that he cannot graduate without taking it
   - Ⓓ To let the student know that it will not be offered until the next year

4. What will the student probably do next?
   - Ⓐ Call the school in France
   - Ⓑ Look at a course catalog
   - Ⓒ Sign up for his classes
   - Ⓓ Complete the application form

5. Listen again to part of the conversation. Then answer the question.

   What can be inferred about the professor when he says this?
   - Ⓐ He was aware that the student had applied to a program.
   - Ⓑ He is disappointed to hear that the student was accepted.
   - Ⓒ He already received an email concerning the student.
   - Ⓓ He feels that the student deserved to be accepted.

Lecture 6~11: Listen to part of a lecture in a zoology class.

Actual Test 09

TOEFL iBT Listening

6. What is the lecture mainly about?
    - Ⓐ The reproductive tendencies of the albatross
    - Ⓑ How the albatross can soar so well
    - Ⓒ Where the albatross typically lives
    - Ⓓ The body structure of the albatross

7. Why does the professor explain the mating habits of the albatross?
    - Ⓐ To explain why the albatross is endangered in some regions
    - Ⓑ To respond to a question that was asked in a previous class
    - Ⓒ To compare them with the mating habits of other birds
    - Ⓓ To provide some background information on the albatross

8. Why does the professor tell the students to look in their textbooks?
    - Ⓐ So that they can follow along as she reads from the book
    - Ⓑ So that they can see some pictures of an albatross's insides
    - Ⓒ So that they can look at the shape of an albatross's wings
    - Ⓓ So that they can look at some photographs of an albatross colony

9. According to the professor, what allows an albatross to glide better than other birds?
    - Ⓐ Its large muscles
    - Ⓑ Its strong bones
    - Ⓒ Its oversized lungs
    - Ⓓ Its reduced weight

10. What is the shape of an albatross's wing?
    - Ⓐ It is straight.
    - Ⓑ It is curved.
    - Ⓒ It is triangular-shaped.
    - Ⓓ It is rectangular.

11. What will the professor probably do next?
    - Ⓐ Talk about a different way that the albatross can soar
    - Ⓑ Discuss the physics involved in how the albatross flies
    - Ⓒ Focus on the shape of the wings of the albatross
    - Ⓓ Have the students begin a discussion on the albatross

Actual Test 10

TOEFL iBT Reading

Reading
Section Directions

This section measures your ability to understand academic passages in English.

In this part, you will read 1 passage and answer reading comprehension questions about the passage. Most questions are worth one point, but the last question is worth more than one point. The directions indicate how many points you may receive.

Some passages include a word or phrase that is underlined in blue. Click on the word or phrase to see a definition or an explanation.

When you want to move on to the next question, click on **Next**. You may skip questions and go back to them later. If you want to return to previous questions, click on **Back**. You can click on **Review** at any time and the review screen will show you which questions you have answered and which you have not answered. From this review screen, you may go directly to any question you have already seen in the Reading section.

You may now begin the Reading section. You will read 1 reading passage. You will have **20 minutes** to read the passage and answer the questions.

Click on **Continue** to go on.

1. The word ultimate in the passage is closest in meaning to
   Ⓐ final
   Ⓑ explanatory
   Ⓒ definitive
   Ⓓ largest

2. The word them in the passage refers to
   Ⓐ many exquisite subway stations
   Ⓑ his dreams
   Ⓒ the Khrushchev and Brezhnev eras
   Ⓓ drab, lifeless buildings

3. In paragraph 1, the author of the passage implies that Joseph Stalin
   Ⓐ became the first leader of the Soviet Union after it was founded
   Ⓑ lived in one of the Seven Sisters for a short period of time
   Ⓒ was proud of his role in designing Moscow's subway system
   Ⓓ played a major role in the development of Soviet architecture

4. The word convergence in the passage is closest in meaning to
   Ⓐ union
   Ⓑ technique
   Ⓒ influence
   Ⓓ disparity

Soviet Classical Architecture

Amidst the Moscow landscape of dull, seemingly endless apartment complexes and modern glass and steel structures, there are seven tall, impressive buildings that rise against the skyline. These buildings, often called the Seven Sisters, are the ultimate example of the era of Soviet classical architecture. This period, which lasted from the 1930s to the 1950s, witnessed the building of numerous great works of Soviet architecture, including many exquisite subway stations. The grand style of Soviet classical architecture was due in part to the vision of Soviet leader Joseph Stalin, but, when he died, his dreams went with him. What followed during the Khrushchev and Brezhnev eras were drab, lifeless buildings that were a stark contrast to those constructed in the time before them.

While the Soviet Union was founded in the early 1920s, what is considered to be Soviet classical architecture did not appear until the 1930s. Previously, Russian architecture had been a convergence of Asian and European styles. But during the Soviet classical period, European influences, particularly Neoclassicism, became more pronounced. Some Soviet architects were influenced by contemporary styles such as Art Deco and Constructivism, yet diverging from the norm was not encouraged during the Stalin Era, so there were few buildings with these styles constructed. In fact, Stalin was so influential in the period during which he led the Soviet Union that many of the building plans required his seal of approval before they could be carried out.

During the pre-war period that ended in 1939, the major project in Moscow, the Soviet Union's capital, was the construction of its subway system. When finished, it became one of the greatest architectural feats of the Soviet period. Construction started in the early 1930s, and the first line was finished and promptly opened in 1935. Each station was designed lavishly and

5. Which of the sentences below best expresses the essential information in the highlighted sentence in the passage? *Incorrect* answer choices change the meaning in important ways or leave out essential information.

   (A) There were many buildings that were made in the Soviet Union during the time that Stalin was in charge.
   (B) Because of Stalin's influence, a lot of buildings were not made until he agreed to their designs.
   (C) There was no one in the Soviet Union who was more influential at any time than Stalin was.
   (D) Joseph Stalin often contributed to the designing of buildings when he was running the Soviet Union.

6. In paragraph 2, the author's description of Soviet classical architecture mentions all of the following EXCEPT:

   (A) Some of it was influenced by the Art Deco and Constructivist movements.
   (B) It stressed European styles much more than it did Asian styles.
   (C) It started during the 1920s and came to an end during the 1930s.
   (D) The opinion of Joseph Stalin was integral during this period of time.

7. The word ornate in the passage is closest in meaning to

   (A) original
   (B) elaborate
   (C) expensive
   (D) outdated

was unique from the other stations. Some were astounding in how ornate they were; frescoes, marble sculptures, massive chandeliers, and other ornaments adorned some stations, making the entire system one of the most beautiful in the world. When World War II began, the building of new lines and stations slowed but did not halt. Yet the war caused disruptions in the completing of other projects as maximum effort was focused on defeating the Germans.

As a general rule during Soviet times, apartment buildings were constructed according to which class of citizen was going to live in them. Party members, high-level bureaucrats, and high-ranking military officers lived in relative luxury while common citizens had to make do with what was available. When World War II ended in 1945, much of the western part of the Soviet Union lay in ruins. A lack of housing was the biggest issue for millions of people—no matter what their class—in the Soviet Union's bombed-out cities. Nevertheless, instead of focusing on building housing for those made homeless by the war, Stalin dreamed of making Moscow an architectural wonder, so he instructed his architects to begin the design and construction of projects such as the Seven Sisters. The erecting of those grandiose buildings started in 1947 and soon resulted in a lack of building materials for other projects. Undeterred, Stalin made sure that the project continued. When completed, the Seven Sisters added a great deal of residential floor space to Moscow. However, each square meter of floor space in them cost more than the equivalent amount of floor space in smaller, less luxurious buildings.

After Stalin died in 1953, many of his ambitious plans took a backseat to the realities of the devastation and destruction that still existed from World War II. An acute housing shortage remained the biggest problem, so endless blocks of similar-looking apartment buildings began swiftly rising

8. In paragraph 3, the author's description of the Moscow subway system mentions which of the following?

   Ⓐ Parts of it were destroyed by the Germans during fighting in World War II.
   Ⓑ Many of the stations were individually approved by Stalin before they opened.
   Ⓒ The first of Moscow's subway lines took more than five years to be built.
   Ⓓ There were many different types of decorations in each of the subway stations.

9. Why does the author mention Party members, high-level bureaucrats, and high-ranking military officers?

   Ⓐ To blame them for the lack of construction immediately after World War II
   Ⓑ To differentiate their housing from that of other people in the Soviet Union
   Ⓒ To declare that they suffered less than others after World War II ended
   Ⓓ To claim that they were responsible for the construction of the Seven Sisters

10. According to paragraph 4, the Soviet Union ran out of building materials because

    Ⓐ construction on one of Stalin's personal projects depleted the country's supplies
    Ⓑ the country was unable to get its factories to produce enough to meet demand
    Ⓒ some countries could not export material to the Soviets after the end of the war
    Ⓓ the country could not afford to purchase many of the required construction supplies

11. The word acute in the passage is closest in meaning to

    Ⓐ severe
    Ⓑ increasing
    Ⓒ discouraging
    Ⓓ problematic

above the landscape. The Khrushchev and Brezhnev eras were noted for their dullness, and this was reflected in the apartments and other buildings constructed during their times. Moreover, the majority of the buildings were shoddily built, and the architects who designed the individual units failed to take the realities of life into account. Most had a single room that doubled as a living room and bedroom, a small kitchen, and a tiny bathroom. Families, no matter how big they were, were forced to live in these cramped quarters. It was decades later, after the Soviet Union came to an end in 1991, that living conditions for most Russians improved even moderately.

Glossary
exquisite: beautiful; wonderful
adorn: to decorate; to put decorations or ornaments on something
grandiose: ostentatious; overdone

12. The word **Most** in the passage refers to
    - Ⓐ The majority of the buildings
    - Ⓑ The architects
    - Ⓒ The individual units
    - Ⓓ The realities of life

13. According to paragraph 5, which of the following is true of the Khrushchev and Brezhnev eras?
    - Ⓐ The designs for Moscow made by Stalin were followed during them.
    - Ⓑ The quality of the buildings that were built during them was low.
    - Ⓒ More apartments than office buildings were constructed during them.
    - Ⓓ They continued the tradition of making ornate buildings from the Stalin Era.

14. **Directions:** An introductory sentence for a brief summary of the passage is provided below. Complete the summary by selecting the THREE answer choices that express the most important ideas of the passage. Some sentences do not belong because they express ideas that are not presented in the passage or are minor ideas in the passage. *This question is worth 2 points.*

The period of Soviet classical architecture during the rule of Joseph Stalin saw many ornate buildings erected and was quite different from Soviet architecture after his death.

- •
- •
- •

Answer Choices

Ⓐ After Stalin's rule ended, most of the buildings that were erected were dull and had no special designs.

Ⓑ A large number of apartment buildings were made during the reigns of Khrushchev and Brezhnev.

Ⓒ Many of the subway stations that were built during Stalin's time were decorated rather elaborately.

Ⓓ Millions of people living in the Soviet Union were without housing when hostilities ceased in World War II.

Ⓔ The Seven Sisters were a personal project of Stalin and added a large amount of residential floor space in Moscow.

Ⓕ Soviet architects from the 1930s to 1950s focused more on European styles such as Neoclassicism.

Drag your answer choices to the spaces where they belong.
To remove an answer choice, click on it. To review the passage, click on **View Text**.

TOEFL iBT Listening

Listening
Section Directions

This section measures your ability to understand conversations and lectures in English.

In this part, you will listen to 1 conversation and 1 lecture. You will hear the conversation or lecture only **one** time. After the conversation or lecture, you will answer some questions about it. The questions typically ask about the main idea and supporting details. Some questions ask about a speaker's purpose or attitude. Answer the questions based on what is stated or implied by the speakers.

You may take notes while you listen. You may use your notes to help you answer the questions. Your notes will **not** be scored.

If you need to change the volume while you listen, click on the **Volume** icon at the top of the screen.

In some questions, you will see this icon: 🎧 This means that you will hear, but not see, part of the question.

Some of the questions have special directions. These directions appear in a gray box on the screen.

Most questions are worth one point. If a question is worth more than one point, it will have special directions that indicate how many points you can receive.

You must answer each question. After you answer, click on **Next**. Then click on **OK** to confirm your answer and go on to the next question. After you click on **OK**, you cannot return to previous questions.

A clock at the top of the screen will show you how much time is remaining. The clock will not count down while you are listening. The clock will count down only while you are answering the questions.

Now you may begin the Listening section.

TOEFL iBT Listening

Conversation 1~5: Listen to part of a conversation between a student and a Registrar's office employee. 10-02

Actual Test 10

TOEFL iBT Listening

1. Why does the student visit the Registrar's office?
   - (A) To request a copy of her transcript
   - (B) To apply to the school as a transfer student
   - (C) To find out how to take time off from school
   - (D) To describe a family problem she has

2. Why is the student unable to get her transcript that day?
   - (A) She does not have enough money to pay for it.
   - (B) The office is unable to process it that quickly.
   - (C) She is not currently enrolled as a student at the school.
   - (D) The office is getting ready to close for the day.

3. What can be inferred about the student's application to the school?
   - (A) It is due soon.
   - (B) It has been accepted.
   - (C) It is complete.
   - (D) It needs a letter of reference.

4. Listen again to part of the conversation. Then answer the question.

   What does the student imply when she says this?
   - (A) She enjoys her life as a student.
   - (B) She is not allowed to change her flight.
   - (C) She is presently attending classes.
   - (D) She lives far away from the school.

5. Listen again to part of the conversation. Then answer the question.

   What can be inferred about the employee when he says this?
   - (A) He is giving the student a discount.
   - (B) He has experience working at a bank.
   - (C) He is used to charging for various services.
   - (D) He expects to be paid immediately.

Lecture 6~11: Listen to part of a lecture in a sociology class.

Actual Test 10

TOEFL iBT Listening

6. What aspect of legal trials does the professor mainly discuss?

   (A) Jury trials
   (B) Lawyers
   (C) Jurors
   (D) Bench trials

7. Why does the professor mention bench trials?

   (A) To stress that they are held for criminal cases
   (B) To explain how they are different from jury trials
   (C) To state that they are less common than other trials
   (D) To focus on how those trials are structured

8. What does the professor say about jury impartiality?

   (A) It is something that both sides hope to avoid.
   (B) Most jurors are able to hide their personal biases.
   (C) Lawyers try to ensure it when selecting jurors.
   (D) It is the major disadvantage of bench trials.

9. What does the professor imply about jurors who are the same race as the defendant?

   (A) They tend to be the most unbiased jurors.
   (B) They are disliked by the defense team.
   (C) They may vote in favor of the defendant.
   (D) They frequently engage in jury nullification.

10. Why does the professor explain jury nullification?

    (A) To describe one drawback of jury trials
    (B) To mention her dislike of the O.J. Simpson verdict
    (C) To state that losing attorneys appeal cases affected by this
    (D) To prove that juries do not frequently use it

11. Listen again to part of the lecture. Then answer the question.

    What does the professor mean when she says this?

    (A) The student has asked an inappropriate question.
    (B) She wants the student to find the answer to his question.
    (C) She cannot answer the student's question for sure.
    (D) The answer to his question is in their textbook.

Compact Actual iBT

Reading & Listening

10 mini TOEFL® Tests

Answer Book

1

DARAKWON

Compact Actual iBT 1
Reading & Listening

Answer Book

DARAKWON

Actual Test 01

Reading Section   p.9

Answers

1. Ⓑ [Vocabulary Question]
2. Ⓓ [Factual Question]
3. Ⓐ [Vocabulary Question]
4. Ⓓ [Negative Factual Question]
5. Ⓑ [Factual Question]
6. Ⓒ [Rhetorical Purpose Question]
7. Ⓐ [Factual Question]
8. Ⓓ [Vocabulary Question]
9. Ⓓ [Reference Question]
10. Ⓑ [Inference Question]
11. Ⓑ [Factual Question]
12. 3rd [Insert Text Question]
13.

	THE INDIAN REBELLION OF 1857
Cause	Ⓑ, Ⓓ, Ⓕ
Effect	Ⓐ, Ⓖ

Translation

1857년 인도 반란 사건

1857년 인도 반란 사건은 인도에서 영국의 통치에 반대하여 일어난 사건이었다. 이는 1857년 5월에 시작되어 1년 이상이 지난 1858년에 끝이 났다. 이 사건은 수많은 원인으로 인해 일어났다. 영국이 동인도 회사를 통해 식민지였던 인도를 통치하던 방식, 영국인들이 인도인들을 영국군으로 편입시켰던 방식, 그리고 인도의 아대륙에 살고 있었던 사람들의 복잡한 사회적 및 종교적 성향이 그러한 원인에 포함되었다. 게다가, 인도의 구귀족 잔존 세력들은, 이들은 영국이 인도를 식민지화했을 때 지배력을 잃게 되었는데, 반란이 일어나는 동안 다시 권력을 획득하려고 했다. 반란은 결국 실패로 끝났지만, 영국인들이 반란을 진압할 당시, 수만 명의 사람들이 목숨을 잃었으며, 양측 모두 끔찍한 잔혹 행위를 저질렀고, 동인도 회사는 인도에서 사라지게 되었다.

1800년대 중반, 영국의 동인도 회사가 인도를 지배했다. 이러한 지위를 확보하기 위해, 동인도 회사는 영국 정부에 해마다 일정 금액을 지급하기로 했는데, 1800년대 중반에는 그 금액이 수십 만 파운드까지 증가했다. 이는 회사에 엄청난 부담이 되었는데, 이 금액을 계속해서 지급하고 세력 기반을 유지하기 위해서는 새로운 수입원이 필요했다. 동인도 회사는 주로 세금을 인상하고 남자 상속인 없이 사망한 인도의 귀족들로부터 토지를 빼앗음으로써 수입원을 마련했다. 아들이 없는 귀족은 상속인을 입양하는 것이 인도의 전통이었지만, 동인도 회사는 그러한 전통을 무시하고 토지를 몰수했다. 이로써 영국에 대한 반감이 일어났다. 법률 제도 또한 지나치게 영국인들에게만 유리하게 되어 있었고, 대부분의 인도인들은 영국인들과의 법적 분쟁에서 자신들이 승소할 가능성이 전혀 없다고 생각했다. 많은 인도인들은 영국인들이 인도의 문화를 억압하고 자신들의 땅으로부터 귀중한 보석, 금, 그리고 그 밖의 유용한 자원을 강탈하는 동시에, 대부분 힌두교도와 이슬람교도인 자신들을 크리스트교로 개종시키려 한다고 의심했다.

어느 정도까지는, 이러한 비난 중 많은 부분이 사실이었다. 종교는 중대한 문제였고, 이는 결국, 인도군에 의한 반란의 촉매제가 되었다. 인도에는 200,000명의 현지인들로 구성된 군인들이 40,000여명의 영국군에게 지원과 지시를 받고 있었는데, 이들은 다시 동인도 회사의 작전 통제를 받았다. '세포이'라고 불렸던 이들 현지인 군대는 힌두교도들과 이슬람교도들로 구성되어 있었으며 실제로 사회의 상위 계층에서 선발된 사람들이었다. 두 종교 집단의 군인들을 같은 부대에 배치함으로써 다소간의 긴장감이 발생했다. (결국, 이슬람교도들과 힌두교도들은 서로 잘 어울리지 못했다.) 낮은 급여와 승진의 지연 등 다른 문제들은 세포이들 사이의 반감을 더욱 심화시켰다. 1857년 봄 예상치 못한 사건으로부터 문제가 시작되었을 때, 이러한 모든 요인들은 극도로 악화되어 있었다.

그 해, 영국인들은 세포이에게 새로운 전장식 소총을 지급했다. 소총에 사용되는 총알과 화약은 종이에 싸여 있었는데, 이것이 약포가 되었다. 약포의 맨 윗부분을 개봉하려면 입으로 물어 뜯어야 했다. 그리고 나서, 소총의 입구에 화약을 넣은 다음, 소총 내부에 화약이 고정되도록 총알을 입구로 밀어 넣은 후에야 총이 발사될 수 있었다. 총알을 쉽게 밀어 넣을 수 있도록 종이와 총알에는 기름이 칠해졌다. 하지만, 영국인들이 약포의 기름칠에 동물의 기름을 사용한다는 소문이 돌았다. 돼지기름을 만지는 것은 이슬람교 세포이들에게 금기시되어 있었고, 쇠기름을 만지는 것은 힌두교 세포이들에게 금기시되어 있었다.

1857년 봄, 약포와 관련된 일련의 사건들은 1857년 5월 10일 메러트에서 세포이들이 영국군에 대항하여 일으킨 반란의 원인이 되었다. 그곳으로부터, 반란은 빠르게 확산되었고, 곧 인도 북부 대부분의 지역에서 영국의 통치에 반대하는 반란이 일어났다. 영국 군인들과 영국 시민들은 포위를 당했고, 포로가 되었으며, 몇몇 경우, 학살을 당하기도 했다. 영국인들은 같은 방법으로 보복을 했다. 수년 동안 격렬한 싸움이 있었지만, 반란은 진압되었다. 영국 정부는 반란의 책임을 주로 동인도 회사에 돌렸기 때문에, 동인도 회사는 해체되었고, 영국의 여왕이 — 민간 행정부를 통하여 — 직접 인도를 통치하게 되었다. 하지만, 반란의 근본적인 원인이 전적으로 해소된 것은 아니었다. 거의 100년이 지난 후, 인도인들은 또 다시 영국인 지배자들에 대항을 했고, 이번에는, 인도에서 영국인들을 몰아내는데 성공했다.

Listening Section   p.15

Answers

1. Ⓒ [Gist-Purpose Question]

2. Ⓑ [Understanding Organization Question]
3. Ⓑ [Understanding Attitude Question]
4. Ⓓ [Making Inferences Question]
5. Ⓐ [Understanding Function Question]
6. Ⓒ [Gist-Content Question]
7. Ⓓ [Understanding Organization Question]
8.

	Remiges	Rectrices
Ⓐ		X
Ⓑ	X	
Ⓒ		X
Ⓓ	X	

[Connecting Content Question]

9. Ⓐ [Detail Question]
10. Ⓑ [Making Inferences Question]
11. Ⓐ [Understanding Function Question]

Script

| 01-02 |

M Student: Good afternoon, Professor Wilson. You, uh, don't happen to be busy right now, do you? Would it be all right with you if I step in for a quick chat?

W Professor: No problem at all, David. Why don't you come on in and tell me about whatever's on your mind . . . ? You know, uh, I really hate to bring this up, but I didn't notice you in your customary seat this morning. What happened?

M: Ah, that's actually the reason why I came here to speak with you right now.

W: All right.

M: You see, um, I had a job interview to go to this morning. That's why I was unable to attend your class. So I wanted to come here to apologize to you in person about not going to class today. I'm so sorry about that. Up until now, I've had perfect attendance, and I really hate to ruin it.

W: Oh, that's all right. Don't worry about it, David. I know that you're a good student, so it's all right if you miss class, especially since you were at a job interview. So your absence today isn't going to count against you on your grade. All right?

M: Wow. I'm so relieved to hear that. I was totally afraid that my grade was going to suffer.

W: There's nothing to be concerned about, David. So, uh, is there anything else that I can do for you?

M: Er, yes, there is one more thing. ⁵About today's class, um . . . what exactly did we go over? I'm pretty sure that I can get the notes from one of my friends in the class. But were there any handouts or anything for us?

W: No, there weren't any handouts today.

M: There weren't? That's unusual.

W: Yeah, I suppose you're right about that.

M: How come there weren't any today?

W: Well, we actually had a guest speaker for most of today's class. His name was Terrance Witherspoon, and he gave a chat about music and how it can be used for therapy. It was a rather fascinating lecture.

M: Oh, no. I can't believe I missed it. I was really looking forward to hearing him speak. In fact, I've been waiting the entire semester for that lecture. I'm so depressed I missed it.

W: I thought you might say that. But . . .

M: But what?

W: Well, it's a good thing for you that Mr. Witherspoon permitted me to record the class. He doesn't normally allow that, but he made an exception in our case since this was a lecture that he gave at a school.

M: No way. You have a video recording of his speech? That's awesome.

W: It's not a video recording, but I did get an audio recording of him.

M: Cool. Can I borrow it?

W: Of course you can. That's why I made the recording. I'm going to put it on reserve in the library's audio-visual room as soon as I can. It should be available either late tonight or early tomorrow. It's a forty-minute talk, so make sure that you have enough time to hear the entire lecture. It will be well worth your time.

M: I can hardly wait. Thanks for the good news, Professor.

W: It's my pleasure.

Translation

M Student: 안녕하세요, Wilson 교수님. 교수님, 어, 지금 바쁘신 것은 아니죠, 그렇죠? 제가 들어가서 교수님과 잠시 말씀을 나누어도 될까요?

W Professor: 물론이에요, David. 들어와서 무슨 이야기든 해볼까요…? 알다시피, 음, 이런 문제를 꺼내기는 싫지만, 오늘 아침 항상 앉던 자리에서 보이지가 않더군요. 무슨 일이죠?

M: 아, 사실 지금 교수님과 말씀을 나누고자 하는 이유가 바로 그것 때문이에요.

W: 좋아요.

M: 그러니까, 음, 저는 오늘 아침 면접에 가야 했어요. 따라서 교수님의 수업에 출석할 수가 없었고요. 그래서 여기에 와서 오늘 수업에 출석하지 못한 것에 대해 직접 사과를 드리고자 했던 것이죠. 지금까지는, 모든 수업에 출석을 했는데, 이제 그렇지 않게 되어 정말 유감이에요.

W: 오, 괜찮아요. 걱정하지 말아요, David. 학생이 우수한 학생이라는 것을 알고 있기 때문에, 수업을 듣지 못했다고 해도 괜찮고, 특히 면접을 보기 위해서였다니, 더욱 괜찮아요. 그래서 오늘 결석한 것은 학생의 성적에 포함시키지 않겠어요. 됐나요?

M: 와. 말씀을 들으니 안심이 되네요. 성적이 깎이는 줄 알고 정말 걱정했거든요.

W: 걱정할 것 없어요, *David*. 그런데, 음, 내가 도와줄 일이 더 있나요?

M: 어, 네, 하나 더 있어요. 오늘 수업에 관한 것인데, 음… 배웠던 내용이 정확히 무엇이었나요? 필기 내용은 수업을 같이 듣는 친구들로부터 구할 수 있을 거에요. 하지만 나누어 주신 보충 자료나 다른 것들은 없었나요?

W: 아니오, 오늘은 보충 자료가 없었어요.

M: 없었다고요? 드문 경우군요.

W: 예, 그 점에 대해서는 학생 말이 맞는 것 같군요.

M: 오늘은 왜 아무 것도 없었나요?

W: 음, 사실 오늘 수업의 대부분은 초청 강연자의 수업으로 이루어졌어요. 그분의 성함은 *Terrance Witherspoon*인데, 음악에 대해서, 그리고 음악을 치료에 사용하는 방법에 대해서 말씀을 해주셨죠. 정말 재미있는 강의였어요.

M: 오, 이런. 그 수업을 놓치다니 믿을 수가 없네요. 정말로 그분의 강연을 기대하고 있었거든요. 사실, 저는 한 학기 내내 그 강의를 기다려왔어요. 강의를 듣지 못하다니 정말 힘이 빠지는군요.

W: 그렇게 말할 거라고 생각했어요. 하지만…

M: 하지만 무엇인가요?

W: 음, 학생에게 좋은 소식인데, *Witherspoon* 선생님께서 강의를 녹음해도 좋다고 허락해 주셨어요. 보통 녹음을 허락하지 않으시지만, 이번 강의는 학교에서 하는 수업이기 때문에 예외로 해주셨죠.

M: 믿기지 않아요. 교수님께서 그분의 강연이 녹화된 테이프를 갖고 계시다고요? 정말 잘 되었군요.

W: 영상 녹화는 아니었고, 그분의 음성을 녹음해 두었죠.

M: 멋지네요. 제가 그것을 대여할 수 있을까요?

W: 물론 대여할 수 있어요. 그렇게 하기 위해서 녹음을 해둔 것이죠. 최대한 빨리 도서관 시청각실에 테이프를 비치해 놓도록 할게요. 오늘 밤 늦게나 내일 이른 시간에 테이프를 빌릴 수 있을 거에요. 약 40분 가량의 강연이라서, 강의 전체를 듣기 위해서는 시간을 충분히 할애해야 할 거에요. 시간을 할애할 만한 충분한 가치가 있을 것이고요.

M: 정말 기다려지네요. 좋은 소식 주셔서 감사합니다, 교수님.

W: 천만에요.

Script

| 01-03 |

W Professor: Of all the animals on the planet, the only ones with feathers are birds. Feathers differ in shape, size, and color among various species. However, most birds use their feathers for the same reasons: to aid them in flight, to protect them from elements such as rain, to insulate their bodies and to provide them with warmth, and either to camouflage themselves so that they can hide from predators or to disguise hunting birds to hide them from their prey.

Birds have two main types of feathers. The first type covers the exterior of a bird's body. These are called vaned feathers. They have the distinctive shape that most people recognize as a feather. Take a look on page 243, and you'll see what I'm talking about . . . See the picture . . . ? There's a long, central shaft with many branches extending from it. Vaned feathers are used for flight. There are, by the way, different types of vaned feathers on the wings and tail. Ah, and vaned feathers also provide an outer protective layer and comprise the colorful parts of a bird's plumage.

¹⁰The second type of feather is the down feather. These are smaller than vaned feathers . . . see the picture in your book next to the vaned feather . . . They're also fluffy, which makes them softer. Down feathers are located beneath vaned feathers and provide most of the insulation for a bird's body.

But right now, I'd like to get back to vaned, or outer, feathers. All right . . . ? Now, as I speak, take a look at the pictures up here on the screen. I'm going to point out some of the different types of feathers. Would someone do me a favor and get the lights, please . . . ? Thank you . . . Now, most birds fly, and, in order to do so, they need special feathers. Flight feathers on the wings are called remiges. That's R-E-M-I-G-E-S. Most birds have three types of remiges. They are primaries, secondaries, and tertials. The primaries are closest to the outer tip of the wing . . . here . . . the secondaries are in the middle of the wing . . . see them here . . . and the tertials are right next to the body, uh . . . here. The primary remiges are the longest and narrowest feathers. Depending on the species, a bird has between nine and sixteen of them. Birds can manipulate them in several ways to aid them in flight. For instance, uh, primary remiges are mainly used to propel the bird by providing thrust and reducing drag. ¹¹Secondary remiges, meanwhile, are shorter and broader than primary remiges. Their main purpose is to provide lift for the wings. Lift, by the way, is the force that enables a bird to fly. While in flight, the secondary remiges remain closed while the primary remiges can rotate and move in different directions. As for tertials, they're not used for flight but serve to protect the other remiges when the bird's wings are folded.

On a bird's tail are more feathers used to control flight. These tail feathers are called rectrices. Here's a picture on the slide, um, along with the spelling as well . . . Okay, so, uh, rectrices are used mainly so that the bird can steer in flight as well as slow down, or brake, as it descends to land somewhere.

As for both rectrices and remiges, they have secondary purposes. As I just mentioned, birds' feathers are used to protect them from the weather and the cold. For that reason, vaned feathers are waterproof for the most part, so they can protect birds from the rain.

Now, many feathers are very colorful as you can clearly see here with these slides of a peacock . . . a parrot . . . a blue jay . . . ah, here's a hawk . . . and this colorful fellow is the beautiful bird of paradise. Color is primarily used for camouflage so that the bird can blend in with either the sky or the ground to remain hidden from predators or prey. Even the hawk, which, as you saw, was brown, uses color for camouflage. Its brown feathers help it blend into the background while it makes low passes as it hunts small land mammals.

Birds, as you would expect, take good care of their feathers. They groom themselves with their beaks on a daily basis. And bird feathers eventually get old and worn out. Thus they must be replaced. This is called molting. Depending on the species, molting can take place, oh, from one to three times a year. Basically, old feathers fall off, and new ones grow to replace them. Since feathers are so vital to birds, the molting period is a vulnerable time for them. Some birds molt all of their feathers at once, which lets them get their molting period over with quickly. But most species molt only a certain type of feather at one time. As a result, a bird may often have some new feathers and some feathers that are about to molt while it's missing feathers that have just molted.

Translation

W Professor: 지구상 모든 동물들 중에서, 깃털을 보유하고 있는 유일한 동물은 새입니다. 깃털은 종에 따라 그 형태와 크기, 그리고 색이 다양합니다. 하지만, 대부분의 새들은 동일한 이유들로 깃털을 사용합니다: 비행에 도움을 얻기 위해, 비와 같은 요인으로부터 보호를 받기 위해, 체온을 유지하고 몸을 따뜻하게 하기 위해, 그리고 포식자로부터 숨을 수 있도록 위장을 하거나 혹은 사냥하는 새들의 경우에는 먹이에게 들키지 않기 위한 위장의 수단으로서 사용됩니다.

새들의 깃털에는 두 가지 주요한 종류가 있습니다. 첫 번째 유형은 새의 몸통의 바깥 부분을 덮고 있는 깃털입니다. 이러한 깃털을 겉깃털이라고 합니다. 이러한 깃털은 대부분의 사람들이 깃털로 인식을 하는 특징적인 형태를 띠고 있습니다. 243페이지를 보시면, 제가 말씀드리고 있는 것을 볼 수 있을 것입니다… 사진이 보이죠…? 길이가 긴, 중앙에 있는 깃대에서 많은 가지들이 뻗어 나와 있습니다. 겉깃털은 비행에 사용됩니다. 그건 그렇고, 날개와 꼬리에 있는 겉깃털의 종류는 이와 다릅니다. 아, 또한 겉깃털은 외부 보호층이 되며 새의 깃털에서 색채를 띠고 있는 부분을 이룹니다.

두 번째 유형의 깃털은 솜깃털입니다. 이 깃털은 겉깃털보다 작습니다… 여러분 교재에서 겉깃털 다음에 있는 사진을 보세요… 이 깃털도 솜털 같아서, 솜깃털을 부드럽게 해줍니다. 솜깃털은 겉깃털 아래에 위치해 있으며 외부 온도를 차단해 주는 역할을 맡고 있습니다.

하지만 이제, 겉깃털의 이야기로 돌아가도록 하겠습니다. 괜찮겠죠…? 자, 제가 말씀드린 것처럼, 화면에 있는 사진을 보세요. 몇 가지 서로 다른 종류의 깃털들을 알려 드리겠습니다. 누가 불 좀 꺼주실래요…? 고마워요… 자, 대부분의 새들은 날아다니는데, 그렇게 하기 위해서는 특별한 깃털이 필요합니다. 날개에 있는 깃털을 날개깃이라고 부릅니다. 철자는 R-E-M-I-G-E-S입니다. 대부분의 새에게는 세 가지 종류의 날개깃이 있습니다. 첫째줄날개깃, 둘째줄날개깃, 그리고 셋째줄날개깃이 그것입니다. 첫째줄날개깃은 날개의 바깥쪽 끝 부분에서 가장 가까운 곳에 있습니다… 이 곳이죠. 둘째줄날개깃은 날개의 가운데 부분에 있습니다… 이곳을 보세요… 그리고 셋째줄날개깃은 몸통 바로 옆에 있습니다, 어… 이곳이지요. 첫째줄날개깃이 가장 길고 가장 폭이 좁은 깃털입니다. 종에 따라, 새들에게는 첫째줄날개깃이 9개 내지 6개 정도가 있습니다. 새들은 다양한 방법으로 이들을 조종하여, 비행에 도움을 얻습니다. 예를 들면, 어, 첫째줄날개깃은 추력을 공급하고 저항을 줄여 줌으로써 새가 추진력을 얻는데 주로 사용됩니다. 반면, 둘째줄날개깃은 첫째줄날개깃보다 길이가 짧고 폭이 넓습니다. 이것의 역할은 날개에 양력을 공급해 주는 것입니다. 그건 그렇고, 양력이란 새가 비행을 할 수 있도록 해주는 힘입니다. 비행을 하는 동안, 둘째줄날개깃은 접혀 있지만 첫째줄날개깃은 여러 방향으로 회전을 하거나 움직일 수 있습니다. 셋째줄날개깃에 대해 말하자면, 이 깃털은 비행에 사용되지는 않지만, 새의 날개가 접혀있을 때 다른 날개깃들을 보호해 주는 역할을 합니다.

새의 꼬리에는 비행을 조종하는데 사용되는 보다 많은 깃털들이 있습니다. 이러한 꼬리 깃털은 꽁지깃이라고 불립니다. 슬라이드에 사진이 있는데, 어, 철자도 같이 있군요… 좋습니다, 그러니까, 어, 꽁지깃은 새가 비행시 방향을 잡는데 사용될 뿐만 아니라 땅으로 하강할 때 속도를 늦추거나 제동을 거는데 주로 사용됩니다.

꽁지깃과 날개깃 모두에 있어서, 부수적인 역할들도 있습니다. 제가 방금 말했던 것처럼, 새의 깃털은 날씨와 추위로부터 새들을 보호하는데 사용됩니다. 이러한 이유로, 대부분의 겉깃털들에는 물이 새어 들지 않아서, 비로부터 새들을 보호해 줄 수 있습니다.

자, 공작새… 앵무새… 큰어치… 아, 여기에 매가 있군요… 그리고 이 화려한 색의 새는 극락조인데, 이들의 슬라이드에서 볼 수 있듯이, 많은 깃털들이 화려한 색채를 가지고 있습니다. 색은 새들이 포식자나 먹이로부터 몸을 숨길 수 있도록 하늘이나 지면에 섞이기 위한 위장용으로 주로 사용됩니다. 심지어 매의 경우도, 여러분들이 보았던 것처럼, 갈색을 띠고 있는데, 위장을 위해 이 색을 사용합니다. 매가 육지에 있는 작은 포유류를 공격하며 저공 비행을 할 때 갈색 깃털은 매가 지면에 섞이도록 도움을 줍니다.

여러분들이 생각하는 것처럼, 새들은 깃털을 잘 관리합니다. 이들은 매일 자신들의 부리로 직접 깃털을 다듬습니다. 결국 새의 깃털도 오래되어 닳아 해집니다. 그래서 새들은 깃털을 교체해야 합니다. 이것이 바로 털갈이입니다. 종에 따라서, 새들은, 오, 일년에 한 번에서 세 번 정도 털갈이를 합니다. 기본적으로, 오래된 깃털들이 빠지고, 새로운 깃털들이 이를 대신하기 위해 그 자리에서 자라납니다. 깃털은 새의 생존에 반드시 필요한 것이기 때문에, 털갈이 기간은 취약한 시기입니다. 몇몇 새들의 경우, 한 번에 모든 깃털이 빠져 버리는데, 이렇게 함으로써 털갈이의 기간을 빠르게 끝낼 수 있습니다. 하지만 대부분의 종들은 한 번에 한 종류의 깃털만 털갈이를 합니다. 그 결과, 빠진 지 얼마 되지 않은 깃털들은 털어내고 새로 난 깃털과 이제 막 빠지려는 깃털들을 가지고 있는 경우도 종종 있을 수 있습니다.

Actual Test 02

Reading Section p.21

Answers

1. C [Vocabulary Question]
2. C [Sentence Simplification Question]
3. A [Vocabulary Question]
4. B [Factual Question]
5. A [Negative Factual Question]
6. D [Rhetorical Purpose Question]
7. C [Reference Question]
8. C [Inference Question]
9. B [Factual Question]
10. C [Vocabulary Question]
11. D [Reference Question]
12. D [Factual Question]
13. A [Rhetorical Purpose Question]
14. C, D, F [Prose Summary Question]

Translation

컴퓨터의 발달

오늘날 컴퓨터는 텔레비전이나 전화기처럼 어느 곳에서나 찾아볼 수 있고, 최신 컴퓨터의 경우에는 휴대가 가능할 뿐만 아니라 실제로 사용자가 지구상 어느 곳에 있더라도 방대한 정보와 즐길 거리를 제공해 줄 수 있다. 최초의 컴퓨터는 그렇지가 못했는데, 최초의 컴퓨터는 계산 능력이 거의 없는, 엄청나게 거대한 기계일 뿐이었다. 현대적인 컴퓨터의 기원은 과거 수십 년 전에서 찾아볼 수 있는데, 그 시기가 확실히 결정지을 수 없을 정도로 그렇게 모호한 것은 아니다. 처음 프로그램 작동을 목적으로 개발된 기계가 이후 군사적 목적의 계산을 수행하기 위해 방 만한 크기로 변화되었고, 그후 1970년대에는 이것이 초기의 개인용 컴퓨터로 변화하였다. 이렇게 보잘것없는 시작으로부터, 현대적인 컴퓨터에는 무수히 많은 발전이 이루어졌다.

19세기 중반, 영국의 찰스 배비지는 천공 카드에 기반한 계산을 수행할 수 있는, 프로그램 실행용 기계에 대한 여러 가지 아이디어들을 떠올렸다. 그가 설계했던 어떤 기기도 성공적으로 완성되지는 않았지만, 그의 선구적인 아이디어와 업적으로 인하여 배비지는 종종 "현대 컴퓨터의 아버지"로 불리고 있다. 배비지와 달리, 이러한 기술을 현실화시켰던 사람은 미국인인 허만 홀러리스였다. 그는 천공 카드의 개념을 활용하여 이 카드로부터 정보를 계산해 낼 수 있는 기계를 개발했다. 홀러리스는 그 후 International Business Machines, 즉 IBM이라고 불리게 된 회사를 설립했다. 또한, 1930년대 후반, 영국의 수학자였던 앨런 튜링은 튜링 기계에 관한 이론을 발표했는데, 실현되지는 않았지만 실질적인 계산 능력을 갖췄던 이 기계는, 현재 사용되는 여러 컴퓨터들의 기능을 예견하고 있었다.

다른 여러 기술 분야들과 마찬가지로, 컴퓨터도 제 2차 세계 대전 중이었던 1940년대에 급속한 발전을 이루었다. 1941년, 독일의 기술자였던 콘래드 주세는 처음으로 앨런 튜링의 이론에 기반한 기계들을 만들어 냈다. 이 기계들은 최초의 현대적인 컴퓨터로서 널리 인정을 받고 있다. 주세는 제 2차 세계 대전 중 독일에서 일을 했기 때문에, 대부분의 그의 연구는, 유도 미사일 프로그램을 위한 컴퓨터 사용을 포함하여, 군사 분야와 관련이 있었다. 반면, 연합군 또한 전쟁 중에 컴퓨터를 이용했다. 이들은 중대한 두 가지 프로젝트에서 컴퓨터를 사용했다: 원자 폭탄의 개발이 목적이었던 미국의 맨해튼 프로젝트에서 계산 업무를 처리하기 위해, 그리고 독일군과 일본군이 서로 교신을 할 때 사용했던 암호를 해독하기 위해서였다. 컴퓨터로 인하여, 두 프로젝트의 복잡한 문제들을 해결하는데 필요한 시간이 단축되어, 전쟁이 보다 신속하게, 그리고 연합군측에 유리한 방향으로 끝날 수 있었다. 예를 들면, 앨런 튜링과 같은 사람들이 지휘했던 영국의 암호 해독가들은, 독일의 암호를 해독하기 위해 "봄브"라는 이름의 기계를 만들었다. 이는 진공관을 사용하여 수많은 계산들을 매우 짧은 시간 안에 처리할 수 있었던, 거대한 기계였다. 미국인들 역시 또 다른 거대한 진공관 컴퓨터를 제작하여 원자 폭탄을 위한 계산 업무를 처리했다.

이들 초기 컴퓨터에 있어서 주요한 문제는 그들의 엄청난 크기와 그들이 진공관에 의존하고 있다는 점이었는데, 진공관은 늘 고장이 나서 교체되어야만 했다. 하지만 1950년대, 트랜지스터가 진공관을 대체하기 시작했다. 이러한 발전으로 보다 작고 보다 신뢰할 수 있는 컴퓨터들이 생산되었다. 그 후 20년 동안, 컴퓨터는 지속적으로 크기가 축소되고 성능은 보다 강력해 졌다. 현대적인 개인용 컴퓨터의 탄생에 있어서 주요한 자극이 되었던 것은 바로 마이크로프로세서 칩의 발명이었다. 1960년대 후반 Intel에서 최초의 마이크로프로세서 칩을 개발하여, 1971년에 이를 판매했다. 작지만 성능이 우수한 이 장치로 인해 컴퓨터의 크기가 작아졌다. 처음에는 비쌌지만, 마이크로프로세서 칩의 가격은 곧 하락했고, 그 결과 현대적인 개인용 컴퓨터의 혁명이 시작되었다.

최초의 개인용 컴퓨터가 무엇인지에 대해서는 많은 논쟁이 있다. 1970년대 동안, 다수의 컴퓨터 기업들이 일부 측면에서 — 모든 측면에서는 아니지만 — 현대적인 컴퓨터의 특징을 가지고 있는 기계들을 개발해 냈다. 캘리포니아에 있는 Xerox PARC 연구소는 1973년에 화면, 키보드, 마우스, 그리고 하드 드라이브가 장착된 최초의 개인용 컴퓨터를 생산했다. 이것이 바로 제록스 알토였는데, 이 기계는, 그래픽 사용자 인터페이스를 활용한 개인 최초의 컴퓨터로서도 주목할 만하다. 이러한 인터페이스는 Microsoft사의 윈도우와 같은, 그 이후에 등장한 다양한 운영 체제의 기초가 되었다. 1980년대 중반에는, 사무실, 학교, 그리고 가정에서 개인용 컴퓨터가 사용되었다. 1990년대 인터넷의 폭발적인 보급으로, 전 세계 수백만 명의 사람들에게 개인용 컴퓨터의 소유와 사용은 일상적인 것이 되었다.

Listening Section

p.27

Answers

1. D [Gist-Content Question]
2. A [Detail Question]
3. B [Understanding Attitude Question]
4. D [Understanding Function Question]
5. B [Making Inferences Question]
6. B [Gist-Purpose Question]
7. C [Gist-Purpose Question]
8. B [Detail Question]
9. B [Understanding Function Question]
10. C [Making Inferences Question]
11. A [Understanding Attitude Question]

Script

| 02-02 |

W1 Student: Good afternoon. Um, I'm sorry to interrupt, but, uh, the woman in the front room told me that I should come back here and talk to you. You're Molly Jenkins, right?

W2 Student Activities Office Employee: That's me. And let me guess . . . You are here about forming some kind of student club. Am I right?

W1: Yes. Yes, you are.

W2: Great. In that case, why don't you have a seat right there and tell me all about the club that you're interested in starting up?

W1: Thanks . . . Okay, uh, you see, I'm hoping to start a film club here on campus.

W2: A film club? But we already have, uh . . . three of them I think. There's the science fiction film club, the blockbuster film club, and . . . uh, there's one more. But I can't come up with it off the top of my head.

W1: I believe that the third one is that group which shows films in the campus center every Wednesday night.

W2: Yeah, that's it. Thanks. Okay, I see that you're already aware of the fact that there are some other film clubs here at the school. So why don't you tell me how your club is going to be different from all of the other three?

W1: Of course. I'd be glad to do that. First, two of the film clubs focus exclusively on modern films. I mean, they only show films that go back to the 1980s or so. And the science fiction movie club just shows, uh, sci-fi films, which is something that I'm definitely not interested in.

W2: Uh-huh.

W1: The film club that I'm hoping to start up would focus exclusively on really old movies. I mean, we'd screen black and white movies. You know, stuff from the 1950s and earlier. And we'd even show movies from the Silent Movie Era. As far as I am aware, none of the other clubs have ever done that.

W2: ⁴Yes, I'm pretty sure that you're right about that.

W1: So, uh, what do you think of my idea?

W2: It's certainly novel. But what I think really isn't important. It's what the students at this school think that actually matters. Do you believe that you can get at least twenty students to join the club? That's the number of members you need to become an official club.

W1: Actually, I have a sign-up sheet right here. I've got thirty-nine names on it. Here you are . . .

W2: Well, that's impressive.

W1: Thank you.

W2: Well, look at that. You even got the students who signed up to include their student numbers so that we can verify they are attending classes this semester. You just made my job a lot easier. Thank you.

W1: So, um, does that mean we can become a club?

W2: ⁵If all of these names are legitimate, then yes. But I'll have to confirm the names first. If you can wait a bit, it should only take me ten minutes to do that. In the meantime, why don't you fill out these forms for me? That's the next step to becoming a club.

W1: Sounds good. Do you mind if I stay right here while I fill out the forms?

W2: Be my guest. Here's a pen if you need one.

Translation

W1 Student: 안녕하세요. 음, 방해해서 죄송하지만, 어, 프론트 룸의 여자분께서 제가 이곳에 다시 와서 선생님께 말씀을 드려야 한다고 하네요. 선생님 성함이 Molly Jenkins죠, 맞나요?

W2 Student Activities Office Employee: 제가 맞아요. 제 생각에는… 동아리를 만들기 위해서 이곳으로 온 것 같군요. 제 말이 맞죠?

W1: 네. 네, 맞아요.

W2: 잘 되었네요. 그렇다면, 그쪽에 앉아서 학생이 만들고 싶어하는 동아리에 대해 말을 해보는 것이 어떨까요?

W1: 감사합니다… 좋아요, 어, 그러니까, 저는 교내에서 영화 동아리를 시작해 보고 싶어요.

W2: 영화 동아리요? 하지만 우리 학교에는 이미, 어… 영화 동아리가 세 개나 있는데요. 공상 과학 영화 동아리, 블록버스터 영화 동아리, 그리고… 어, 그리고 하나 더 있어요. 하지만 생각이 날 듯 말 듯 하군요.

W1: 세 번째 동아리는 매주 수요일 밤 캠퍼스 센터에서 영화를 상영하는 동아리인 것 같아요.

W2: 예, 맞아요. 고마워요. 그래요, 학생은 이미 우리 학교에 다른 영화 동아리들이 있다는 사실을 알고 있는 것 같군요. 그렇다면 학생이 시작하려고 하는 동아리가 나머지 세 동아리와 어

W1: 물론이죠. 기꺼이 말씀해 드릴게요. 우선, 영화 동아리 중 두 개는 현대적인 영화에만 초점을 맞추고 있어요. 1980년대 정도까지의 영화들만을 상영을 하고 있죠. 그리고 공상 과학 영화 동아리에서는 단지, 어, 공상 과학 영화만을 상영하는데, 저는 그러한 영화에 전혀 관심이 없어요.

W2: 그렇군요.

W1: 제가 시작하고자 하는 영화 동아리는 정말로 오래된 영화들에만 초점을 맞출 거에요. 제 말은, 흑백 영화를 상영할 것이라는 점이죠. 그러니까, 1950년대와 그 이전의 영화들을요. 그리고 무성 영화 시대의 영화들도 상영하려고 해요. 제가 알기로는, 다른 동아리들 중에 그렇게 하고 있는 곳은 없어요.

W2: 네, 학생의 말이 분명히 맞아요.

W1: 그렇다면, 어, 제 생각에 대해 어떻게 생각하시나요?

W2: 정말로 참신하군요. 하지만 제 생각이 그렇게 중요한 것은 아니에요. 여기 학생들의 생각이 정말로 중요하죠. 그 동아리에 최소한 20명의 회원을 가입시킬 수 있을 것이라고 생각하나요? 공식적인 동아리가 되기 위해 필요한 최소한의 인원이 그 정도거든요.

W1: 실은, 가입 신청서를 가지고 왔어요. 여기에는 39명의 이름이 적혀 있어요. 받으세요…

W2: 와, 인상적이군요.

W1: 감사합니다.

W2: 음, 여기를 좀 봐요. 서명한 학생들이 이번 학기에 등록을 했는지 확인할 수 있도록 학생들의 학번도 적어 두었군요. 제 일을 훨씬 더 쉽게 해주었네요.

W1: 그렇다면, 음, 우리가 동아리가 될 수 있다는 뜻인가요?

W2: 이 이름들이 모두 적절한 것이라면, 그렇죠. 하지만 우선 이 이름들을 확인해 보아야 해요. 잠시 기다려 줄 수 있다면, 확인하는데 10분 정도만 걸릴 거에요. 그러는 동안, 이 양식들을 작성하는 것이 어떨까요? 동아리가 되기 위한 그 다음 단계죠.

W1: 좋아요. 여기에서 양식을 작성해도 되나요?

W2: 물론이에요. 필요하다면 이 펜을 사용하세요.

Script

| 02-03 |

W Professor: Continuing our discussion on natural phenomena associated with storms, it's only natural to talk about lightning and thunder. Lightning, of course, is a bright flash of light while thunder is the sound that's, um, produced by lightning. Right now, we need to cover the physics of both lightning and thunder.

Lightning is merely a form of electricity. It's primarily created in three places: storm clouds, volcanic ash clouds, and large dust storms. Storm clouds, as you can probably guess, are the most common sources for lightning of the three. Yes, David?

M Student: How common is lightning? I mean, we don't get it very often here. How about everywhere else?

W: Hmm . . . I have the number right here . . . Ah, yes, here it is. It's estimated that, at any given second, around 100 bolts of lightning strike somewhere on the Earth. So, as you can see, it's quite common.

Now, as for how lightning is created . . . well, that's still something of a mystery. The most probable theory is that of electrostatic induction. Let me explain that briefly. Within a storm cloud, there are strong updrafts and downdrafts of wind. These help separate oppositely charged particles of ice, snow, and water. Why these particles separate into positive and negative groups is still one of the mysteries of lightning formation though. Nevertheless, it's believed that, uh, when particles with opposite charges collide with one another, lightning results. Yet how exactly this happens is still unknown. What we do know is that positively charged particles are lighter, so they rise with the updrafts. Meanwhile, negatively charged particles are heavier, so they—as you can surely guess—fall with the downdrafts.

What happens is that, at some point, a massive buildup of positively charged particles is at the top of the storm cloud while a similarly massive buildup of negatively charged particles is at the bottom of the cloud. Between these two areas lies a strong electric field. This field provides a, uh . . . a pathway, or conduit, from the top of the cloud to its bottom. Simultaneously, there's an electrical charge on the ground below the cloud. As the cloud moves, the charge on the ground follows it. This ground charge is positive since it's in opposition to the negatively charged bottom of the cloud.

[11]While this is happening, the air around the cloud becomes extremely ionized. **This means . . . well, it would take a long time to explain ionization, and we're running out of it.** But, for the purposes of our study of lightning, be aware that ionization makes it easier for lightning to occur. All right, so here's what we have so far . . . The air is ionized. There are positive charges at the top of the cloud and on the ground. And the bottom of the cloud is negatively charged. Got it . . . ? Good.

What occurs next is the creation of step leaders. These are discharges of ionized air. Step leaders aren't always noticeable. They can be small or very long, and they can branch out in many directions within the cloud. What they do is stretch toward the ground or other parts of the cloud. Then, a huge discharge occurs. This happens either within the cloud or between the cloud and the ground. This is lightning as we normally see it. Oh, and the same basic principles apply to lightning formation within volcanic ash clouds and dust storms except that the separation of charges is created by dust particles rather than ice, snow, or water.

M: Professor Devers, I have another question if you don't mind . . . I read somewhere that lightning can travel from the ground to a cloud. Is that true?

W: It sure is. Lightning can flow from the ground to a cloud if the step leaders originate at ground level and move toward the bottom of a cloud. However, that's much rarer than cloud-to-ground strikes.

Okay, as for thunder . . . It's the noise produced

by the rapid ionization of the air. It's created by the expansion of the air due to changes in both pressure and temperature when lightning discharges. Just so you know, the average temperature of a lightning bolt is around 20,000 degrees Celsius, and it can get up to around 30,000 degrees Celsius in some cases. That, by way of comparison, is hotter than the sun's surface, which is only around 5,500 degrees Celsius. Anyway, uh, the lightning superheats the air and causes a shock wave to form as the heated air expands into the surrounding cooler air. When the shock wave expands the air, sound is produced. That's thunder. Now, as you should already know, sound travels much slower than light. That's why you see the lightning first and then hear the thunder. So, um, if you see lightning and almost immediately hear thunder, be aware that the strike was close. Okay. In our remaining time, uh, let's look at some different types of lightning, shall we?

Translation

W Professor: 폭풍과 관련된 자연 현상에 대한 논의를 계속하고 있기 때문에, 번개와 천둥에 대해서 이야기를 하는 것은 당연한 일입니다. 물론, 번개는 밝은 빛의 섬광이며, 반면 천둥은, 음, 번개에 의해 생겨나는 소리입니다. 지금부터는, 번개와 천둥에 관한 물리학을 다루어야 할 것 같군요.

번개는 단지 전기의 한 형태일 뿐입니다. 주로 세 곳에서 발생하죠: 먹구름, 화산재 구름, 그리고 거대한 모래 폭풍이 그러한 곳입니다. 먹구름은, 여러분들이 추측할 수 있듯이, 셋 중에서 번개가 가장 흔하게 발생하는 곳입니다. 네, *David*?

M Student: 번개는 얼마나 흔히 발생하나요? 제 말은, 여기서 번개를 그렇게 자주 볼 수가 없는 것 같아서요. 다른 곳들은 어떤가요?

W: 흠… 여기에 그 수치가 있는데… 아, 네, 여기에 있군요. 초당 약 100볼트의 번개가 지구상의 어딘가를 치고 있다고 추정됩니다. 그러므로, 여러분도 알다시피, 번개는 상당히 흔한 것이죠.

자, 번개가 어떻게 만들어 지는지에 대해 이야기해 보면… 음, 이는 여전히 미스터리로 남아 있습니다. 가장 그럴듯한 이론은 정전기 유도 이론입니다. 간단하게 설명을 하도록 하죠. 먹구름 내부에는, 강력한 상승 기류와 강력한 하강 기류가 존재합니다. 이러한 현상은 얼음, 눈, 그리고 물 입자들로 하여금 극에 따라 서로 분리되도록 합니다. 왜 이러한 입자들이 음극과 양극으로 분리되는지는 번개 생성에 관한 미스터리 중 하나입니다. 그럼에도 불구하고, 어, 서로 다른 극을 지닌 입자들이 충돌하여 번개가 생성된다고 생각되고 있습니다. 하지만 정확히 어떻게 이러한 현상이 발생하는지는 여전히 알려져 있지 않습니다. 우리가 알고 있는 것은, 양극을 띤 입자들이 더 가볍기 때문에, 이들이 상승 기류와 함께 떠오른다는 점입니다. 반면에, 음극을 띤 입자들은 더 무겁기 때문에, 이 입자들은 — 여러분들이 추측할 수 있는 것처럼 — 하강 기류와 함께 아래로 내려갑니다.

그래서, 어떤 시점에 이르게 되면, 양극을 띤 상당한 양의 입자가 먹구름의 맨 위에 쌓이는 동안, 이와 비슷한 양의 음극 입자들이 구름의 가장 아래쪽에 쌓이게 됩니다. 이 두 부분 사이에서는 강력한 전자기장이 형성됩니다. 이러한 전자기장은, 어… 구름의 윗부분으로부터 아랫부분까지의 경로, 즉 전선관이 됩니다. 이와 동시에, 구름 아래의 지면에서 전기적인 충전이 발생합니다. 구름이 움직임에 따라, 지면의 전하는 구름을 따라갑니다. 지면의 전하는 구름 아랫층의 음극에 반대되기 때문에 양극을 띠고 있습니다.

이러한 현상이 발생하는 동안, 구름 주위의 대기는 극도로 이온화됩니다. 이것의 의미는… 그러니까, 이온화를 설명하기 위해서는 오랜 시간이 필요하기 때문에, 이에 대해서는 다루지 않겠습니다. 하지만, 번개에 대한 공부의 목적에 국한한다면, 이 온화가 번개의 발생을 보다 쉽게 만들어 준다는 점은 알아 두십시오. 좋아요, 그렇다면 우리가 지금까지 이야기한 것은 다음과 같습니다… 대기가 이온화됩니다. 구름의 윗부분과 지면이 양극을 띱니다. 그리고 구름의 아랫부분은 음극을 띱니다. 이해하셨나요…? 좋습니다.

다음으로 일어나는 현상은 선행 방전의 생성입니다. 이는 이 온화된 대기가 방전된 것입니다. 선행 방전이 항상 관측 가능한 것은 아닙니다. 작을 수도 있고 매우 길 수도 있으며 구름 내에서 여러 방향으로 뻗어나갈 수도 있습니다. 이들이 하는 일은 지면을 향해, 혹은 구름의 다른 부분을 향해 뻗어나가는 것입니다. 그런 다음, 대규모의 방전이 발생합니다. 이러한 현상은 구름의 내부나 구름과 지면 사이에서 발생합니다. 이것이 우리가 보통 보게 되는 번개입니다. 오, 그리고 얼음, 눈, 또는 물 입자가 아닌, 먼지 입자에 의해 전하의 분리 현상이 발생한다는 사실을 제외하면, 화산재 구름과 모래 폭풍 내부에서 발생하는 번개에도 동일한 원리가 적용됩니다.

M: *Devers* 교수님, 괜찮으시다면 질문이 하나 더 있는데요… 번개가 지면으로부터 구름으로 이동할 수도 있다는 내용을 어디선가 읽어본 적이 있습니다. 사실인가요?

W: 물론 사실입니다. 만약 선행 방전이 지면에서 발생하여 구름의 아랫부분으로 이동한다면 지면에서 구름 쪽으로 번개가 칠 수도 있습니다. 하지만 구름에서 지면으로 향하는 번개에 비하면, 훨씬 더 드문 경우죠.

좋습니다, 천둥에 대해 이야기하자면… 이는 대기가 빠르게 이온화됨으로써 생성되는 소리입니다. 번개가 방전될 때의 압력 및 온도의 변화로 대기가 팽창하며 천둥이 발생하게 됩니다. 여러분들이 알고 있는 것처럼, 번갯불의 평균 온도는 약 섭씨 20,000도로, 몇몇 경우에는 섭씨 30,000도까지 올라갈 수 있습니다. 비교를 해보면, 이는 태양 표면보다도 더 뜨거운 것인데, 태양 표면의 온도는 섭씨 5,500도 정도입니다. 어쨌든, 어, 번개는 대기를 과열시키는데, 가열된 대기는 보다 더 차가운 주변의 대기 쪽으로 팽창해 나가면서 충격파를 형성시킵니다. 충격파가 대기를 팽창시킬 때, 소리가 생성됩니다. 이것이 바로 천둥입니다. 자, 여러분들이 이미 알고 있는 것처럼, 소리는 빛보다 훨씬 느린 속도로 이동합니다. 번개를 먼저 본 다음 천둥 소리를 듣게 되는 이유인 것이죠. 자, 음, 만일 여러분들이 번개를 보고 곧바로 천둥 소리를 들었다면, 번개가 가까운 곳에 있다는 점을 명심하십시오. 좋습니다. 남은 시간에는, 어, 몇 가지 다른 종류의 번개에 대해서 알아보도록 하겠습니다, 그럴까요?

Actual Test 03

Reading Section   p.33

Answers

1. Ⓐ [Vocabulary Question]
2. Ⓒ [Negative Factual Question]
3. Ⓒ [Reference Question]
4. Ⓑ [Factual Question]
5. Ⓓ [Vocabulary Question]
6. Ⓓ [Vocabulary Question]
7. Ⓐ [Sentence Simplification Question]
8. Ⓒ [Factual Questionn]
9. Ⓒ [Rhetorical Purpose Question]
10. Ⓑ [Vocabulary Question]
11. Ⓓ [Inference Question]
12. Ⓑ [Factual Question]
13.

DATING METHOD	
Carbon-14 Dating Method	Ⓑ, Ⓓ, Ⓕ
Potassium-Argon Dating Method	Ⓒ, Ⓖ

[Fill in a Table Question]

Translation

역사적 유물들의 연대 측정

어떠한 물체가 매우 오래되면, 이것이 만들어진 정확한 시기를 알아내는 것이 어려운 경우가 종종 있다. 몇몇 경우, 그 제작에 사용되었던 재료나 스타일뿐만 아니라 물건에 적혀 있는 문자나 표식과 같은 특정한 단서들이 물체의 제작 연대를 알려줄 수 있는 정보를 나타내 줄 수도 있다. 하지만, 이들 방법들이 수많은 오래된 물건들의 제작 연대를 항상 확인시켜 줄 수 있는 것은 아니다. 따라서, 전문가들은, 탄소 14 연대 측정법과 칼륨-아르곤 연대 측정법을 포함한, 다양한 테스트들을 개발해서 물체의 화학적인 구성 성분을 검사함으로써 그 연대를 알아내고 있다. 두 연대 측정법 모두 일부 측면에서는 한계를 보이지만, 이 방법들로 인하여 학자들은 과거 인류에 대해 보다 많이 알게 되었다.

탄소에는 세 가지 주요한 동위 원소가 있다: 탄소 12, 탄소 13, 탄소 14가 그것이다. 처음 두 동위 원소는 안정적이지만, 탄소 14는 결국 분해되어, 시간이 흐르면서, 질소 14로 변하게 된다. 우주선이 대기 상층부에 부딪쳐 탄소와 산소가 혼합되어 이산화탄소가 생성될 때 탄소 14가 만들어 진다. 이는 식물에 의하여 흡수되는데, 식물은 또 다시 동물과 인간에 의해 섭취된다. 식물, 동물, 그리고 인간이 죽으면, 그 안에 있는 탄소 14 동위 원소는 일정한 속도로 분해되기 시작한다. 과학자들은 탄소 14의 반감기가 5,730년이라는 사실을 알고 있기 때문에, 대기 내에 존재하는 안정적인 탄소 12의 수준과 어떤 물건에 함유된 탄소 14의 분해 속도를 비교할 수 있고, 이를 통해 특정한 물체의 연대를 측정할 수 있다.

그럼에도 불구하고, 탄소 14 연대 측정법에는 몇 가지 한계가 있다. 예를 들면, 나무, 석탄, 해양 생물의 껍질, 동물 및 인간의 뼈, 그리고 토탄과 같은 자연계의 유기 물질에만 사용될 수 있다. 이 연대 측정법의 또 다른 문제는 대기에 존재했던 탄소 14와 탄소 12의 양에 대한 역사적인 기록이 존재하지 않는다는 점이다. 우주선의 강도 및 화산 활동의 변화로, 과거 대기 탄소량에 변동이 생겼을 수도 있기 때문에, 정확한 연대를 측정하는 것은 어렵다. 게다가, 다양한 종의 식물들은 서로 다른 양의 탄소 14를 흡수하는데, 이 때문에 탄소 14를 이용하여 식물의 연대를 측정하는 것은, 식물을 섭취한 동물과 인간들은 물론이거니와, 부정확하게 된다. 어떤 물체가 발견된 지역의 환경적 요인들 또한 정확한 측정에 있어서 중요한 역할을 한다. 특히 화산 활동이 많은 지역에서는 인근에 탄소의 양이 많기 때문에, 탄소 14 연대 측정이 잘못될 수도 있다. 이러한 모든 요인들로 인하여 연대 측정법으로 특정 연도를 측정해 낼 수는 없지만, 다만 40년이라는 오차 범위로는 측정이 가능하다.

탄소 14 연대 측정법의 또 다른 한계는 60,000년 안쪽의 물체에 대해서만 이 방법을 쓸 수 있다는 점인데, 그 이유는 그보다 더 오래된 물건에 함유된 탄소 14가 거의 모두 분해되어 있기 때문이다. 이로 인하여 정말로 오래된 물품의 연대 측정은 사실상 불가능하다. 이 때문에, 학자들은 또 다른 방법에 의지하고 있다: 칼륨-아르곤 연대 측정법이 그것이다. 이 연대 측정법은 100,000년 이상 오래된 화성암의 연대를 측정하는데 유용하다. 이 방법은 화성암을 분석하는데, 그 이유는 용융된 암석이 특정 온도에 다다르면 그 안에 있는 아르곤 기체가 모두 방출되기 때문이다. 그 후, 화산에서 분출된 용암이 빠르게 식어서 굳어지면, 암석은 아르곤이 침투할 수 없는 상태가 된다. 따라서, 대기 중의 새로운 아르곤이 암석으로 스며들 수 없게 된다. 대부분의 암석에는 소량의 칼륨 40이 들어 있는데, 이는 결국 분해되어 아르곤 40이 된다. 학자들은 칼륨 40 동위 원소의 반감기를 알고 있고, 암석이 냉각된 후 새로운 아르곤이 스며들 수 없다는 사실을 알고 있기 때문에, 암석 내의 칼륨 40과 아르곤 40을 비교함으로써 암석의 연대를 대략적으로 추정할 수 있다.

칼륨-아르곤 연대 측정법은 탄소 14 연대 측정법만큼 정확하지는 않지만, 여전히 유용한 방법이다. 인간과 동물의 잔해와 같은 물체가 발견되는 지층의 암석의 연대를 측정함으로써, 학자들은 보다 확실한 암석의 연대를 추정할 수 있으며, 더 나아가, 다른 물체들의 연대도 추정할 수 있다. 칼륨-아르곤 연대 측정법의 주요한 한계는 화산 활동이 있었던 지역에서 발견되는 물체에 대해서만 연대 측정이 가능하다는 점이다. 하지만, 칼륨-아르곤 연대 측정법을 사용하여 40억 년 이상 오래된 암석의 연대를 측정할 수 있는데, 이는 거의 지구 자체만큼이나 오래된 것이다.

Listening Section

p.39

Answers

1. B [Gist-Content Question]
2. A [Gist-Content Question]
3. A, C [Detail Question]
4. C [Making Inferences Question]
5. A [Understanding Function Question]
6. B [Gist-Content Question]
7. D [Understanding Organization Question]
8. A [Gist-Purpose Question]
9. B, C [Detail Question]
10. C [Understanding Attitude Question]
11. B [Understanding Function Question]

Script

| 03-02 |

M Professor: Ah, Melissa. Thank you for dropping by before I leave for the day. I assume that you got my voice message, right?

W Student: Yes, sir. I did. It sounded sort of urgent when I heard it, so I came here straight from the library as soon as I got the message.

M: Oh, I see . . . Um, I hope that I didn't interrupt your studies.

W: Not really. I was mostly just hanging out with a couple of my friends there. I can always go back and meet them after we're done anyway. So, uh, what do you need to see me about? Is there a problem?

M: There may very well be one.

W: Oh . . . I don't like the sound of that. Did I mess up on a homework assignment or something?

M: Homework? No. Your homework is totally fine. This possible problem has to do with your upcoming schedule. You see, I was going over the list of classes that you gave me that you're considering taking next semester . . .

W: Yes? And?

M: Well, I'm curious why you are going to enroll in Advanced Microeconomics. According to your transcript, you've only taken Basic Microeconomics. ⁵Do you really think that you're qualified to take an advanced class in microeconomics? I mean, I realize that you are a junior and that this is a junior-level class, but you simply don't have the prerequisites for it. According to the student catalog, you should have at least already taken Intermediate Microeconomics, but I don't see that class listed anywhere on your transcript.

W: You don't? But I took that course last summer.

M: Not according to this transcript you didn't.

W: That's odd. I took the course at Western University in the summer, and the secretary in the Economics Department here told me that the course would transfer.

M: But, uh, did you actually go ahead and fill out the paperwork to get the class transferred so that you'd get credit for it?

W: Paperwork? What paperwork?

M: Melissa, any class that you take at another school doesn't automatically get transferred here. You have to fill out some forms before it gets approved.

W: Oh . . . I see. So, uh, what do I need to do?

M: All right. It's actually not that complicated. Do you have a copy of your transcript from Western University?

W: Not with me, but I've got a copy back at my dormitory.

M: Good. You need to go back and get that transcript. Then, take it to the Economics Department and ask the secretary there for a course transfer form. Fill it out, and be sure to give her a copy of that transcript with the economics course on it, too.

W: That's it?

M: Well, that's all you have to do. After the paperwork gets filed, a committee of three Economics professors will either approve or disapprove the class for transfer credit here. It should take just a few days.

W: You mean that they might not let me transfer the credits? That would be awful.

M: It happens sometimes, but, in your case, I wouldn't be too worried. We have a good relationship with Western University, so almost all of their classes get approved for transfer here. If that happens, then you'll be allowed to take the advanced class that you're interested in.

W: Okay. Thanks. I'll get on it right away then.

Translation

M Professor: 아, Melissa. 퇴근 시간 전에 들려줘서 고맙네요. 내가 남긴 음성 메시지를 들은 것 같군요, 그렇죠?

W Student: 네, 교수님. 들었어요. 제가 듣기에는 긴급한 사안이 었던 것 같아서, 메시지를 확인하자마자 도서관에서 바로 이리로 왔어요.

M: 오, 그랬군요… 음, 학생의 공부에 방해가 되지 않았기를 바라요.

W: 방해가 된 것은 아니었어요. 단지 그곳에서 친구들하고 시간을 보내고 있었을 뿐이었죠. 교수님과 말씀을 나눈 다음 다시 가서 친구들을 만나면 되니까요. 그런데, 어, 어떤 일 때문에 저를 만나고자 하신 건가요? 무슨 문제라도 있나요?

M: 문제가 하나 있는 것 같군요.

W: 오… 그런 말씀을 들으니 걱정이 되네요. 제가 숙제 같은 것을 잘 하지 못했나요?

M: 숙제라고요? 아니에요. 학생의 숙제는 정말로 훌륭했어요. 문제의 소지가 있는 것은 학생의 다음 학기 시간표와 관련이 있어요. 그러니까, 나는 학생이 제출한, 다음 학기에 수강하고자 하는 과목의 목록을 살펴보고 있었는데…

W: 네? 그런데요?

M: 음, 학생이 왜 고급 미시경제학 수업을 신청을 하려는지 궁금하네요. 성적증명서를 보면, 학생은 초급 미시경제학 과목만 수강했더군요. 본인이 고급 과정의 미시경제학 수업을 들을 준비가 되어있다고 생각하나요? 내 말은, 학생이 3학년이기 때문에 3학년 과정의 수업을 선택한 것이라고 생각하지만, 학생은 이 과목을 수강하는데 필요한 필수 과목을 수강하지 않았어요. 학생 요람에 따르면, 학생은 우선 중급 미시경제학 수업을 수강했어야 하는데, 학생의 성적증명서 어디에서도 그 과목을 찾아볼 수가 없네요.

W: 없다고요? 하지만 저는 지난 여름 학기에 수강을 했는걸요.

M: 이 성적증명서에 의하면 그렇지 않아요.

W: 이상하네요. 저는 여름 학기 때 Western 대학교에서 그 과목을 수강했고, 그 학교 경제학과장님께서는 그 과목을 수강한 기록이 이전될 것이라고 말씀해 주셨어요.

M: 하지만, 어, 학생은 그 학점을 인정받기 위해 수강 기록 이전에 관한 서류를 작성했나요?

W: 서류라고요? 어떤 서류 말씀이신가요?

M: Melissa, 다른 학교에서 어떤 수업을 들었더라도, 그 과목을 수강한 기록이 우리 학교에 자동으로 이전되는 것은 아니에요. 수강한 사실을 인정받기 전에 몇 가지 양식을 작성해야만 하죠.

W: 오… 알겠어요. 그러니까, 어, 제가 무엇을 해야 하나요?

M: 좋아요. 사실 그렇게 복잡한 것은 아니에요. Western 대학에서 준 성적증명서 사본을 가지고 있나요?

W: 지금은 없지만, 기숙사에 가서 가지고 올 수는 있어요.

M: 좋아요. 기숙사에 가서 성적증명서 사본을 가지고 오도록 해요. 그리고 나서, 사본을 경제학과로 가지고 가서 그곳 학과장님께 수강 기록 이전 신청서를 달라고 하세요. 신청서를 작성해서, 경제학 과목이 기재되어있는 성적증명서 사본과 함께 제출하세요.

W: 그렇게만 하면 되나요?

M: 음, 학생이 해야 할 일은 그것이 전부에요. 서류를 제출하고 난 뒤, 세 분의 경제학과 교수님으로 구성된 위원회가 수강 기록 이전을 승인할 것인지 아닐지를 판단할 거예요. 단 며칠만 걸릴 뿐이죠.

W: 그분들께서 학점을 이전해 주지 않을 수도 있다는 말씀인가요? 그렇게 되면 정말 큰일이에요.

M: 그런 경우가 가끔 있지만, 학생의 경우에는 그렇게 걱정할 필요가 없어요. 우리 학교는 Western 대학과 좋은 관계를 유지하고 있어서, 거의 모든 과목에 대해 수강 기록 이전을 승인하고 있으니까요. 승인을 받게 되면, 학생이 수강하고자 하는 고급 과정의 수업을 들을 수 있을 거예요.

W: 알겠습니다. 감사합니다. 그러면 지금 바로 시작하도록 할게요.

Script

| 3-03 |

M Professor: Among the greatest of all Russian writers was Alexander Pushkin. Pushkin's work was part of the great outpouring of Russian literature that took place from, oh, the early eighteenth century to the early twentieth century. Prior to that period, literature had been virtually absent because Russian society had been, uh, pretty much closed to the outside world. In the early eighteenth century, however, Tsar Peter the Great opened Russia to the world. This paved the way for the beginning of Russian literature.

I'd like to give you a brief biography of Pushkin followed by a short description on how he influenced other writers. Then, I'll discuss some of his most famous works. Ready . . . ? Okay, let's begin. Pushkin was born in 1799 in Moscow. His family belonged to the Russian nobility but wasn't particularly well off. Despite his family's relative lack of money, Pushkin was educated in style. He attended a famous school in the town of Tsarskoe Selo, which was located near St. Petersburg. As a youth, Pushkin wrote poetry and published his first work when he was twenty years old. He would, of course, later write many poems, plays, and short stories in prose. [10]Pushkin had many radical political leanings and was dedicated to social reform. However, while he spent years on the fringes of various Russian revolutionary movements, he never wholeheartedly committed himself to any of them. That's perhaps what spared him from imprisonment or even execution when the Russian government easily quashed these revolutionary movements.

Nevertheless, because many of Pushkin's writings served as sources of inspiration to the revolutionaries, he was forced into exile away from the capital of St. Petersburg for several years. Pushkin spent much of this time traveling in southern Russia and writing. Eventually, he returned to St. Petersburg, fell in love, and got married in 1831. His wife's name was Natalya, and she and Pushkin had four children together. Unfortunately, their marriage wasn't a happy one. Natalya was young and beautiful and enjoyed living the high life. To make matters worse, Pushkin was something of a heavy gambler, so the two soon found themselves deep in debt. In 1837, rumors spread that Natalya was having an affair. Pushkin challenged the man rumored to be her lover to a duel with pistols. During the ensuing duel, both men were wounded. Pushkin, sadly, succumbed two days later.

During his lifetime, Pushkin achieved a great measure of fame. However, due to their radical nature, some of his writings were censored during his lifetime. The works of his that were published before his death included various long poems, plays with historical themes, and short stories. As for Pushkin's works, well, they greatly influenced many Russian writers.

W Student: Why is that? Because he was such a great writer?

M: Well, that's definitely one reason. But there was another one as well. You see, Russian writers were heavily influenced by the French. Yes, that's right . . .
The French. The reason is that they had no Russian examples to follow. Here's why: Most Russian writers came from the upper classes. Those writers were not

educated in Russian. They were instead educated in French, which was, during Pushkin's time, the language of academia and the educated. Oddly, many Russian nobles could barely speak the native language of their own country. Some couldn't speak it all. Imagine that. As a result, the members of the upper class . . . these were the people who bought books and supported writers by the way . . . wanted their literature in French.

Pushkin could, naturally, speak French, but he also spoke Russian. He learned it during his childhood as the members of the household staff that lived on his parents' small estate only spoke Russian. [11]Pushkin actually wrote some early works in French, but then he began to write exclusively in Russian. And, let me tell you . . . If there's a better writer in the Russian language, I've yet to read his—or her—work. Oh, also, at that time, the Russian language wasn't fully developed as a tool for writing. Russian writing existed in an archaic form called Slavonic and, for centuries, had mainly been used for church services. The uneducated masses spoke Russian, but, for the most part, they were illiterate. So in order to express his thoughts in Russian, Pushkin frequently resorted to creating new words. In this regard, you could say that he was like William Shakespeare. By that I mean that Pushkin helped create modern written Russian.

As for his work, Pushkin wrote about Russians, both historical and fictional figures. The people reading his writing recognized these characters as their fellow countrymen. This greatly influenced later writers. In fact, I strongly believe it's impossible to underestimate Pushkin's influence on Russian literature. Everyone who came after him—including Gogol, Turgenev, and Tolstoy, owed a tremendous debt to Pushkin. For that reason, it's easy to understand why Pushkin is considered the father of modern Russian literature.

Translation

M Professor: 모든 러시아 작가 중에 가장 뛰어난 사람 중의 하나가 알렉산더 푸쉬킨이었습니다. 푸쉬킨의 작품은, 어, 18세기 초반에서 20세기 초반까지 쏟아져 나왔던 러시아 문학의 일부분이었습니다. 그 이전에는, 러시아 사회가, 어, 외부에 대해 상당히 폐쇄적이었기 때문에, 문학이 사실상 존재하지 않았습니다. 하지만, 18세기 초반, 표트르 대제가 러시아의 문호를 개방했습니다. 이로써 러시아 문학이 탄생할 수 있는 길이 열렸던 것이었습니다.

푸쉬킨의 생애에 대해 간단히 언급을 한 후, 그가 다른 작가들에게 어떠한 영향을 미쳤는지에 대해 짧게 설명해 드리겠습니다. 그리고 나서, 그의 가장 유명한 몇몇 작품들에 대해서 논의해 보도록 하죠. 준비되었나요… ? 좋아요, 시작해 봅시다. 푸쉬킨은 1799년 모스크바에서 태어났습니다. 그의 가족은 러시아 귀족이였지만 특별히 부유했던 것은 아니었습니다. 그의 집에 비교적 돈은 없었지만, 푸쉬킨은 교육을 잘 받았습니다. 그는 차르스코예셀로라는 마을의 유명한 학교에 다녔는데, 이 마을은 상트페테르부르크 인근에 위치해 있었습니다. 젊은 시절, 푸쉬킨은 시를 썼고 20세의 나이에 첫 번째 작품을 출간했습니다. 물론, 이후 여러 편의 시, 희곡, 그리고 산문 형태의 단편 소설을 썼습니다. 푸쉬킨은 매우 급진적인 정치적 성향을 가지고 있었고 사회 개혁에 전념했습니다. 하지만, 다양한 러시아 혁명 운동에서 수년간 비주류로 활동을 하면서도, 어떠한 혁명 운동에 전적으로 헌신한 것은 아니었습니다. 러시아 정부가 이러한 혁명 운동들을 쉽게 진압했을 때 그가 수감되거나 처형을 당하지 않았던 이유는 아마도 이러한 점 때문이었을 것입니다.

그럼에도 불구하고, 푸쉬킨의 여러 작품들이 혁명에 영감을 주었기 때문에, 그는 수년 동안 수도인 상트페테르부르크에서 추방을 당해야 했습니다. 푸쉬킨은 러시아 남부 지방을 여행하고 글을 쓰면서 이 시기의 대부분을 보냈습니다. 결국, 상트페테르부르크로 돌아온 후, 그는 사랑에 빠지게 되었고, 1831년에는 결혼을 했습니다. 부인의 이름은 나탈리아였는데, 그녀와 푸쉬킨 사이에는 네 명의 아이들이 있었습니다. 불행하게도, 그들의 결혼은 행복하지 않았습니다. 나탈리아는 젊고 아름다웠으며 상류층의 삶을 즐겼습니다. 설상가상으로, 푸쉬킨은 도박에 빠져서, 두 사람은 곧 심각한 부채를 떠안게 되었습니다. 1837년, 나탈리아가 외도를 하고 있다는 소문이 퍼졌습니다. 푸쉬킨은 그녀의 연인이라고 소문이 난 남자에게 권총 결투를 신청했습니다. 결투 도중, 두 사람 모두 부상을 당했습니다. 안타깝게도, 푸쉬킨은 이틀 후 사망했습니다.

생전에, 푸쉬킨은 상당한 명성을 얻었습니다. 하지만, 그의 급진적인 성향으로 인하여, 몇몇 작품들은 일생 동안 검열을 받았습니다. 그가 사망하기 전 출판된 작품에는 다양한 장편의 시, 역사적인 주제가 담긴 희곡, 그리고 단편 소설이 포함되어 있었습니다. 푸쉬킨의 작품들에 대해서 이야기를 해보면, 음, 그의 작품들은 수많은 러시아 작가들에게 막대한 영향을 주었습니다.

W Student: 왜 그렇죠? 그가 너무나 뛰어난 작가였기 때문이었나요?

M: 글쎄요, 그것도 분명히 하나의 원인이었겠죠. 하지만 또 다른 이유가 있었습니다. 그러니까, 러시아 작가들은 프랑스 작가들의 영향을 많이 받았습니다. 네, 맞습니다… 프랑스 작가들입니다. 그들에게 모범으로 삼아야 할 러시아 작가가 없었기 때문입니다. 그 이유는 이렇습니다: 대부분의 러시아 작가들은 상류층 출신들이었습니다. 이러한 작가들은 러시아어 교육을 받지 않았습니다. 대신 프랑스어 교육은 잘 되어 있었는데, 푸시킨이 살았던 당시 프랑스어는 학문 언어이자 교양 있는 사람들의 언어였습니다. 이상하게도, 많은 러시아 귀족들이 자신의 모국어를 거의 사용하지 못했습니다. 일부는 전혀 러시아어를 하지 못했죠. 상상을 해보세요. 그 결과, 상류층 사람들은… 어쨌든 이들이 책을 사고 작가들을 후원해 주는 사람들이었는데… 자신들의 문학이 프랑스어로 쓰여지기를 원했습니다.

푸쉬킨도 물론 프랑스어를 구사할 수 있었지만, 러시아어도 사용했습니다. 그는 어린 시절 부모님 소유의 작은 주택에서 러시아어만을 사용했던, 집안일을 하는 사람들과 함께 살며 러시아어를 배웠습니다. 푸쉬킨이 초기 작품 중 일부를 프랑스어로 쓴 것은 사실이지만, 이후 러시아어만을 사용하여 글을 쓰기 시작했습니다. 그리고, 말하자면… 러시아어로 글을 쓴 더 훌륭한 작가가 있을지도 모르지만, 저는 아직까지 그러한 작가의 작품은 읽어보지 못했습니다. 오, 또한, 당시에는 러시아어가 글을 쓰기에 적합한 수단으로 완전히 발달해 있지도 않았습니다. 러시아 문자는 슬라브어라 불리던 원시 언어의 형태였고, 수세기 동안, 주로 교회 예배에서만 사용되었습니다. 교육받지 못한 일반 대중들은 러시아어를 사용했지만, 이들 대부분은 문맹이었습니다. 그래서 러시아어로 자신의 생각을 표현하기 위해, 푸쉬킨은 종종 새로운 단어를 만들어 내야 했습니다. 이러한 점에서 볼 때, 여러분들은 그가 윌리엄 셰익스피어와 같다고 할 수도 있겠습니다. 제 말은 푸쉬킨이 현대 러시아 문자의 발전에 도움을 주었다는 것입니다.

그의 작품에 대해 이야기하자면, 푸쉬킨은 러시아인에 관한 작품을 썼는데, 여기에는 역사적 인물과 가상의 인물 모두가 포함됩니다. 그의 작품을 읽은 사람들은 이러한 인물들을 자신들 주변 사람들로 인식했습니다. 이는 이후의 작가들에게 막대한 영향을 끼쳤습니다. 사실, 저는 러시아 문학에 미친 푸쉬킨의 영향을 과소평가하는 것은 불가능한 일이라고 생각합니다. 고골리, 투르게네프, 그리고 톨스토이 등 푸쉬킨 이후의 모든 작가들이 푸쉬킨으로부터 막대한 영향을 받았습니다. 이러한 이유로, 푸쉬킨이 현대 러시아 문학의 아버지로 간주되는 이유를 이해하는 것은 어렵지 않습니다.

Actual Test 04

Reading Section   p.45

Answers

1. C [Vocabulary Question]
2. A [Reference Question]
3. B [Negative Factual Question]
4. B [Vocabulary Question]
5. A [Factual Question]
6. C [Sentence Simplification Question]
7. D [Inference Question]
8. D [Rhetorical Purpose Question]
9. C [Vocabulary Question]
10. B [Factual Question]
11. D [Factual Question]
12. B [Factual Question]
13. 2nd [Insert Text Question]
14. C, D, E [Prose Summary Question]

Translation

매머드

매머드는 수만 년 동안 여러 북부 지역에 서식하던 거대한 육상 포유류였다. 코끼리와 비슷하게 생긴 이 종은 현재 멸종 상태이다; 하지만, 매머드가 죽은 방식과 죽은 장소 덕분에 멸종된 모든 동물들 중에서 매머드가 가장 잘 알려지고 연구될 수 있었다. 그 이유는 다수의 매머드가 극한의 진흙 강둑과 호수의 바닥에서 죽었기 때문인데, 이 곳에서는 매머드의 잔해가 잘 보존될 수 있었다. 수천 년이 지난 후, 러시아의 시베리아 북부와 다른 극한의 툰드라 지역에서 많은 잔해들이 발견되었다. 조심스럽게 발굴되어 연구 시설로 옮겨진 후, 이들은 과학자들이 종과 환경에 대한 귀중한 통찰력을 가질 수 있도록 해주었다.

외양을 살펴보면, 매머드는 현대의 코끼리와 상당히 닮아 있었는데, 몸의 크기도 코끼리와 비슷했으며, 몇 가지 예외적인 점들을 제외하면, 체형도 거의 비슷했다. 예외적인 점들에 대해 알아보면, 매머드는 현대의 코끼리에 비해서 귀가 훨씬 작았지만 엄니는 훨씬 더 크고 확연하게 휘어져 있었다. 또한 매머드의 몸은, 그들이 서식하던 추운 환경에서 체온을 유지하는데 도움을 주고 그 길이가 1미터까지 자랄 수 있는, 두껍고 텁수룩한 털로 덮여 있었다. 매머드는 식물을 먹었는데, 이는 주로 툰드라 지역에서 자라는 짧은 풀이었다. 매머드는 그들의 거대한 엄니로 눈을 치워서 그 아래에 자라고 있던 풀을 뜯어먹었을 것으로 생각된다. 코끼리와 마찬가지로, 매머드도 무리를 지어 이동을 했고 그들이 지키던 사회적 구조가 존재했다는 점은 거의 확실하다.

매머드와 다른 코끼리 종들이 과거 수백만 년 전 동일한 조상으로부터 진화되었다는 점은 일반적으로 인정되고 있다. 약 4백만 년 전, 매머드가 된 한 분파가 북아프리카 코끼리로부터 떨어져 나왔고 이들은 북쪽으로 가서, 시간이 지남에 따라, 추운 기후에 적응하게 되었다. 매머드는 유럽과 아시아에 주로 서식했을 뿐만 아니라 현대의 알래스카, 캐나다, 그리고 미국의 대부분 지역에서도 서식했다. 완전히 진화된 모습으로서의 매머드는 기원전 400,000년 무렵 최초로 등장하여, 이 때부터 기원전 1700년경 멸종할 때까지 번성하였다. 수만 년 동안, 지구의 북쪽 지역에는 일련의 빙하기가 나타났고, 이는 매머드에게 다른 종들을 뛰어넘는 한 가지 이점을 가져다 주었는데, 그것은 극한 추위에서도 생존할 수 있는 매머드의 능력 때문이었다.

인간이 매머드의 영역에 최초로 모습을 보였던 시기는 마지막 대빙하기가 끝날 무렵이었다. 빙원의 감소와 인간 사냥꾼들의 수적 증가로부터 오는 압박감 때문에, 매머드는 계속해서 더욱 좁은 지역으로 밀려났다. 기원전 40,000년부터 기원전 14,000년 사이, 엄청난 수의 매머드가 죽었다; 사냥꾼들에 의해서 죽거나 한정된 양의 먹이 때문에 굶어 죽기도 했다. 결국, 북극해의 몇몇 섬에 겨우 몇 마리의 매머드만이 살아남게 되었다. 최후의 매머드는 기원전 1700년 렝겔 섬에서 죽은 것으로 생각되고 있다. 몇몇 매머드들은 죽으면서 강이나 호수의 바닥에 쓰러졌는데, 이곳에서 그들의 몸은 흙으로 뒤덮였다. 이로 인하여 청소 동물들이 그들의 사체를 먹지 못하게 되었고, 추위와 진흙으로 인해 그들의 유기 물질은 수천 년 동안 보존될 수 있었다.

매머드가 멸종되고 나서 오랜 시간이 지난 후 여러 북쪽 지역의 문화에 거대하고 털이 많은 짐승에 대한 전설이 나타났다. 시베리아에서는, 사냥꾼들과 덫 사냥꾼들이 때로 지표면이나 혹은 그

바로 아래의 층에서 엄니와 뼈를 발견해 냈다. 사냥꾼들은 이것들을 상인에게 팔았는데, 상인들은 특히 상아에 관심을 가졌다. (그 거대한 크기 때문에 상아는 매우 가치가 높았다.) 18세기 무렵, 화석화된 이 동물의 이야기들이 유럽 과학자들의 귀에 들어갔다. 처음에는, 이 화석들이 지구가 따뜻했던 시기에 북쪽 지역에서 서식하던 코끼리의 화석이라고 생각되었다. 하지만 몇몇 시베리아인들이 피부, 털, 뼈, 그리고 내부 장기가 모두 보존되어 있는, 완전한 상태의 매머드를 발견하기 시작했으며, 전문가들은 이러한 동물들이 코끼리와 완전히 다른 새로운 종의 동물이라는 것을 알게 되었다. 흥미롭게도, 오늘날 몇몇 학자들은 이러한 동물의 유해만을 연구하는 것에 만족하지 않고 있다. 이들 중 일부는 보존이 잘 된 여러 표본으로부터 매머드의 DNA를 추출하여 암컷 코끼리에 수정을 시도함으로써 매머드를 복제해 낼 수 있기를 기대하고 있다. 몇 세대의 매머드-코끼리 이종 생물들을 교배시킨 후, 최대한 원래의 매머드에 가까운 종의 동물을 만들어 내는 것이 그들의 바람이다.

Listening Section p.51

Answers

1. B [Gist-Purpose Question]
2. D [Detail Question]
3. B [Making Inferences Question]
4. A [Understanding Attitude Question]
5. C [Understanding Function Question]
6. A [Detail Question]
7. B [Gist-Content Question]
8. D [Understanding Organization Question]
9. B [Detail Question]
10.

	High Blood Pressure	Low Blood Pressure
A		X
B		X
C	X	
D	X	

[Connecting Content Question]

11. C [Making Inferences Question]

Script

| 04-02 |

W Student: Uh, hi . . . I've got this, um, really huge problem, and I hope that you can help me out with it.

M Librarian: Sure thing. I'll do the best that I can to assist you.

W: That's great because this problem absolutely has to be solved as soon as possible.

M: All right. In that case, why don't you tell me what it is? Do you need to find a book or something? I can take care of that for you.

W: No, I don't need to find a book. I've already got the book. See . . . It's right here. It's this book on the Great Depression.

M: All right then . . . If you already have the book, uh, I'm not quite sure what you need me for. I work at the circulation desk here, so all that I do is check out books, renew them, and return them. ⁴If you require a reference librarian to provide some information about that book, you can go to that desk and talk to Wayne. Wayne is the man standing over there. He can help you out.

W: I don't need to talk to Wayne. Just bear with me for a minute, please.

M: Okay. Sure.

W: I checked out this book because I'm writing my senior thesis on the Great Depression. This happens to be one of the most important books on that period of time, but it's extremely hard to find.

M: In that case, it's a good thing for you that we have it here.

W: Yeah. Right . . . Anyway, I need to check a reference on page thirty-eight in this book. Without that reference, I can't prove that the argument in my thesis is correct. So, uh, why don't you go ahead and turn the book to page thirty-eight?

M: Uh, sure. I can do that . . . Thirty-three . . . Thirty-five . . . Thirty-nine . . . Huh? That's weird. Where are pages thirty-seven and thirty-eight?

W: Yeah, that's exactly what I asked. That page is missing from the book. Look here. Someone just ripped it out. Can you believe that? I'm totally doomed if I don't get a hold of that page.

M: All right. Calm down, miss. Let me get on the computer here and see which area libraries have it.

W: None of them do. I already checked.

M: Hold on. I've got access to a bigger list of libraries on this database . . . Hmm . . . There are actually several libraries that have the book.

W: ⁵Really? Where?

M: One's in Texas. Another's in Alabama . . . Er, two are in California.

W: It's too bad that we're hundreds of miles away from all of them.

M: Yeah, that's true, but this book is also available at a school in New York City. And, fortunately for you, I happen to know the head librarian there. So I'll give her a call and ask her to photocopy the page and then email it to me. Would you be satisfied with that?

W: Would I? It would be amazing if you could do that.

M: All right. But I don't know if she can do that today since it's getting near the end of the workday for her. Why don't you give me your name and email address?

15

As soon as I get the page, I'll forward it to you. Then, you'll be able to get your research done. How does that sound to you?

Translation

W Student: 어, 안녕하세요… 저에게, 음, 정말 큰 문제가 생겼는데, 선생님께서 이 문제에 관해 저를 도와주셨으면 해요.

M Librarian: 물론이죠. 최선을 다해 도움을 드리도록 할게요.

W: 정말로 가능한 빨리 해결되어야만 하는 문제라서요. 잘 됐군요.

M: 좋아요. 그런 경우라면, 문제가 무엇인지 저에게 말씀해 주시겠어요? 책이나 다른 무언가를 찾아야 하나요? 그런 건 제가 처리해 드릴 수 있어요.

W: 아니오. 책을 찾을 필요는 없어요. 이미 찾았거든요. 보세요… 여기에 있어요. 대공황에 대한 책이에요.

M: 그렇군요… 이미 책을 찾았다면, 어, 제가 무엇을 해야 할 지 확신이 서지 않는군요. 이곳 대출 창구에서 일을 하고 있기 때문에, 제가 하는 업무는 책을 대출해 주고, 기한을 연장해 주고, 책을 다시 갖다 놓는 일들이 전부예요. 만일 학생이 책에 대한 정보를 얻기 위해 참고 사서를 만나고 싶다면, 저쪽에 있는 데스크로 가서 Wayne씨에게 말을 해보세요. Wayne씨는 저쪽에 서 있는 남자예요. 그가 도와줄 수 있을 거예요.

W: Wayne씨와 이야기를 할 필요는 없어요. 잠시만 참고 들어주세요.

M: 좋아요. 알았어요.

W: 저는 대공황에 대한 졸업 논문을 작성하기 위해 이 책을 대출했어요. 이 책은 그 시기와 관련된 가장 중요한 책 중의 하나인데, 찾기가 매우 힘들죠.

M: 그런 경우라면, 우리가 그 책을 소장하고 있다는 사실이 학생에게 좋은 일이군요.

W: 네. 그래요… 어쨌든, 저는 이 책의 38쪽에 있는 참고 사항을 확인해 보아야 해요. 그 참고 사항이 없으면, 제 논문의 주장이 옳다는 것을 증명할 수가 없어요. 그러니까, 어, 이쪽으로 오셔서 38쪽을 펴 보시겠어요?

M: 음, 좋아요. 그렇게 하죠… 33쪽… 35쪽… 39쪽… 어? 그것 참 이상하군요. 37쪽과 38쪽이 어디에 있죠?

W: 네, 제가 묻고 싶었던 것이 바로 그것이에요. 그 페이지가 떨어져 나갔어요. 여기를 보세요. 누군가가 그 부분을 찢어 버렸어요. 믿어지세요? 그 부분이 없으면 저는 완전히 끝이에요.

M: 알겠어요. 진정해요, 학생. 컴퓨터를 확인해 보고 어느 도서관에 이 책이 있는지 알아볼게요.

W: 어느 도서관에도 없어요. 제가 이미 확인했어요.

M: 기다려 봐요. 이 데이터베이스에 있는 보다 많은 도서관들의 목록에 접속했어요… 흠… 실제 그 책을 소장하고 있는 도서관들이 몇몇 있군요.

W: 정말이요? 어디인가요?

M: 텍사스에 한 곳. 앨라배마에 또 한 곳… 음, 캘리포니아에 두 곳이 있고요.

W: 그 모든 도서관이 여기에서 수백 마일 떨어진 곳에 있다니 정말 좋지 않네요.

M: 네, 그건 사실이지만, 이 책은 뉴욕 시의 한 학교에서도 찾을 수 있어요. 그리고, 학생에게는 좋은 일인데, 제가 그 도서관의 책임 사서를 알고 있어요. 그래서 그분에게 전화를 해서 그 부분을 복사하여 전자 우편으로 보내 달라고 부탁할게요. 그렇게 하면 만족하시겠어요?

W: 만족하겠냐고요? 그렇게 해주신다면 정말 감동할 것 같아요.

M: 좋아요. 하지만 근무 시간이 거의 다 끝났기 때문에 그분이 오늘 해줄 수 있는지는 잘 모르겠어요. 학생의 이름과 이메일 주소를 알려 줄 수 있나요? 그 페이지를 받자마자, 학생에게 전달해 줄게요. 그러면, 조사를 끝낼 수 있을 거예요. 어때요?

Script

| 04-03 |

M1 Professor: Okay. Break's over, so we need to get started again . . . Let's continue examining the human circulatory system. We know that the heart pumps blood throughout the body. Blood carries oxygen and nutrients to cells, removes waste from cells, and keeps the body functioning. To circulate through the body, blood must be maintained at a certain pressure. If the pressure gets either too high or too low, it can cause health problems.

There are two types of blood pressure: systolic and diastolic. Systolic blood pressure is taken when the heart contracts, uh, pumps, and is the maximum—or highest—rate of blood pressure. Diastolic blood pressure is taken when the heart relaxes between beats. It's the lowest—or minimum—rate of blood pressure. Just so you know, blood pressure is measured in millimeters of mercury. And there are many devices able to measure it. The most common is the blood pressure cuff. I'm sure everyone's familiar with it. The doctor wraps it around the patient's upper left arm and then pumps air until it's inflated. Then, the air is slowly released. While doing that, the doctor uses a stethoscope to listen to the patient's pulse. The doctor simultaneously reads a device which measures the millimeters of mercury. Oh, in case you're curious, the upper left arm is the best place to get an accurate blood pressure reading because it's a convenient part of the body where major arteries and veins are near the heart. I bet you didn't know that, did you?

Anyway, when recording a patient's blood pressure, the doctor notes the systolic measurement first and the diastolic measurement second. So a blood pressure of one hundred twenty systolic and eighty diastolic would be expressed as one hundred twenty over eighty. When it's written, therefore, it looks like a fraction.

M2 Student: Professor Kent, what's normal blood pressure?

M1: Ah, you must have read my mind, Tim. I was just about to get to that. In fact, the measurement I just cited—one hundred twenty over eighty—is considered to be normal. Anything measuring much higher or lower than those two numbers can be indicative of a health problem. Now, uh, since high blood pressure is the more common of the two, let's go over it first.

High blood pressure can be considered dangerous if it's consistently above one hundred forty over ninety. This is called stage one hypertension. Please note that I said consistently. During times of stress or extreme physical activity, a person's blood pressure may reach this level or even rise above it. That's why, uh, to be completely accurate, blood pressure measurements should be taken when a person is resting. Ideally, a person should take his or her blood pressure twice a day for a month to determine what it really is.

Also, when people visit the doctor, they tend to have higher blood pressure than normal. After all, simply visiting a clinic or hospital can cause stress for some people. So it's best for a person to measure his or her blood pressure at home with a device that's available in virtually any neighborhood drugstore. After a month of testing, if the person determines that the average is too high, he or she most likely has high blood pressure. For most people, their lifestyles are why they have this condition. Being overweight is the most common cause of high blood pressure. Additionally, let's see . . . a lack of regular exercise . . . smoking . . . drinking too much . . . and, um, stress, both at work and home, may contribute to high blood pressure.

The health effects of high blood pressure can be serious. Remember that as blood gets pumped through the arteries, the artery walls expand. But, if the walls expand too much and too consistently, then some small tears can appear in them. These tears can trap particles of different substances that are in the bloodstream. The most common particles are lipids of cholesterol. Over the course of several years, these particles can build up and eventually block the blood vessels they're in. [11]This may result in heart attacks or strokes. Additionally, high blood pressure is a leading cause of kidney problems. To avoid these problems, reducing blood pressure is essential. There are some medicines that can do this. But, you know what . . . ? Losing weight, reducing drinking and smoking, and decreasing the stress in one's life are all essential to reducing blood pressure.

Of course, you don't want your blood pressure to be too low either. Low blood pressure, called hypotension, is a serious problem for some people. If a person's blood pressure is below ninety over sixty, it may result in dizziness and fainting. The reason is that there's not enough blood reaching the person's brain. Low blood pressure is much rarer than high blood pressure though. It's typically caused by hormonal problems such as, uh, Addison's disease. Other causes are toxins in the blood and the loss of blood due to an accident.

Translation

M1 Professor: 좋습니다. 쉬는 시간이 끝났으니, 다시 시작을 하도록 합시다… 인간의 순환계에 대해 계속해서 알아보도록 하죠. 우리는 심장이 신체의 곳곳으로 혈액을 보낸다는 사실을 알고 있습니다. 혈액은 산소와 영양분을 세포에 전달하고, 세포의 노폐물을 제거하며, 신체 기능이 유지될 수 있도록 합니다. 체내를 순환하기 위해, 혈액은 일정한 압력을 받아야만 합니다. 이러한 압력이 너무 높거나 낮으면, 건강상의 문제가 일어날 수 있습니다.

혈압에는 두 종류가 있습니다: 수축기 혈압과 확장기 혈압입니다. 수축기 혈압은 심장이 수축하여, 어, 혈액을 뿜어낼 때의, 최대치 — 즉 가장 높은 수치의 — 혈압을 의미합니다. 확장기 혈압은 심장 박동 사이에 심장이 이완될 때의 혈압입니다. 이는 최저치의 — 즉 가장 낮은 수치의 — 혈압을 의미합니다. 여러분들이 알고 있는 것처럼, 혈압은 mmHg라는 단위로 측정됩니다. 그리고 혈압을 측정할 수 있는 여러 장비들이 있습니다. 가장 흔한 것은 혈압계 밴드입니다. 여러분 모두가 이것에 친숙할 것으로 생각합니다. 의사가 환자의 왼쪽 팔 위에 이 장비를 감고, 부풀어 오를 때까지 공기를 주입합니다. 그리고 나서, 공기가 천천히 빠져나옵니다. 이렇게 하는 동안, 의사는 청진기를 사용하여 환자의 맥박을 듣습니다. 그와 동시에 의사는 측정된 mmHg를 확인합니다. 오, 여러분들이 궁금해 할 것 같아서 말씀을 드리면, 왼쪽 팔의 윗부분은 정확한 혈압을 측정할 수 있는 가장 좋은 곳인데, 그 이유는 이 부분이 심장 가까이 있는 주요 동맥과 정맥이 있는 부분 중에서 혈압을 측정하기에 편한 곳이기 때문입니다. 여러분들이 모르고 있었을 것이라고 생각하는데, 그런가요?

어쨌든, 환자의 혈압을 기록할 때, 의사는 확장기 혈압을 먼저 기록한 후 수축기 혈압을 기록합니다. 그래서 확장기 혈압 120과 수축기 혈압 80은 120/80이라고 표현됩니다. 그렇기 때문에, 혈압을 적으면, 마치 분수처럼 보이는 것이죠.

M2 Student: Kent 교수님, 정상 혈압은 어느 정도인가요?

M1: 아, 제 마음을 읽은 것 같군요, Tim. 지금 막 이야기 하려던 참이었거든요. 사실, 제가 방금 언급한 수치가 — 120/80이 — 정상이라고 간주됩니다. 이 두 수치보다 높거나 낮게 측정이 되면 건강에 문제가 있다는 신호가 될 수 있습니다. 자, 어, 이 두 경우 중에서 고혈압이 더 흔하기 대문에, 우선 고혈압을 먼저 다루어 보도록 하죠.

지속적으로 140/90 이상의 수준이 나타날 경우 고혈압이 위험한 것으로 간주될 수 있습니다. 이러한 상태를 고혈압증이라고 부릅니다. 제가 지속적이라고 말했던 점에 주목해 주세요. 스트레스를 받거나 격한 신체적 활동을 하는 동안에는, 사람의 혈압이 그 정도에 도달하거나 그 정도를 넘어설 수도 있습니다. 그렇기 때문에, 어, 혈압을 철저하게 정확히 측정하기 위해서는 휴식을 취하고 있을 때 측정해야 합니다. 이상적으로, 자신의 실제 정확한 혈압을 측정하기 위해서는 한 달 동안 하루에 두 번씩 혈압을 측정해야 합니다.

또한, 의사를 찾아갈 때, 평상시에 비해서 혈압이 높아지는 경향이 있습니다. 결국, 단순히 진료소나 병원을 방문하는 것만으로도 어떤 사람들은 스트레스를 받을 수 있습니다. 그래서 인근 약국에서 구입할 수 있는 장비를 사용하여 집에서 자신의 혈압을 측정하는 것이 가장 좋습니다. 한 달 동안 측정을 한 후, 자신의 혈압이 정상 수치보다 높다면, 고혈압일 가능성이 상당히 높습니다. 대부분의 사람들의 경우, 이러한 상태가 되는 원인은 생활 방식에서 찾을 수 있습니다. 과체중은 고혈압의 가장 일반적인 원인입니다. 게다가, 어디 봅시다… 규칙적인 운동의 부족… 흡연… 과음… 그리고, 음, 가정과 직장에서의 스트레스 등이 고혈압을 일으킬 수 있습니다.

　고혈압이 건강이 미치는 영향은 심각할 수 있습니다. 혈액이 동맥을 통해서 흘러나갈 때, 동맥의 벽이 확장된다는 사실을 기억해 두십시오. 하지만, 이 벽이 너무 많이 그리고 너무 지속적으로 팽창되면, 벽이 찢어질 수도 있습니다. 이렇게 찢어진 곳에는 혈류에 존재하는 다른 물질들의 입자가 끼게 됩니다. 가장 흔한 입자들은 지질과 콜레스테롤입니다. 이러한 상태로 몇 년이 지나면, 입자들이 쌓여서 결국 혈관을 막아버립니다. 이로써 심장 마비나 뇌졸중이 일어날 수도 있습니다. 게다가, 고혈압은 신장 질환의 주요 원인이 되기도 합니다. 이러한 문제들을 피하기 위해서, 혈압을 낮추는 것이 필수적입니다. 혈압을 낮출 수 있는 약들이 몇몇 있습니다. 하지만, 알고 있나요…? 체중을 줄이고, 음주량과 흡연량을 줄이고, 일상 생활에서 스트레스를 줄이는 것 모두가 혈압을 낮추는데 필수적입니다.

　물론, 여러분들은 자신의 혈압이 너무 낮아지는 것도 원치 않을 것입니다. 혈압이 낮은 상태를 저혈압이라고 부르는데, 몇몇 사람들에게는 심각한 문제가 됩니다. 만일 혈압이 90/60 이하로 내려가면, 어지럼증이나 기절을 경험하기도 합니다. 그 이유는 충분한 혈액이 뇌에 도달하지 못하기 때문입니다. 하지만 저혈압은 고혈압에 비해 훨씬 드뭅니다. 저혈압은 일반적으로, 어, 애디슨병과 같이 호르몬의 문제로 인하여 발생합니다. 그 밖의 원인으로는 혈액 내의 독소와 사고로 인한 혈액의 손실 등이 있습니다.

Actual Test 05

Reading Section   p.57

Answers

1. D [Vocabulary Question]
2. B [Factual Question]
3. A [Rhetorical Purpose Question]
4. B [Vocabulary Question]
5. C [Negative Factual Question]
6. C [Sentence Simplification Question]
7. A [Vocabulary Question]
8. D [Inference Question]
9. D [Factual Question]
10. B [Factual Question]
11. C [Vocabulary Question]
12. D [Reference Question]
13. A [Factual Question]
14. C, D, F [Prose Summary Question]

Translation

몽타주

　몽타주란, 종종 대사가 전혀 없거나 거의 없지만 음악은 삽입되어 있는 짧은 단편적인 장면들을 사용하여, 사건을 연속적으로 빠르게 보여 주는 것이다. 몽타주의 목적은 시간의 경과에 따라 사건들을 연속적으로 보여 주는 것이다. 주인공과 관련이 있는 경우가 많지만, 이야기의 배경에 해당되는 특정한 사건들이 일어나는 과정을 보여 줄 수도 있다. 또한, 처음에는 관객들에게 지적인 내용을 전달하고자 하는 것이 몽타주 사용의 의도였으나, 대체적으로, 현대의 영화 제작자들은 이 기법을 다양한 방법으로 사용하고 있다.

　몽타주 기법은 1920년대 소련 영화에서 최초로 사용되었는데, 특히 영화 감독 세르게이 에이젠슈타인에 의해서 사용되었다. 그는 몽타주가 관객들에게, 지적인 성격의 메시지를 전달해 주는, 이미지들의 충돌을 보여 줄 수 있는 방법이라고 생각했다. 예를 들면 그의 영화 중 한 편에서, 파업을 하고 있는 노동자들이 경찰에게 공격을 받는다. 이 사건의 장면들에는 황소를 도살하는 장면이 함께 삽입되어 있다. 노동자들이 도살장의 동물들과 다를 바 없는 대우를 받고 있다는 메시지를 전달할 의도에서였다. 그는 영화 제작에 있어서 몽타주의 다섯 가지 기본적인 방법들을 포함하는 – 이 모두는 자신의 영화에서 사용되었다 – 하나의 몽타주 이론을 정립했다.

　에이젠슈타인은 영화계에서 지적인 거장으로 여겨지고 있지만, 몽타주에 대한 그의 견해는 다른 국가의 주류 영화계에 잘 전파되지 않았다. 특히 미국에서 제작되는 할리우드 영화의 경우가 그러했다. 몽타주 기법이 할리우드 영화 제작자들에 의해 도입되었을 때, 이 기법은 시간이나 사건의 흐름을 보여 주는 방법이 되었다. 몽타주 기법에는 관객들의 사고를 이끌어 낼 목적으로, 연기 보다는 연속된 행동의 장면들이 포함되었다. 1930년대, 몽타주 기법은 할리우드 영화에서 널리 쓰였다. 몽타주의 한 유형은 신문이 빠르게 돌아가다가 갑자기 정지하면서 카메라가 헤드라인에 초점을 맞추는 기법을 활용했다. 많은 경우에는, 신문들이 연속적으로 빠르게 보여 지는 장면들이 있었는데, 모든 신문에서 사건 발생과 관련된 헤드라인들이 나타났고 관객들이 줄거리를 이해하는데 필요한 중요 정보들도 나타나 있었다. 자주 사용되었던 또 다른 몽타주 종류는 여행 몽타주 기법이었다. 여러 장소에서 다양한 활동을 하는 많은 장면들을 보여 줌으로써 극중 인물들의 여행이 묘사되었다. 일반적으로 배경에는 지도가 있었는데, 이는 등장 인물들이 장소를 이동하는 경로를 보여 주었다.

　할리우드 영화에서 몽타주 기법의 또 다른 용도는 절정에 다가가는 동안 긴장감을 형성하는 것이었다. 서로 다른 등장 인물들 사이의 모습을 연속적으로 빠르게 보여 주거나 한 장면을 다양한 각도에서 보여 주는 기법이 긴장감을 조성하는데 이용되었다. 적절한 음악을 — 그리고 적절한 사건을 — 사용하여, 영화 제작자는 인상적인 순간을 만들어 낼 수 있었다. 아마도 이러한 몽타주 기법의 가장 좋은 사례는, 세르지오 레오네가 1966년에 제작한 영화 석양의 무법자에서 세 명의 주인공이 벌이는 권총 결투 장면일 것이다. 인상 깊은 음악과 등장 인물들의 눈, 총, 그리고 손이 나오는 장면을 빠르게 보여 줌으로써 긴장감이 고조되는데, 이러한 긴장감은 영화

사에서 가장 뛰어난 클라이맥스 장면에서 해소된다.

현재, 몽타주 기법은 사실상 모든 장르의 영화에서 다양한 방법으로 사용되고 있다. 영화의 첫 자막 장면이나 마지막 자막이 올라가는 장면에서도 종종 이 기법이 사용된다. 몽타주 기법은 많은 스포츠 영화에서 특히 효과적으로 사용된다. 예를 들면, 운동선수가 중요한 대회를 준비할 때 훈련 장면들을 연속적으로 보여 주는 경우가 많다. 1976년에 제작된 영화 록키에서는, 승리할 가능성이 없어 보이는 권투 선수인 록키 발보아가 챔피언 아폴로 크리드와의 경기를 준비하기 위해 훈련을 하는 과정이 몽타주 기법을 통해 보여 진다. 몽타주 장면이 시작되기 전, 몸도 만들어 지지 않은 상태로 계단을 잘 오르지 못하는 록키의 모습이 보여 진다. 하지만, 몽타주 기법을 사용한 장면에서, 그는 늠름하게 자기 자신을 싸우는 기계로 변화시킨다. 모든 장면들은 실제로 아무런 대사 없이 분위기를 고조시키는 음악만을 포함하고 있다. 이는 관객들에게 록키가 아폴로의 호적수이며 한판 승부에서 승리할 수도 있다는 의미를 전달해 준다. 결국, 록키는 패배하지만, 몽타주 기법이 없었다면, 관객들은 록키가 챔피언과 마지막 라운드까지 경기를 할 수 있었다는 사실을 믿을 수 없었을 것이다.

Listening Section   p.63

Answers

1. Ⓓ [Gist-Content Question]
2. Ⓓ [Understanding Attitude Question]
3. Ⓒ, Ⓓ [Detail Question]
4. Ⓐ [Understanding Function Question]
5. Ⓒ [Making Inferences Question]
6. Ⓑ [Gist-Content Question]
7. Ⓒ [Detail Question]
8. Ⓐ [Understanding Organization Question]
9.

	Tadpole Stage	Metamorphic Stage
Ⓐ		X
Ⓑ	X	
Ⓒ		X
Ⓓ		X

[Connecting Content Question]

10. Ⓒ [Understanding Function Question]
11. Ⓓ [Understanding Attitude Question]

Script

| 05-02 |

M Professor: Okay, Kate. I believe we have your class schedule for next semester all settled. Is there anything else you need to discuss right now? If not, I've got to get going. I have a staff meeting in a few minutes that I have to attend.

W Student: Oh, actually, yes, Professor Gibbons. If you've got a couple more moments to spare, I've got something that really can't wait.

M: It can't wait? All right. I suppose I can't turn you down if it's that important. But I've only got about three or four minutes. Anything you want to chat about which takes longer than that is going to have to wait until after the meeting's over.

W: I see. Well, okay. I'll make this as fast as possible.

M: Great.

W: It's about the research paper that we need to write for your class.

M: You're talking about the paper that's due in about five weeks?

W: Er, yes. I thought that I'd get an early start on things.

M: That's a good attitude. So, uh, what exactly are you thinking of writing for the paper?

W: Well, to be honest, I've never read too many children's books before. Uh, at least not since I was a kid. That's why I find this class on children's literature to be, um, totally fascinating.

M: Okay.

W: I mean, I'd heard about books such as the *Harry Potter* series. I've seen the movies, too. But I'd never actually gotten around to reading them.

M: Does that mean you're considering writing your paper on some of the more modern works of children's literature? If yes, I can recommend quite a large number of books for you to read.

W: Uh, actually, no. I was thinking of going back to the past. But this is where I need your assistance.

M: How so?

W: Well, like I said, I don't know that much about children's literature. So I thought it might be nice—and interesting—to go back to the nineteenth century and look at some of the works of children's literature from that period. I remember you saying in class that there were several influential authors of children's books during that century.

M: That's correct.

W: So, what I'd like to know from you is which children's authors I should concentrate on.

M: Ah, I see. Hmm . . . There are quite a few of them. Lewis Carroll is definitely one you ought to look at.

W: He wrote *Alice in Wonderland*, right?

M: That's correct. Be sure to read it. And another author you simply have to research is George MacDonald.

W: George MacDonald? Sorry, but I'm not familiar with him. What makes him so important?

M: Ah, you ought to know about him. He wrote several important books in that genre. *The Princess and the Goblin* is the most famous of them. Take a look at it. MacDonald wrote many fairy tales and works of a religious nature as well. But, more importantly, his stories influenced numerous modern authors of children's literature. C.S. Lewis, who wrote *The Chronicles of Narnia*, cited MacDonald as a major influence. And today's lecture, as I hope you recall, focused on some of the authors that Lewis's writing influenced. I think you can see the connection there. So I highly recommend that you check out some of George MacDonald's writings, too. Come to think of it, he would make a fascinating topic for a paper.

W: Great. Thanks for the advice, sir.

Translation

M Professor: 좋아요, Kate. 학생의 다음 학기 수업 시간표가 모두 결정된 것 같군요. 이야기할 것이 더 남아 있나요? 없다면, 나는 이제 가봐야겠어요. 잠시 후에 참석해야 하는 교직원 회의가 있어서요.

W Student: 오, 사실은, 드릴 말씀이 더 있어요, Gibbons 교수님. 몇 분만 시간을 더 내주실 수 있다면, 꼭 말씀드릴 것이 있어요.

M: 꼭 해야 할 이야기요? 좋아요. 그렇게 중요한 문제라면 거절을 할 수 없을 것 같네요. 하지만 3, 4분 정도의 시간밖에 없어요. 그보다 오래 걸리는 이야기라면 회의가 끝난 뒤로 미루도록 해야 할 거예요.

W: 알겠어요. 음, 좋아요. 최대한 빠르게 말씀 드릴게요.

M: 그래요.

W: 교수님 수업 시간에 작성해야 하는 연구 보고서에 관한 것이에요.

M: 5주 후에 제출해야 하는 보고서를 말하고 있는 건가요?

W: 어, 맞아요. 빨리 시작해야겠다고 생각했어요.

M: 좋은 태도군요. 그렇다면, 어, 학생이 보고서에 쓰려고 생각하고 있는 것이 정확히 무엇이죠?

W: 음, 솔직히 말씀을 드리면, 저는 예전에 동화책을 많이 읽어 보지 못했어요. 어, 적어도 어린 시절 이후로는요. 그렇기 때문에 저는 아동 문학을 다루고 있는 이번 수업이, 음, 정말로 재미있어요.

M: 좋아요.

W: 제 말씀은, 저도 해리 포터 시리즈와 같은 책에 대해서는 들어본 적이 있어요. 영화도 물론 봤죠. 하지만 실제로 책을 읽어 볼 기회는 없었어요.

M: 현대적인 아동 문학 작품들에 대한 보고서를 작성하려고 생각하고 있다는 뜻인가요? 만일 그렇다면, 읽어야 할 수많은 책들을 추천해 줄 수 있어요.

W: 어, 사실은, 그렇지 않아요. 저는 과거로 거슬러 올라가 볼 생각이에요. 하지만 그 때문에 교수님의 도움이 필요해요.

M: 어떻게요?

W: 음, 말씀을 드렸다시피, 저는 아동 문학에 대해서 많이 알고 있지 않아요. 그래서 19세기로 거슬러 올라가서 그 시기의 아동 문학 작품들을 살펴보는 것이 재미있고 흥미로울 것이라고 생각했어요. 교수님께서 19세기에 영향력이 있었던 몇몇 아동 문학 작가들이 있다고 수업 시간에 말씀하셨던 것을 기억하고 있어요.

M: 맞아요.

W: 그래서, 제가 어떤 아동 문학 작가에 초점을 맞춰야 하는지 교수님께서 알려 주셨으면 해요.

M: 아, 알겠어요. 흠… 상당히 여러 명인데요. 루이스 캐롤은 꼭 살펴보아야 할 작가 중의 한 명이죠.

W: 이상한 나라의 앨리스를 쓴 사람이죠, 그렇죠?

M: 맞아요. 그 책은 꼭 읽어 보세요. 그리고 살펴봐야 할 또 다른 작가는 조지 맥도날드에요.

W: 조지 맥도날드라고요? 죄송하지만, 익숙하지 않군요. 그 작가는 무엇 때문에 유명해졌나요?

M: 아, 그에 대해서는 알고 있어야 해요. 아동 문학 장르에서 몇몇 중요한 책을 썼죠. 공주님과 난쟁이가 그 중 가장 유명한 책이고요. 그 책을 살펴봐요. 또한 맥도날드는 많은 동화와 종교적 성향의 작품들도 썼어요. 하지만, 보다 중요한 것은, 그의 작품들이 현대의 수많은 아동 문학 작가들에게 영향을 주었다는 점이죠. 나니아 연대기를 쓴 C.S. 루이스는 자신에게 가장 큰 영향을 준 작가로 맥도날드를 언급했어요. 그리고, 학생이 기억하고 있었으면 좋겠는데, 오늘 강의에서는 루이스의 작품에 영향을 받은 몇몇 작가들에 초점을 맞췄죠. 학생이 거기에서 연관성을 찾을 수 있을 거예요. 따라서 조지 맥도날드의 작품들도 몇 권 찾아볼 것을 강력히 추천해요. 그러고 보니, 그가 훌륭한 논문 주제가 될 수도 있겠군요.

W: 정말 그렇겠어요. 조언해 주셔서 감사합니다, 교수님.

Script

| 05-03 |

W Professor: Moving on, it's time to discuss amphibians. Although they look like reptiles, amphibians are different from reptiles in a number of ways. Additionally, since amphibians are born in the water but then leave the water to live on land, they cannot be considered fish either. Without a doubt, amphibians comprise one of the more, well, unusual classes of animals. One of their most unique features is the fact that they change from being water-dwelling creatures that breathe with gills to being land-living creatures with both lungs and legs.

As for the number of amphibians . . . There are fewer than 6,500 known species of amphibians. They're divided into three main groups. The largest is composed of frogs and toads and contains more than 5,500 species. Second in size are salamanders and newts, of which there are around 500 species. Finally, there are also fewer than 200 species of caecilians. Now, let's look at the life cycle of . . . hmm . . . I see some frowns on your faces. What's up?

M Student: [11]I'm sorry, Professor Burgess, but, uh, what's a caecilian? I've never heard that word before.

W: Is that a fact . . . ? Oh, I see most of you nodding your heads. Er, okay. Well, I suppose it's true that caecilians are not particularly well known. What are they? They're legless amphibians that resemble earthworms or small snakes. They reside in the tropics and spend most of their time underground. I guess that's why they aren't well known. I'll go over them in detail a little later. Okay?

Now, as for the life cycle of a typical amphibian . . . I'm going to use the frog as an example since most of you should be roughly familiar with it already. A frog goes through four main stages in its life. These are the egg stage, the tadpole stage, the metamorphic stage, and the adult stage. Frogs breed in fresh water and lay their eggs in ponds, lakes, puddles, or virtually any other place that contains fairly stagnant fresh water. Most frogs lay thousands of eggs at a time. This ensures that at least a few survive since insects, snakes, and other creatures frequently eat frog eggs. Oh, diseases can also kill large numbers of them. So, about a week after being laid, the eggs hatch. The frog then enters the tadpole stage.

A tadpole . . . You've all seen tadpoles before, right . . . ? Good. Well, the tadpole is the frog's larva stage. A tadpole spends its time in the water feeding and growing. It breathes with gills and has a long tail but no legs. For some frogs, the tadpole stage lasts as little as one week, but this time varies from species to species. As a general rule though, frogs spend a fairly short amount of time as tadpoles since they're vulnerable to predators during this stage.

The third stage in a frog's life is the metamorphic stage. During this period, the frog is undergoing the changes that will take it from being a tadpole to an adult frog. It grows hind legs first . . . then front legs . . . and also develops lungs. The tail doesn't drop off but is actually absorbed by the body. The eyes transform rather dramatically as well. They move up and toward the front of the head and grow eyelids. This change signifies that the frog has become a predator rather than a prey animal. You see, tadpoles survive by consuming algae or very small creatures in the water, but adult frogs are hunters, uh, predators. They mostly eat insects that they catch. So, once the metamorphosis stage is complete, the frog becomes an adult. As adults, many species leave the water and live most of their lives on land, but they typically remain close to some source of water even though they don't necessarily live in it like they did as tadpoles.

Please remember that not all amphibians follow this life path, but, as a general rule, most do. Just so you know, um, amphibians may differ in where and how they breed, how their breathing systems develop, and how their legs grow—if they even grow at all. Additionally, most amphibians require fresh water to breed in, but some species can breed in salt water. And some amphibians that live in the tropics don't need water to breed at all. For these amphibians, the animal inside the egg transforms to the tadpole stage prior to being born. So, when the eggs finally hatch, the amphibian is closer to being an adult. Finally, some amphibians never reach the stage where they rely solely on their lungs to breathe. Some species retain gills as adults. Even rarer are species that breathe through their skin . . . yes, their skin . . . and have the ability to take oxygen out of both the air and water.

So, that's a general overview of amphibians. Are there any questions . . . ? Not yet I see. Okay, now it's time to go over the three major groups of amphibians in detail. I'm going to get pretty technical, so be sure to take good notes.

Translation

W Professor: 주제를 바꿔서, 양서류에 대해 알아볼 시간이군요. 양서류는 파충류와 비슷하게 생겼지만, 여러 가지 측면에서 파충류와 다릅니다. 게다가, 양서류는 물에서 태어나지만 육지에서 살기 위해 물을 떠나기 때문에, 어류라고 볼 수도 없습니다. 의심할 여지 없이, 양서류는, 음, 보다 특이한 동물의 강(綱)을 구성하고 있습니다. 가장 독특한 특징은 이들이 아가미로 호흡하는 수중 생물에서 폐와 다리를 갖춘 육상 생물로 변화한다는 점입니다.

양서류의 수에 대해서 이야기하자면… 6,500종 이하의 양서류가 있는 것으로 알려져 있습니다. 이들은 세 가지 주요한 종류로 나누어 집니다. 가장 큰 종류는 개구리와 두꺼비로 이루어져 있는데 5,500여종 이상의 종이 여기에 포함됩니다. 두 번째로 큰 종류는 도롱뇽과 영원으로, 여기에는 약 500종이 속해 있습니다. 마지막으로, 200여종 이하의 나사를 포함하는 종류가 있습니다. 자, 그렇다면 이들의 라이프 사이클에 대해 살펴보죠… 흠… 얼굴을 찌푸리는 모습이 보이는군요. 무슨 일이죠?

M Student: 죄송합니다, *Burgess* 교수님, 하지만, 나사가 무엇인가요? 예전에 들어본 적이 없는 단어라서요.

W: 정말인가요…? 오, 대부분의 학생들이 고개를 끄덕이는군요. 어, 좋습니다. 그렇다면, 나사가 특별히 알려져 있는 동물은 아니라고 생각해야겠군요. 이들은 무엇일까요? 나사는 지렁이나 작은 뱀처럼 생긴, 다리가 없는 양서류입니다. 열대 지방에서 서식하며 대부분의 시간을 땅 속에서 보냅니다. 이들이 잘 알려져 있지 않은 이유가 짐작이 가는군요. 잠시 후 이들에 대해서 자세히 알아보도록 하겠습니다. 괜찮죠?

자, 전형적인 양서류의 라이프 사이클에 대해 이야기를 해보면… 여러분 대부분에게 친숙한 개구리를 예로 들어 보겠습니다. 개구리는 일생 동안 네 번의 주요 단계를 거칩니다. 알, 올챙이, 변태, 그리고 성체 단계가 그것이죠. 개구리는 담수에서 번식하여 연못, 호수, 웅덩이, 또는 지속적으로 물이 고여 있는, 사실상 모든 장소에서 알을 낳습니다. 대부분의 개구리들은 한 번에 수천 개의 알을 낳습니다. 곤충, 뱀, 그리고 기타 생물들이 종종 개구리 알을 먹기 때문에 이러한 사실은 최소한 몇 마리만이라도 살아남을 수 있게 해줍니다. 오, 이들 중 상당수는 병에 걸려 죽기도 합니다. 어쨌든, 알을 낳고 1주일 정도가 지나면, 알이 부화합니다. 그런 다음 개구리는 올챙이 단계로 들어갑니다.

올챙이는… 여러분들 모두는 올챙이를 본 적이 있을 것입니다. 그렇죠…? 좋아요. 음, 올챙이는 개구리의 유충 단계입니다. 물속에서 시간을 보내며 먹이를 먹고 성장합니다. 아가미로 호흡을 하고 긴 꼬리가 있지만 다리는 없습니다. 몇몇 개구리의 경우, 올챙이 단계가 1주일 정도 지속되는데, 하지만 이러한 시간은 종에 따라 다릅니다. 그러나 일반적으로, 개구리는 상당히 짧은 시간 동안에 올챙이 단계를 마치는데, 이 단계는 개구리들이 포식자로부터 공격을 받기 쉬운 단계이기 때문입니다.

개구리의 세 번째 생애 단계는 변태 단계입니다. 이 기간 동안, 개구리는 올챙이에서 개구리로 변화하게 됩니다. 뒷다리가 먼저 생기고… 그 다음에는 앞다리가… 그리고 허파도 생깁니다. 꼬리는 떨어져 나가는 것이 아니라 몸 속으로 흡수됩니다. 눈 또한 상당히 극적으로 변합니다. 위쪽으로 올라가서 머리의 앞쪽으로 이동하며 눈꺼풀이 생깁니다. 이러한 변화는 개구리가 피식 동물이 아닌 포식 동물이 되었다는 점을 의미합니다. 알다시피, 올챙이는 조류나 매우 작은 수중 생물들을 먹고 살지만, 개구리는 사냥을 하는, 어, 포식 동물입니다. 주로 곤충을 잡아먹습니다. 그래서, 변태 단계가 끝나면, 개구리는 성체가 되는 것이죠. 다 자라면, 많은 종들이 물을 떠나 주로 육지에서 살아가지만, 올챙이처럼 물속에서 살 필요가 없음에도 불구하고, 보통 물가에서 가까운 곳에 남아 있습니다.

모든 양서류들이 이러한 생애 과정을 따르는 것은 아니라고 기억해 두어야겠지만, 일반적으로는 대부분이 이를 따릅니다. 여러분들이 알고 있는 것처럼, 음, 양서류들은 번식을 하는 장소와 방법, 호흡기의 발달 과정, 그리고 — 만약 다리가 자란다면 — 다리가 자라는 과정까지도 모두 다를 수 있습니다. 게다가, 대부분의 양서류들이 번식을 하기 위해 민물을 필요로 하지만, 몇몇 종들은 바닷물에서 번식을 하기도 합니다. 그리고 열대 지방에 서식하는 몇몇 양서류들은 번식을 할 때 전혀 물을 필요로 하지 않습니다. 이러한 양서류들의 경우에는, 태어나기 전 알 내부에서 올챙이 단계를 겪게 됩니다. 따라서, 알이 부화할 때, 성체에 가까운 상태가 됩니다. 마지막으로, 일부 양서류들은, 허파에만 의존하여 호흡을 하는 단계에 도달하지 않는 경우도 있습니다. 몇몇 종들은 성체가 되어서도 아가미를 보유하고 있습니다. 더욱 희귀한 종들은 피부로 호흡을 하기도 하고… 네, 피부입니다… 공기뿐만 아니라 물에서도 산소를 얻을 수 있는 능력을 가지고 있습니다.

자, 양서류에 대한 일반적인 개요였습니다. 질문이 있나요…? 없는 것 같군요. 좋습니다, 이제 양서류의 주요한 세 종류에 관해 검토해 볼 시간이군요. 상당히 전문적인 내용을 다룰 것이기 때문에, 필기를 잘 해두시길 바랍니다.

Actual Test 06

Reading Section p.69

Answers

1. Ⓓ [Vocabulary Question]
2. Ⓑ [Reference Question]
3. Ⓒ [Factual Question]
4. Ⓐ [Vocabulary Question]
5. Ⓒ [Negative Factual Question]
6. Ⓐ [Factual Question]
7. Ⓒ [Rhetorical Purpose Question]
8. Ⓒ [Vocabulary Question]
9. Ⓓ [Factual Question]
10. Ⓑ [Vocabulary Question]
11. Ⓑ [Inference Question]
12. Ⓑ [Vocabulary Question]
13. Ⓓ [Inference Question]
14. Ⓑ, Ⓓ, Ⓕ [Prose Summary Question]

Translation

치명적 가족성 불면증

수년간 연구를 해왔음에도 불구하고, 전문가들은 수면이 인간에게 왜 필요한지에 대해 정확하게 알지 못하고 있다. 하지만, 알고 있는 것은, 적당한 수면이 없으면, 사람은 결국 사망할 것이라는 점이다. 이러한 사실은 치명적 가족성 불면증이라고 알려진 매우 희귀한 질병에서 명백히 드러난다. 이 질병을 겪는 사람들은 처음에는 낮잠을 못 자고, 그 다음에는 밤새도록 잠을 이루지 못하며, 결국 전혀 잠을 잘 수가 없게 된다. 이 질병에는 네 개의 주요 단계가 있는데, 대부분의 환자들이 발병 후 6개월 이내에 마지막 단계에 진입한다. 아직까지, 이 병에 걸린 후 3년 이상 생존한 사람이 없다. 의사들과 과학자들은 이 질병의 원인을 알고 있다고 확신하지만, 현재에도 그 치료법은 알아내지 못하고 있다.

치명적 가족성 불면증은 한 세대에서 다음 세대로 이어지는 유전 질환으로, 전세계적으로 약 40여 가족들에게서 발견되고 있다. 부모 중 한 명이 치명적 가족성 불면증의 돌연변이 유전자를 가지고 있는 경우, 아이가 이 병에 걸릴 확률은 50%이다. 몇몇 사람들의 경우 빠르면 30세 늦으면 60세에 발병이 될 수도 있지만, 대부분의 환자들의 경우에는 50대에 질병의 징후가 나타나기 시작한다.

어떤 사람에게서 질병의 증상이 나타나면 학자들은 네 개의 특징적인 단계를 확인한다. 4개월 가량 지속되는 첫 번째 단계에서, 환자는 미미한 수준의 불면증을 경험하기 시작할 뿐만 아니라 편집증, 공황 발작, 그리고 다양한 공포증으로 인한 고통을 겪게 된다. 두 번째 단계는 5개월 가량 지속되고 환각 증세 및 심해지는 공황 발작과 함께 심각한 불면증의 징후를 나타낸다. 세 번째 단계는 3개월 정도만 지속되며 전혀 잠을 이루지 못하는 불면증이 시작된다. 이때의 가장 눈에 띄는 새로운 증상은 급격한 체중 감소이다. 마지막 단계에서는 환자가 완전한 치매 증상을 보이며, 결국, 말을 하지 못하는 것을 포함하여, 외부의 자극에 전혀 반응을 하지 못한다. 이 단계는 6개월까지 지속될 수 있는데, 항상 사망으로 끝을 맺는다. 몇몇 이차적 증상으로, 심해지는 발한, 심장 박동의 증가, 그리고 혈압의 증가 및 비교적 단기간에 나타나는 급격한 노화 현상이 나타난다.

뇌의 한 부분인 시상은 치명적 가족성 불면증을 이해하는데 있어서 중요한 단서로 알려져 왔다. 학자들은 이 질병을 앓고 있는 사람들의 경우, 기형적인 단백질이 시상을 공격하여 시상을 손상시킨다는 점을 밝혀냈다. 플라크가 시상에 쌓이기 시작하면서, 시상의 기능이 정지된다. 몇 가지 면에서 완전히 이해되고 있지는 않지만, 이 단백질 플라크가 쌓이면서 사람의 수면 능력이 방해를 받게 된다. 하지만, 이는 아마도 시상이 뇌로부터 신체의 나머지 부분에 신호를 전달하는 메시지 센터라는 사실과 관련이 있을 것이다. 과학자들은, 시상이 많은 시간 동안 지속적인 활동을 한 후, 신호를 효과적으로 전달하지 못하게 되어, 수면을 유발하는 단계로 진입하게 된다고 믿는다. 하지만, 단백질 플라크가 축적됨으로써 시상은 이러한 단계에 진입하지 못하고, 결국 환자들은 수면에 이를 수 없게 된다.

치명적 가족성 불면증의 한 가지 불행한 측면은, 대부분의 사람들의 경우 통상 아이를 나은 후가 되는 인생 후반기에 들어서야 그 징후가 나타난다는 점이다. 그렇기 때문에, 자신도 모르게 질병의 유전자를 자손에게 물려주는 경우가 많다. 그럼에도 불구하고, 모든 사람들이 그러한 유전자와 질병을 물려받는 것은 아니다. 돌연변이 유전자를 보유하고 있는 이탈리아 가정에 대한 사례 연구에 따르면, 6세대에 걸친 228명의 가족 중에서 29명만이 돌연변이 유전자와 질병을 가지고 있었다. 게다가, 현재 체내에 변형된 유전자를 보유하고 있는지를 알아낼 수 있는 테스트들이 존재한다. 양성 반응을 보인 사람들에게는 이것이 딜레마가 될 수도 있다: 자신의 아이들이 이러한 유전자를 물려받을 가능성이 있기 때문에, 아이를 낳을 것인지에 대한 여부를 결정해야만 할 수도 있는 것이다.

돌연변이 유전자에 대한 검사를 어린 나이에 받는 것이 보균자가 일정한 치료를 받을 수 있는 유일한 희망이 될 수 있다. 현재, 학자들은 유전자 대체 치료법을 개발하고 있다. 학자들 중 일부는 치명적 가족성 불면증과 같은 유전 질환을 가지고 있는 사람들의 몸속에서 돌연변이 유전자를 대체시킬 수 있기를 바라고 있다. 만약 이 치료법이 효과가 있다면, 그러한 유전자를 보유하고 있는 사람들의 몸속에서 마침내 질병을 제거시킬 수도 있을 것이다. 그리고 나면, 미래에는, 환자들과 환자들의 아이들이 편안한 수면을 취할 수 있을지에 대해 걱정할 필요가 없을 것이다.

Listening Section p.75

Answers

1. Ⓐ [Understanding Function Question]
2. Ⓑ, Ⓓ [Detail Question]
3. Ⓑ [Making Inferences Question]
4. Ⓓ [Gist-Purpose Question]
5. Ⓒ [Understanding Attitude Question]
6. Ⓓ [Detail Question]
7. Ⓑ [Understanding Organization Question]
8. Ⓐ [Making Inferences Question]
9.

Event	Order
Ⓐ	2
Ⓑ	1
Ⓒ	3
Ⓓ	4

[Connecting Content Question]

10. Ⓒ [Understanding Attitude Question]
11. Ⓑ [Understanding Function Question]

Script

| 06-02 |

W Museum Employee: So, Larry, are you ready for your first day on the job?

M Student: Uh, I'm not sure. I mean, I've been to lots of museums in the past, but, uh, I was always a visitor. ⁵I've never done anything like this before.

W: Well, don't worry about it. I have faith in you.

M: I'm glad that you do because I can't say the same about myself.

W: Oh, I think you're just worrying a bit too much. Say, I've got an idea . . . Why don't we go over your job duties to make sure you know exactly what you're supposed to do? How does that sound to you?

M: I think that's perfect, Rebecca. That way, I'll be sure I haven't forgotten anything.

W: Great. Why don't you tell me everything you need to do during your shift?

M: Sure thing . . . Well, the first thing I'm supposed to do is monitor the museum's galleries. I guess that I should just, uh, walk around through all of the exhibits and make sure that none of the visitors here is doing anything, uh, improper, I guess.

W: Correct. And that's a very important part of your job, Larry. Some of these items on exhibit cost the university a lot of money to acquire. Others have been donated or lent to the university museum by some very rich and influential people. We wouldn't want anything bad to happen to them. That would be, um, unforgivable really.

M: But don't we have security cameras and other stuff?

W: Sure, but a human presence is also important. After all, cameras can only observe. They can't tell someone to back away from a painting or to get his hands off an exhibit. We have a couple of guards, too, but they can't be everywhere at once. You're not a security guard, of course, but, by keeping an eye out, you can help them do their jobs.

M: That makes sense.

W: Good. Now, what about your other duties?

M: All right . . . I'm supposed to answer any questions that visitors ask about the exhibits. You know, um . . . I've been studying the brochures you gave me, so I think I have a decent knowledge of most of the exhibits. But . . .

W: Yes . . . ?

M: I'm an art history major, right? So, uh, talking about artwork won't be a problem. I mean, we have a few Picassos here at the museum, and he happens to be one of my personal favorites. I know a great deal about his work.

W: Outstanding. The Picassos we have displayed are some of the museum's most popular exhibits.

M: I can understand why. But, uh . . . some of the other exhibits are going to be harder for me to explain.

W: Such as what?

M: Okay. I noticed that we have a fairly large display on the Native American artifacts which some archaeologists dug up around this area. I guess there used to be a lot of Native American tribes living here or something. Uh, I don't know too much about that. I'm not an archaeologist.

W: Hmm . . . I guess you're just going to have to learn. That's what you're at college for, isn't it? To learn?

M: Yeah, I see your point. Okay, I think I can do it.

Translation

W Museum Employee: 자, *Larry*, 출근 첫 날에 대한 준비는 다 되었나요?

M Student: 어, 잘 모르겠어요. 제 말은, 전에 여러 박물관을 다녀본 적은 있지만, 하지만, 어, 항상 관람객일 뿐이었죠. 전에는 이러한 일을 해본 적이 없어요.

W: 음, 그 점에 대해서는 걱정하지 말아요. 나는 학생을 믿고 있어요.

M: 저는 제 자신에 대해 그렇게 말할 수 없는데, 믿어 주신다니 기쁘네요.

W: 오, 나는 학생이 너무 많은 걱정을 하고 있다고 생각해요. 자, 내게 생각이 있어요… 학생이 해야 할 일을 정확하게 알고 있는지 확인하기 위해 학생의 직무에 대해서 같이 살펴보는 것이 어떨까요? 어떻게 생각해요?

M: 그러면 정말 좋을 것 같아요, *Rebecca* 선생님. 그러면, 분명 어떠한 사항도 잊어버리지 않을 거예요.

W: 좋아요. 근무 시간 동안에 학생이 해야 하는 모든 업무에 대해서 말해 줄 수 있나요?

M: 물론이죠… 음, 제가 해야 할 첫 번째 일은 박물관의 전시장을 감시하는 것이에요. 제 생각에는 제가, 음, 전시품들이 있는 모든 곳을 돌아다니면서 방문객들 중 어느 누구도, 음, 부적절한 행동을 하지 못하도록 하는 것이죠.

W: 맞아요. 그리고 그것이 매우 중요한 부분이에요, *Larry*. 전시회장의 일부 물품들은 우리 대학교가 상당한 액수의 비용을 들여서 구입한 것이죠. 다른 물품들은 몇몇 부유층 인사들과 영향력 있는 분들께서 기증을 해주시거나 대여를 해주셨어요. 우리는 그 물품들에 어떠한 좋지 않은 일도 일어나지 않기를 바라고 있어요. 그러한 일은, 음, 정말로 용서받을 수 없을 거예요.

M: 하지만 감시 카메라와 다른 직원들도 있지 않나요?

W: 물론 그렇지만, 사람이 있다는 사실이 중요해요. 결국, 카메라는 단지 감시만을 할 수 있을 뿐이죠. 사람들에게 그림 뒤로 물러나라던가 전시물품에 손을 대지 말라고 말을 할 수는 없어요. 경비원도 두 분이 있기는 하지만, 모든 곳에 있을 수는 없죠. 물론, 학생이 경비원은 아니지만, 주변을 면밀히 주시함으로써, 그 분들의 일을 도와 드릴 수는 있어요.

M: 이해가 가네요.

W: 잘 되었군요. 자, 다른 일들은 어떤가요?

M: 좋아요… 저는 방문객들이 전시품들에 대해서 물어보는 모든 질문에 답을 해야 해요. 그러니까, 음… 선생님께서 제게 주신 책자에 대해 공부를 하고 있기 때문에, 대부분의 전시품들에 대해서는 어느 정도 알고 있다고 생각해요. 하지만…

W: 네…?

M: 저는 미술사 전공이에요, 그렇죠? 그래서, 어, 미술 작품들에 대해 이야기하는 것은 문제가 없을 거예요. 제 말은, 여기 박물관에는 피카소의 작품들이 몇 점 있는데, 피카소는 제가 개인적으로 가장 좋아하는 화가 중 한 명이에요. 그의 작품에 대해서는 상당히 많이 알고 있죠.

W: 훌륭하군요. 우리가 전시한 피카소의 작품들은 박물관에서 가장 인기가 좋은 작품 중에 속하죠.

M: 그 이유를 이해할 수 있어요. 하지만, 어… 다른 몇몇 전시품들은 제가 설명하기에 어려울 것 같아요.

W: 이를테면 어떤 것들인가요?

M: 좋아요. 여기에는 몇몇 고고학자들이 이 지역에서 발굴한 아메리카 인디언들의 유물이 상당히 많이 소장되어 있더군요. 제 생각에 수많은 아메리카 인디언 부족들이 이곳에서 살았던 것 같아요. 어, 제가 그에 대해서 많이 알고 있지는 못해요. 저는 고고학자가 아니거든요.

W: 흠… 학생이 공부를 해야 할 것 같군요. 그것이 바로 학생이 대학에 다니는 이유죠, 그렇지 않나요? 배우기 위해서?

M: 네, 무슨 말씀인지 알겠어요. 좋아요, 할 수 있을 것 같아요.

Script

| 06-03 |

M Professor: One of the most integral figures in South American history is Simon Bolivar. He's important because his leadership helped to, uh, to bring about independence for a number of South American states that were under Spanish rule. Among these states were Venezuela, Bolivia, Peru, and Columbia.

As for the man himself, Simon Bolivar was born in Venezuela in 1783. His family belonged to the nobility and was quite wealthy. But Bolivar's parents died when he was a young boy, so he was raised by a series of nannies and educated by private tutors. During his education, he learned about the principles of liberty, which would fuel his desire for independence from Spanish rule. Bolivar's father had been a military officer, so Bolivar followed in his father's footsteps and entered a military academy when he was a teenager.

During Bolivar's early life, Spain controlled Venezuela, but it was weak and beset by numerous problems at home. In the decades following the discovery of the Americas, Spain became the world's largest and richest empire, but, well, let's see . . . bad management, overspending, and countless military failures in Europe and abroad greatly weakened it by the 1800s. In addition, the late 1700s and early 1800s were a time of revolution in the New World. For instance, America gained its independence from England in 1783, and

Haiti became free from French rule in 1804 after a long war.

Across the Atlantic Ocean, France had its own revolution in 1789. But by the beginning of the 1800s, Napoleon was leading armies through much of Europe, including Spain. French soldiers invaded Spain in 1808 but could never quite conquer the Spanish. [10]As a result, a drawn-out war occurred. This weakened Spain even further. After some time, the Spanish king abdicated, leaving Spain without a central government. Napoleon attempted to provide one by making his brother the king of Spain, but many Spanish colonists abroad refused to accept his legitimacy to rule.

As you can see, revolution was in the air. In fact, revolutionary sentiment had long been stirring in Spain's American colonies because of various political and economic grievances. Then, in Venezuela in 1811, some rebels took advantage of this period of Spanish weakness and declared independence from Spain. But colonists who remained loyal to Spain fought the rebels. They won an early victory, but the rebels continued fighting. The civil war that took place lasted off and on for almost a decade.

As for Bolivar, he was at the forefront fighting with the rebels. He didn't begin as the leader of the movement although he was a colonel and one of its best officers. However, this changed early in the revolution. In 1813, Bolivar led forces under his control in the capture of the Venezuelan capital of Caracas. Upon doing so, he declared himself the military leader of Venezuela.

W Student: Was Bolivar elected by the people of Venezuela?

M: Not at all. There were no elections. But no one really expected that. Remember, uh, that elections weren't particularly common in most countries until the twentieth century. Anyway, back to Bolivar . . . Not everyone supported his rule, but the other rebel military commanders did nothing to stop him. Yet the situation soon changed, and, in 1814, royalist forces pushed Bolivar and his troops out of Venezuela. Bolivar himself was arrested and forced into exile. Soon afterward, the Napoleonic Wars in Europe ended, and the Spanish crown was restored. Spain subsequently sent a force of 10,000 men to restore order in its colonies.

For the next several years, Bolivar and others like him attempted to restart the revolution from abroad. They encountered setbacks but also won some victories. I don't want to get into the minutiae of those individual battles though. [11]Just know that it wasn't until 1821 that Bolivar emerged victorious in Venezuela. As an added bonus, his forces also liberated Columbia. Victory wasn't easy though. There were many battles, large numbers of people died, and Bolivar faced several challenges to his leadership, all of which he ruthlessly put down.

After winning in Venezuela, Bolivar set out to fulfill his dream of creating one large state in South America. It was to be called Gran Colombia. His idea was to form a state so powerful that the Spanish—or other Europeans for that matter—could never reconquer the continent. Between 1821 and 1824, Bolivar led forces that achieved the independence of Peru and Bolivia. These lands became part of Gran Colombia.

But the newly unified state didn't last long. By 1826, there were signs of an impending breakup, and, by 1828, people were opening calling for an end to the experiment. To retain his cherished dream, Bolivar declared himself dictator and violently suppressed any opposition. Bolivar truly believed he was doing what was best for South America's former Spanish colonies. But the people disagreed. There was even a failed assassination attempt in 1828. Bolivar soon fell ill with tuberculosis. As he died in 1830, so too did his dream of a unified state. Despite the fact that Gran Colombia fell apart, Bolivar's lasting legacy endures as he's without a doubt South America's greatest hero.

Translation

M Professor: 남아메리카 역사에서 가장 중요한 인물 중 한 명은 시몬 볼리바르입니다. 그는 자신의 지도력으로, 어, 당시 스페인의 지배를 받고 있었던 남아메리카의 수많은 국가들에 독립을 안겨다 주었습니다. 이러한 국가들에는 베네수엘라, 볼리비아, 페루, 그리고 콜롬비아가 있습니다.

그 사람 자신에 대해서 말을 해보면, 시몬 볼리바르는 1793년 베네수엘라에서 태어났습니다. 집안은 귀족에 속했고 상당히 부유했습니다. 하지만 볼리바르가 소년이었을 때 부모님이 사망했기 때문에, 그는 여러 명의 유모에 의해 길러졌고 가정 교사들에 의해 교육을 받았습니다. 교육을 받는 동안, 그는 자유의 원칙에 대해 알게 되었는데, 이 원칙들은 스페인의 지배로부터 독립을 얻고자 하는 그의 열망에 불을 붙여 주었습니다. 볼리바르의 아버지는 군사 장교였기 때문에, 볼리바르는 십대 때 아버지의 뒤를 따라 육군 사관 학교에 입학했습니다.

볼리바르가 어렸을 당시, 스페인이 베네수엘라를 지배하고 있었지만, 스페인은 약했고 본국에서의 수많은 문제로 어려움을 겪고 있었습니다. 미 대륙을 발견한 후 수십 년 동안, 스페인은 세상에서 가장 크고 가장 부유한 제국이 되었지만, 음, 어디 봅시다… 잘못된 행정, 낭비, 그리고 유럽과 해외에서의 셀 수 없을 정도의 군사적 실패로 1800년대에는 매우 약해졌습니다. 게다가, 1700년대 후반과 1800년대 초반은 신대륙에서 혁명이 일어났던 시기였습니다. 예를 들면, 미국은 1783년에 영국으로부터 독립을 얻어냈고, 아이티는 오랜 전쟁 끝에 1804년 프랑스의 지배로부터 해방되었습니다.

대서양의 맞은편, 프랑스에서는 1789년에 혁명이 발생했습니다. 하지만 1800년대가 시작될 무렵, 나폴레옹은 스페인을 포함한 유럽 대부분의 지역으로 군대를 이끌고 진군했습니다. 1808년 프랑스 군대가 스페인을 침공했지만 스페인을 완전히 점령하지는 못했습니다. 그 결과, 전쟁이 장기화되었습니다. 이로 인해 스페인은 훨씬 더 약해졌습니다. 얼마 후, 스페인 국왕이 퇴위했는데, 이로써 스페인에는 중앙 정부가 존재하지 않게 되었습니다. 나폴레옹은 자신의 동생을 스페인 국왕으로 만듦으로써 정부를 세우려고 했지만, 해외의 많은 스페인 식민지 사람들은 그러한 통치의 정당성을 인정하지 않았습니다.

짐작할 수 있듯이, 혁명의 분위기가 감돌게 되었습니다. 사실, 미국에 있는 스페인의 식민지에서는 오랫동안 혁명의 분위기가 감돌고 있었는데, 이는 다양한 정치적, 경제적인 불만들 때문이었습니다. 그러자, 1811년 베네수엘라에서, 스페인이 약해진 틈을 타서 일부 반란 세력들이 스페인으로부터의 독립을 선언했습니다. 하지만 스페인에 대한 충성심이 남아 있던 식민지 사람들은 반란군과 맞서 싸웠습니다. 처음에는 그들이 승리했지만, 반란군들은 싸움을 계속했습니다. 이렇게 발생한 내전은 거의 10년 동안 지속되었습니다.

볼리바르에 대해 말하자면, 그는 반란군과 함께 선두에 서서 싸웠습니다. 그는 대령이었고 선임 장교 중 한 명이었으나, 처음부터 혁명의 지도자는 아니었습니다. 하지만, 혁명의 초기에 이러한 상황은 바뀌었습니다. 1813년, 볼리바르는 자신의 지휘 하에 군대를 이끌고 베네수엘라의 수도인 카라카스를 점령했습니다. 점령을 하자마자, 그는 자신이 베네수엘라군의 지도자라고 선언을 했습니다.

W Student: 볼리바르가 베네수엘라 국민들에 의해서 선출되었나요?

M: 결코 그렇지 않습니다. 선거는 없었습니다. 하지만 어느 누구도 선거를 기대하지는 않았습니다. 20세기가 될 때 까지는, 어, 선거가 대부분의 국가에서 그렇게 일반적인 것이 아니었다는 점을 기억해 두십시오. 어쨌든, 볼리바르에 대한 이야기로 돌아와서… 모든 사람들이 그의 통치를 지지했던 것은 아니었지만, 다른 반란군 지도자들이 그를 막을 수는 없었습니다. 하지만 곧 상황이 바뀌었고, 1814년, 왕당파의 군대가 볼리바르와 그의 군대를 베네수엘라에서 몰아냈습니다. 볼리바르는 체포되었고 강제 추방을 당했습니다. 얼마 후, 유럽에서는 나폴레옹 전쟁이 끝나고, 스페인 왕이 복위되었습니다. 스페인은 그 후 식민지의 질서를 회복하기 위해서 식민지에 10,000명의 군대를 파병했습니다.

그 후로 몇 년 동안, 볼리바르와 그와 같은 사람들은 해외에서 혁명을 재개하려고 시도했습니다. 패배를 하기도 했지만 몇 차례의 승리도 거두었습니다. 하지만 이러한 전투에 대해서 상세히 설명하고 싶지는 않군요. 1821년이 되어서야 볼리바르가 베네수엘라에서 승리를 하게 되었다는 사실만 알아 두십시오. 부수적인 결과로, 그의 군대는 콜롬비아 역시 해방시켰습니다. 하지만 승리는 쉽지 않았습니다. 많은 전투가 있었고, 수많은 사람들이 사망했으며, 볼리바르는 자신의 지도력에 대항하는 몇 차례의 도전을 받았는데, 그는 이러한 것들을 무자비하게 진압했습니다.

베네수엘라에서의 승리 후, 볼리바르는 남아메리카에 거대한 국가를 세우려는 자신의 꿈을 성취하고자 했습니다. 그란 콜롬비아라 불리는 것이었죠. 스페인 사람들이 — 또는 이 문제에 대해서는 다른 유럽인들도 — 결코 남미 대륙을 다시 침략하지 못하도록 강력한 국가를 세우는 것이 그의 생각이었습니다. 1821년에서 1824년 사이에, 볼리바르는 페루와 콜롬비아의 독립을 이루어 냈던 군대를 이끌었습니다. 이 지역들은 그란 콜롬비아의 일부가 되었습니다.

하지만 새롭게 통합된 국가는 오래 지속되지 않았습니다. 1826년경, 해체가 임박했다는 징후들이 나타났고, 1828년경에는, 사람들이 그러한 실험을 중단할 것을 요구하기 시작했습니다. 자신이 간직해 왔던 꿈을 이어가기 위해, 볼리바르는 스스로를 절대 권력자라 칭하고 모든 반대 세력을 폭력적으로 억압했습니다. 볼리바르는 자신의 행동이 이전 스페인 식민지였던 남미 국가들에게 최선의 것이라고 굳게 믿었습니다. 하지만 사람들은 그렇게 생각하지 않았습니다. 1828년에는 한 차례의 암살 시도가 실패로 끝나기도 했습니다. 볼리바르는 곧 폐결핵에 걸렸습니다. 1830년 그가 사망함에 따라, 통합된 국가를 세우려는 그의 꿈도 함께 사라졌습니다. 그란 콜롬비아는 해체되었지만, 볼리바르가 의심할 바 없이 남미에서 가장 위대한 영웅으로 남아 있기 때문에, 그의 유산은 지속되고 있습니다.

Actual Test 07

Reading Section   p.81

Answers

1. Ⓑ [Factual Question]
2. Ⓑ [Vocabulary Question]
3. Ⓑ [Rhetorical Purpose Question]
4. Ⓒ [Sentence Simplification Question]
5. Ⓒ [Reference Question]
6. Ⓐ [Vocabulary Question]
7. Ⓓ [Vocabulary Question]
8. Ⓑ [Factual Question]
9. Ⓐ [Inference Question]
10. Ⓐ [Vocabulary Question]
11. Ⓓ [Factual Question]
12. Ⓒ [Negative Factual Question]
13. 1st [Insert Text Question]
14. Ⓐ, Ⓒ, Ⓕ [Prose Summary Question]

Translation

산불 통제

산불은 특정한 나무들이 열과 불에 의해 손상을 입지 않고 성장할 수 있도록 하며, 동시에 산림의 성장을 조절해 주는 하나의 자연적인 방법이다. (이는 미국 이외의 지역에서도 마찬가지이다.) 하지만 인간의 활동에 의해 미국 서부의 몇몇 지역에서는 이러한 균형이 무너졌다. 여러 가지 요인으로 인하여, 이는 현재 발생하고 있는 산불의 강도 및 지속 기간을 수십 년 전 보다 증대시키는 상황을 초래했다. 그 결과, 오랜 기간에 걸쳐, 넓은 지역을 뒤덮는 보다 빈번하고 강력한 산불이 일어나게 될 것으로 예상되고 있다.

이러한 현상에 대한 하나의 사례는 비터루트 산의 숲에서 찾아볼 수 있는데, 이 산은 미 서부의 몬태나 주에 위치해 있다. 20세기 초반, 산불 진압과 관련된 기관들은 모든 산불을 발생하자마자 진화하는 것을 그 목표로 삼았다. 하지만, 1945년 제 2차 세계 대전이 끝난 이후에야 이러한 목표가 성취될 수 있었다. 그 이유는, 전쟁이 끝난 후, 도로망이 개선되었는데, 이로 인하여 소방관들은 보다 쉽게 화재 현장에 도착할 수 있었고, 여분의 전투기는 소방용 항공기로 활용될 수 있었다. 수 년이 흐른 뒤, 화재가 발생하는 즉시 진화를 하는 것이 가능해 졌다. 수십 년 동안 아무런 문제도 없었다. 그 후, 갑자기, 1980년대에, 비터루트 산에서 화재 발생이 더욱 빈번해 지고 그 강도도 강해졌는데, 그 확산 속도가 너무나 빨라서 일부 산불은 비가 충분히 내린 뒤에야 진화될 수 있었다. 이러한 추세는 1990년대와 2010년까지 계속되었다.

산불 전문가들에 의해 가장 널리 인정받고 있는 이론은, 지난 수십 년 동안 모든 산불을 너무 빠르게 진화함으로써, 인간이 몬태나 주의 숲의 자연적인 균형을 무너뜨렸다는 것이다. 과거, 대부분의 산불은 번개에 의해 발생했으며 대략 10년 주기로 숲의 일정한 지역을 태웠다. 몬태나 주의 숲에는 쉽게 불이 붙는 키 작은 전나무들과, 껍질이 두꺼워서 불에 상당히 잘 견디는 키 큰 소나무들이 섞여 있다. 대부분의 장소에서 평균적으로 10년에 한 번 정도 화재가 발생하기 때문에, 전나무들과 다른 작은 나무들이 높이 자랄 수 있는 시간은 충분치 않다. 대신, 이 나무들은 불에 타 죽지만, 나무들의 씨앗이 땅에 묻혀 싹이 터서 다음 번의 화재가 발생하기 전까지 또 다시 자라기 시작한다. 반면, 소나무는 높이 강하게 자라서 산불을 막아 주는 방화벽 역할을 한다; 이들이 불에 잘 견디기 때문에 산불의 확산이 차단된다. 하지만 인간이 산불을 진화하기 시작하면서 상황이 달라졌다. 인간의 행동으로 전나무가 높이 자라게 되었고, 곧 소나무 주변은 전나무로 빽빽하게 되었다.

이 때문에, 1980년대 몬태나 주에서 산불이 발생했을 때, 불길이 점점 높이 치솟아서 높이 자란 전나무의 가지에 불이 붙었다. 불길은 전나무와 소나무의 꼭대기까지 퍼졌다. 이러한 화재는 너무나 강력하게 타올라서 때때로 불길이 수백 미터까지 타올라 다른 나무에 옮겨 붙기도 했다. 몇몇 경우에는, 사실상 화재 폭풍이 일어나 불길이 너무 빠르게 확산되어, 자연적인 진화, 즉 비가 내리기 전까지는 진화가 불가능했다.

산불의 강도에 영향을 미치는 또 다른 요인은 벌목 회사의 행태이다. 이 회사들은 가장 크고 가장 좋은 소나무를 벌목했는데, 이로 인하여 내화성이 강한 나무 중 일부가 숲에서 사라졌다. 게다가, 벌목업자들은 나무를 벌목한 후 가지를 쳐내어 이를 숲의 바닥에 남겨 두었다. 이러한 가지들은 불쏘시개 역할을 했고 번개에 의해 발생하는 산불이 빠르게 확산되도록 만들었다.

이러한 산불들은 너무도 강력했기 때문에, 몬태나 주의 숲에 살고 있는 많은 주택 소유자들은 자신의 집이 불에 타는 것을 지켜볼 수 밖에 없었다. 게다가, 귀중한 목재들도 함께 타버렸다. 개인들과 벌목 회사 모두 정부를 비판하면서 정책의 변화를 요구했다. 하지만 규모가 작은 산불을 통제하여 자연의 균형을 복원하려는 정부의 계획은 일부 사람들의 강력한 반대에 직면하고 있다. 앞으로 어떠한 일이 발생하더라도, 한 가지는 확실하다: 앞으로도 산불이 계속 존재할 것이라는 점이다. 알 수 없는 한 가지는, 산불이 어느 정도까지 강력해 질 것인가이다.

Listening Section p.87

Answers

1. B [Gist-Purpose Question]
2. A [Making Inferences Question]
3. C [Detail Question]
4. C [Understanding Attitude Question]
5. D [Understanding Function Question]
6. B [Gist-Content Question]
7. D [Detail Question]
8. B [Understanding Organization Question]
9. C [Making Inferences Question]
10. A [Understanding Function Question]
11. C [Making Inferences Question]

Script

| 07-02 |

W1 Student: Knock, knock. Professor Reeves, may I come in now?

W2 Professor: Of course, Cindy. I did, after all, call and ask you to drop by my office today.

W1: Yes, ma'am. I would have been here earlier in the day, but I had a couple of classes to attend. One was my seminar, and you know how long those classes can run.

W2: I sure do. I'm teaching one this semester. Sometimes it seems like they last all afternoon long. Anyway, I didn't ask you here to talk about our schedules. I have something more important to discuss.

W1: Really? What's that?

W2: Well, as you know, I'm currently conducting research on dolphins. I'm doing some studies of them in the wild, so I spend lots of time on the ocean. Well, I just received some really good news . . . I applied for a grant from the government, and it was accepted. It's a, uh, well, a rather sizable amount of money that I'm being given.

W1: ⁵Congratulations. That's wonderful news.

W2: Ah, yes. Thank you. Anyway, you're probably wondering what this has to do with you, aren't you?

W1: Uh, yes, but I think I might see what you're getting at.

W2: Yeah, I figured that you would. So, uh, this grant is going to enable me to expand the amount of work I'm doing. In order to do that, I'm going to have to hire at least one—but probably two—students to assist me with my work. And I'd like for you to be one of my student assistants.

W1: Seriously?

W2: Sure. Why not? You're not only a hard worker, but you're also one of the top students in the Biology Department. I also know that you're interested in attending graduate school, so this would look really good on your applications.

W1: This sounds great, but, uh, don't you have to be a graduate student to work on one of these projects? I mean, I'm not really qualified for this, am I?

W2: Hmm . . . As a general rule, most professors hire graduate students to do this kind of work. However, I don't think that any of the graduate students in this department are qualified for the work that I need done.

W1: But you think that I am?

W2: Sure. You know, Cindy, I'm quite familiar with your work. I do have firsthand experience with it you know. And the other professors in the department speak rather glowingly about you as well. Even if you don't know it, you've got quite a good reputation in the Biology Department.

W1: Uh . . . Actually, I had no clue. But . . .

W2: But what?

W1: Well, I'm totally flattered, but I've been offered a job by a company that's doing research on humpback whales. It's a marine lab located fairly near my house. If I take that job, I don't believe I'll have time to do your work for you.

W2: Oh . . . I had no idea. That's something of a problem.

W1: Yeah, so what do you think I should do?

W2: Well, you've got to go with the better offer. Let me write down the description of the job I want you to do—as well as the salary I can pay you—and then you can compare the two offers. After that, choose the one you want. How does that sound?

W1: Great. I appreciate that a lot, Professor Reeves.

Translation

W1 Student: 똑, 똑, *Reeves* 교수님, 지금 들어가도 될까요?

W2 Professor: 물론이죠, *Cindy*. 전화해서 오늘 내 사무실에 들러 달라고 한 것은 바로 저니까요.

W1: 네, 교수님. 오늘 더 일찍 오려고 했지만, 들어야 할 수업이 두 개가 있었어요. 한 수업은 세미나였는데, 그러한 수업들이 얼마나 오래 걸리는지 교수님도 아실 거예요.

W2: 물론 잘 알아요. 나도 이번 학기에 한 과목을 가르치고 있는걸요. 때로는 오후 내내 진행되는 것 같기도 해요. 어쨌든, 시간표에 대해서 이야기를 하려고 학생을 부른 것은 아니에요. 논의해야 할 보다 중요한 사안이 있어요.

W1: 정말이요? 무엇인가요?

W2: 음, 학생도 알고 있는 것처럼, 나는 최근에 돌고래에 대한 연구를 하고 있어요. 야생 돌고래에 대한 몇 가지 연구를 진행하고 있어서, 많은 시간을 바다에서 보내고 있죠. 그런데, 정말 좋은 소식을 들었어요… 정부에 보조금을 신청했는데, 그것이 승인되었죠. 받게 될 보조금은, 어, 그러니까, 상당한 금액이 될 거예요.

W1: 축하드립니다. 정말 좋은 소식이네요.

W2: 아, 네, 고마워요 어쨌든, 학생은 아마도 이번 일이 본인과 어떤 관련이 있는지 궁금해 할 것 같군요, 그렇지 않나요?

W1: 어, 네, 하지만 교수님께서 하시려는 말씀을 알 것 같아요.

W2: 네, 그러리라고 생각해요. 그러니까, 어, 이번 보조금을 통해서 내가 수행하고 있는 연구를 확장시킬 수 있게 되었어요. 그렇게 하기 위해, 연구를 보조해 줄 최소한 한 명 — 혹은 두 명 정도의 학생을 채용할 예정이에요. 그리고 학생이 연구 보조 학생 중 한 명이 되었으면 좋겠고요.

W1: 정말이세요?

W2: 물론이죠. 왜 아니겠어요? 학생은 성실할 뿐만 아니라, 생물 학과에서 가장 뛰어난 학생 중 한 명이잖아요. 또한 학생이 대학원 진학에 관심을 가지고 있는 것으로 알고 있는데, 이번 일은 대학원 지원에 정말로 도움이 될 거예요.

W1: 정말 좋게 들리지만, 어, 이러한 프로젝트를 수행하려면 대학원생이어야 하지 않나요? 저는 자격이 되지 않는다고 생각하는데, 제가 자격이 되나요?

W2: 흠… 일반적으로, 대부분의 교수님들은 대학원생들을 고용해서 이러한 종류의 연구를 하죠. 하지만, 나는 우리 학과의 어떤 대학원생들도 내가 하는 연구에 적임이라고 생각하지 않아요.

W1: 하지만 저는 적임이라고 생각하시는 건가요?

W2: 물론이에요. 그러니까, *Cindy*, 나는 학생의 노력에 대해 잘 알고 있어요. 알겠지만 내가 직접 경험한 걸요. 그리고 우리 학과의 다른 교수님들도 학생을 좋게 생각하고 있어요. 학생은 잘 모르겠지만, 학생은 생물학과 내에서 평판이 상당히 좋아요.

W1: 어… 실은, 전혀 모르고 있었어요. 하지만…

W2: 하지만 무엇인가요?

W1: 그러니까, 정말 영광이지만, 저는 한 회사에서 혹등고래의 연구와 관련된 일을 제안받았어요. 저의 집에서 상당히 가까운 곳에 있는 해양 연구소죠. 만약 그 일을 하게 된다면, 교수님께서 제안하신 일을 할 수 있는 시간이 있을지 모르겠어요.

W2: 오… 제가 몰랐네요. 문제가 되긴 하겠군요.

W1: 네, 제가 어떻게 하면 좋을까요?

W2: 음, 보다 좋은 제안을 받아 들여야 해요. 학생이 해야 할 업무를 — 학생에게 지급할 급여도 포함해서 — 적어 줄 테니, 두 가지 제안을 비교해 볼 수 있을 거예요. 그리고 나서, 학생이 원하는 하나를 선택하도록 해요. 어떤가요?

W1: 좋아요. 정말 감사합니다, *Reeves* 교수님.

Script

| 07-03 |

W Professor: We often think of art as something that's painted on canvas or sculpted from marble. But art comes in many forms. As we saw in an earlier class, numerous illuminated manuscripts were produced during the Middle Ages. In my opinion, those books contain some of the most beautiful artwork ever produced.

Well, there are some books from relatively recent times that can also be considered works of art. One was by John James Audubon. You probably know the name from the Audubon Society. But you may or may not know that Audubon was one of the greatest figures in the study of birds. [10]Today, we're going to focus on the famous book of bird illustrations he made in the nineteenth century. **This collection of colored illustrations is arguably the best example we have of the methods of collecting and making images of birds in the time before photography became commonplace.** Not only that, but, as you will see in a couple of minutes, many of his pictures can also be considered literal works of art.

Audubon was a Frenchman—born in Haiti in 1785—but later became an American. As a child, Audubon moved to France with his father. However, in 1803, his father sent him to live in America.

M Student: That's peculiar. Why did he do that?

W: Well, in 1803, Napoleon was sending his armies to fight wars in Europe. Audubon was eligible to be drafted, which his father didn't want. So he sent his son to America to escape from the wars. As for Audubon, in America, he tried his hand at a number of businesses, but he was pretty much unsuccessful at everything. He married and had four children, but two died in infancy. His wife was a school teacher, and it was she who primarily supported the family while Audubon was preparing his massive work on birds.

[11]Audubon was fascinated by birds for most of his life. He studied them while living in France and America, and he even picked up various skills as an artist and taxidermist. **Er, that's a person who stuffs and mounts dead animals.** So, at an early age, Audubon began drawing birds. It was around 1820 when he set himself the task of making a book of illustrations of American birds, which he, appropriately enough, called *Birds of America*. Between 1820 and 1826, he drew hundreds of illustrations of a wide variety of American birds from many parts of the country. Here are some of the more famous ones . . . here . . . another . . . and another. There are lots more, but I'll show them to you after I finish my chat about Audubon.

Anyway, ultimately, 435 illustrations were included in the book. Audubon tried to get his work published in America, but it was rejected by every publisher he visited.

M: People rejected his book? Why? Those pictures were beautiful. I can't believe an editor would turn an entire book of them down.

W: I agree, but they had a good reason: the price. You see, at that time, producing a work such as Audubon's required the use of engraved copper plates. And they were incredibly expensive then. American publishers couldn't afford the plates, so Audubon set off for England. There, he presented himself as an American frontiersman. He quickly captured the attention of the English, which enabled him to snare a publisher. In 1827, the book started being published in sections. It wasn't until 1838 that the last part of it was actually printed.

Now, we're interested in this book for its artistic value. It was, you see, a tremendous work of art. The realism of the illustrations is startling. Yes?

M: How did Audubon manage to get such close views of the birds if he didn't have a camera?

W: Oh, that's easy. He shot the birds.

M: Huh? Like, uh, with a gun?

W: Of course. That's how they did things back during his time. Anyway, Audubon shot the birds with buckshot so as not to damage them too much. He actually spent lots of time in the field hunting various birds. After he brought them back home, he would string them into various poses by using wire. He tried to put them into natural positions, such as, uh, eating, grooming, or flying. Then, he spent several hours a day drawing or painting his illustrations. Audubon used watercolors, chalk, and pastels for his works. And many of his pictures included drawings of eggs, birds' nests, trees, branches, and other objects that were found in nature. Finally, he strove to draw each bird as close to life size as possible. In short, it was the realism of Audubon's work that set him apart from the other bird artists of his time.

Well, I believe that's enough background. Why don't we take a short break now before we look at some of his illustrations, and then you can judge the quality of his work for yourself? I believe most of you will be quite impressed.

Translation

W Professor: 우리는 종종 캔버스에 그린 그림이나 대리석을 조각한 것을 미술이라고 생각합니다. 하지만 미술은 여러 가지 형태를 지니고 있습니다. 이전 수업에서 본 것처럼, 중세 시대에는 수많은 채색 필사본이 제작되었습니다. 제 의견이지만, 지금까지 제작되었던 것 중 가장 아름다운 미술 작품들이 이러한 책들에 포함되어 있습니다.

음, 미술 작품으로 간주될 수 있는 비교적 최근의 책들이 몇 권 있습니다. 그 중 하나가 존 제임스 오듀본의 책입니다. 여러분은 아마도 오듀본 협회를 통해서 그의 이름을 알고 있을 것입니다. 하지만 오듀본이 조류 연구 분야에 있어서 가장 뛰어난 인물 중 한 명이었다는 사실은 알고 있을 수도, 모르고 있을 수도 있겠군요. 오늘은, 그가 19세기에 그린 새들의 그림이 포함된 유명한 책에 초점을 맞추어 보고자 합니다. 컬러 그림이 실려 있는 이 서적은 사진술이 널리 퍼지기 전에 당시의 새들의 모습을 수집하고 그 이미지를 알아 볼 수 있는, 가장 좋은 본보기가 될 수 있을 것입니다. 뿐만 아니라, 잠시 후에 알게 되겠지만, 그의 많은 그림은 두 말할 틈없는 미술 작품으로 간주될 수 있을 것입니다.

오듀본은 — 아이티 출생의 — 프랑스인이었지만, 이후 미국인이 되었습니다. 어렸을 때, 오듀본은 아버지와 함께 프랑스로

떠났습니다. 그러나, 1803년, 그의 아버지는 그를 미국으로 보냈습니다.

M Student: 그것 참 이상하군요. 왜 그랬던 것인가요?

W: 음, 1803년, 나폴레옹은 유럽에서의 전쟁을 위해 자신의 군대를 보냈습니다. 오듀본은 징병의 대상이 되었는데, 그의 아버지는 이를 원치 않았습니다. 그래서 자신의 아들을 전쟁으로부터 빼내기 위해 아들을 미국으로 보냈던 것이었죠. 오듀본에 대해 이야기하면, 미국에서, 그는 여러 사업에 손을 댔으나, 모든 것에서 막대한 실패를 맛보았습니다. 그는 결혼을 했고 네 명의 아이들을 얻었지만, 두 아이들은 유아기에 사망했습니다. 그의 아내는 학교 선생님이었는데, 오듀본이 새에 관한 방대한 작업을 준비하는 동안 가족을 부양한 것은 바로 그녀였습니다.

오듀본은 거의 평생 동안 새에 매료되어 있었습니다. 그는 프랑스와 미국에 살면서 새를 연구했고, 심지어 화가와 박제사로서의 다양한 기술도 습득했습니다. 어, 박제사는 죽은 동물의 몸에 속을 채워서 박제를 하는 사람입니다. 그리고, 어린 시절에, 오듀본은 새의 그림을 그리기 시작했습니다. 미국의 새의 그림이 실려 있는 서적을 제작하는 일은 1820년 무렵에 시작되었는데, 그는 이 책을, 상당히 적절하게, *미국의 새들*이라고 이름 붙였습니다. 1820년과 1826년 사이, 그는 여러 지역의 다양한 미국 새들에 대해 수백여 점의 그림을 그렸습니다. 여기에 보다 유명한 그림들이 있는데… 여기… 또 다른 그림… 그리고 또 다른 그림입니다. 많은 그림들이 더 있지만, 오듀본에 대한 이야기를 끝낸 후 보여 드리도록 하죠.

어쨌든, 모두 다 해서, 435점의 그림이 책에 실려 있습니다. 오듀본은 미국에서 자신의 책을 출판하려고 했지만, 그가 방문했던 모든 출판사들이 출판을 거절했습니다.

M: 그의 책을 거절했다고요? 왜요? 이 그림들은 아름다운데요. 편집자가 책 전부를 출판하지 않겠다고 했다니 믿을 수가 없네요.

W: 저도 그렇게 생각합니다만, 그럴만한 이유가 있었죠: 바로 가격이었습니다. 그러니까, 당시, 오듀본이 그린 그림과 같은 작품을 제작하려면 음각 동판을 사용해야 했습니다. 그리고 당시에 이 판들의 가격은 꽤 높았습니다. 미국의 출판사들은 이러한 판을 구입할 여력이 없었기 때문에, 오듀본은 영국으로 갔습니다. 그곳에서, 그는 자신을 미국의 개척자로 소개했습니다. 그는 빠르게 영국인들의 관심을 받았는데, 이로 인하여 출판사를 설득할 수가 있었습니다. 1827년, 이 책은 부분적으로 출판되기 시작했습니다. 1838년이 되어서야 비로소 책의 마지막 부분이 인쇄되었습니다.

자, 우리는 예술적인 가치 때문에 이 책에 관심을 가지고 있습니다. 이 책은, 정말이지, 대단한 미술 작품집입니다. 그림의 사실성은 놀랍습니다. 네?

M: 오듀본은 사진기도 없이 어떻게 이렇게 새를 가까이서 볼 수 있었나요?

W: 오, 그것은 쉬웠습니다. 새를 사냥했던 것이었죠.

M: 네? 그러니까, 어, 총으로요?

W: 물론입니다. 그 당시에는 그런 식으로 했습니다. 어쨌든, 오듀본은 새에게 너무 많은 손상이 가지 않도록 산탄으로 새를 쏘았습니다. 실제로 그는 다양한 새를 사냥하기 위해 들판에서 많은 시간을 보냈습니다. 새들을 집으로 가져온 후에는, 철사로 묶어서 다양한 자세를 만들었습니다. 그는 새들을 자연스러운 모습으로 만들려고 했는데, 예를 들면, 어, 먹이를 먹거나, 깃털을 손질하거나, 날아가는 모습으로 말이죠. 그리고 나서, 하루에 몇 시간 동안 밑그림을 그리고 채색을 했습니다. 오듀본은 자신의 작품에 물감, 초크, 그리고 파스텔을 사용했습니다. 그리고 그의 많은 그림에는 알, 새의 둥지, 나무, 나뭇가지, 그리고 자연에서 찾아볼 수 있는 여러 가지 사물들이 포함되었습니다. 마지막으로, 그는 각각의 새를 최대한 실물 크기와 비슷하게 그리려고 노력했습니다. 요컨대, 그가 당시의 다른 조류 화가들과 다른 점은 바로 오듀본 작품에 나타나 있는 사실성 때문이었습니다.

자, 이제 배경 지식은 충분하다고 생각합니다. 그의 그림들을 보기 전에 잠시 휴식을 취한 후, 작품의 우수성을 여러분이 직접 판단해 보는 것이 어떨까요? 여러분 대부분이 깊은 인상을 받게 될 것이라고 생각합니다.

Actual Test 08

Reading Section p.93

Answers

1. Ⓐ [Negative Factual Question]
2. Ⓓ [Factual Question]
3. Ⓒ [Rhetorical Purpose Question]
4. Ⓓ [Inference Question]
5. Ⓑ [Factual Question]
6. Ⓑ [Reference Question]
7. Ⓑ [Vocabulary Question]
8. Ⓒ [Rhetorical Purpose Question]
9. Ⓐ [Factual Question]
10. Ⓓ [Vocabulary Question]
11. Ⓐ [Factual Question]
12. 2nd [Insert Text Question]
13.

	PHENOMENON
Pulsar	Ⓕ, Ⓖ
Quasar	Ⓐ, Ⓑ, Ⓓ

Translation

펄서와 퀘이서

우주에서 발생하는 가장 독특한 현상 중 두 가지는 펄서와 퀘이서이다. 이들의 명칭이 비슷하고 이 둘 모두 다 잘 이해되고 있지는 않지만, 펄서와 퀘이서에는 공통점이 거의 없다. 펄서는 전파를 방출하는 소멸된 별인 반면, 은하 중심부에 있는 블랙홀의 활동에 의해서 생성되는 퀘이서는 우주에서 가장 밝은 물체이다. 덧붙여 말하자면, 이들은 생성 과정, 방출하는 빛과 전파의 양, 그리고 지구로부터의 거리에 있어서도 서로 다르다.

1967년, 두 명의 천문학자가 전적으로 우연히 펄서를 발견했다. 그들은 밤 하늘을 관찰하는 동안, 초당 일정한 간격으로 날아오는 전파의 진원지를 발견했다. 곧 이어, 천문학자들은 이러한 진동 전파의 진원지를 더 많이 발견하기 시작했고, 이들의 명칭을 펄서라고 정했다. 이때부터 대략 300개의 펄서가 발견되었다. 펄서는 거대한 초신성의 폭발로 별이 소멸할 때 생성된다. 이러한 일이 발생하면, — 중성자 별이라고 불리는 — 압축된 핵이 남겨진다. 중성자 별에는 엄청난 자기장이 존재하는데, 이로 인하여 전파를 포함한 상당한 양의 전자기파가 방출된다. 중성자의 극지방이 지구 쪽으로 일직선 상에 놓여지면, 중성자 별이 회전할 때 마다 지구에서 전파를 감지할 수 있게 된다. 천문학자들은 이를 등대 효과라고 부르는데, 중성자 별에서 방출되는 전파가 등대 및 등대에서 회전하는 등과 비슷하기 때문이다.

반면, 퀘이서는 은하 중심부에 있는 블랙홀 주변의 밀집 영역에 존재한다. 퀘이서는 우주에서 가장 밝은 물체이지만, 이러한 밝기에도 불구하고, 지구로부터의 거리가 너무 멀어서 가장 성능이 좋은 망원경을 통해서만 관측이 가능하다. 실제로, 퀘이서는 너무 밝아서, 그 밝기 때문에 퀘이서가 위치해 있는 은하가 보이지 않을 정도다. 퀘이서의 엄청난 광도에는 이유가 있다. 어떠한 물체도 — 빛을 포함하여 — 블랙홀로부터 벗어날 수가 없기 때문에, 블랙홀로 빨려 들어가는 물체에서 방출되는 에너지는, 그 물체가 블랙홀로 빨려 들어가기 전에 블랙홀 주변에서 응축 원반을 형성한다는 이론이 제시되었다. 은하 중심부에 있는 블랙홀의 크기가 상당할 것으로 여겨지고 있기 때문에, 응축 원반에서는 전파와 광파를 포함한 상당한 양의 에너지가 방출되고, 이로 인하여 응축 원반은 상당히 밝아진다. (퀘이서가 블랙홀을 감싸고 있기 때문에 이는 그 크기가 상당하다는 것을 의미한다.) 퀘이서가 항성인지 그렇지 않은 지에 대한 논쟁이 계속되고 있다; 하지만, 오늘날, 대부분의 천문학자들은 퀘이서가 단지 빛을 방출하고 은하 중심의 블랙홀 주변을 감싸고 있는 거대한 물체라고 생각한다. 게다가, 중심에 있는 블랙홀에서 충분한 양의 전자기 에너지가 방출되지 않는 경우가 있기 때문에, 모든 은하에 퀘이서가 존재하는 것은 아니다. 예를 들면, 지구의 태양이 위치해 있는 은하수뿐만 아니라, 비교적 가까운 거리에 있는 은하인 안드로메다 은하에도 퀘이서는 존재하지 않는다.

펄서와 퀘이서는 생성 연대에서도 상당한 차이를 보인다. 퀘이서는 빅뱅 직후에 생성되었다고 생각되는데, 빅뱅은 수십억 년 전에 우주의 탄생을 야기했던 사건이다. 하지만, 펄서는 어느 때라도 생성될 수 있다. 퀘이서는 또한 지구에서 상당히 멀고 — 일부 퀘이서는 100억 광년의 거리에 있다 — 지구 반대편으로 빠르게 이동한다. 지구에서 가장 가까운 거리에 있는 펄서는, 약 280광년의 거리에 있다.

퀘이서와 펄서의 한 가지 공통점은 이들이 깊은 방법으로 관측될 수 있다는 점이다. 이들 모두 전파를 방출하기 때문에 천문학자들은 초기에 전파 망원경을 사용하여 관측을 했다; 하지만, 퀘이서에서 밝은 빛이 방출되기 때문에, 멀리 떨어진 은하의 적색 편이를 분석하여 퀘이서의 존재 여부를 알 수도 있다. 적색 편이란 광파에서 붉은 빛이 보다 선명하게 나타나는 도플러 효과의 산물이다. 붉은 빛의 광파가 더 많다는 것은 어떠한 물체가 지구로부터 멀어지고 있다는 사실을 나타낸다. 물체의 광도 또한 적색 편이를 분석해 봄으로써 확인할 수 있다. 하지만, 지난 수십 년이 될 때까지, 퀘이서를 실제로 관측하는 것은 불가능했다. 지구에 거대한 망원경이 설치되고 지구 궤도에 허블 우주 망원경이 설치된 후에야, 과학자들은 멀리 떨어진 곳의 은하에서 퀘이서를 관측할 수 있게 되었다.

Listening Section p.99

Answers

1. Ⓑ [Gist-Purpose Question]
2. Ⓓ [Making Inferences Question]
3. Ⓐ [Understanding Attitude Question]
4. Ⓑ, Ⓓ [Detail Question]
5. Ⓒ [Understanding Function Question]
6. Ⓒ [Gist-Content Question]
7. Ⓐ [Detail Question]
8. Ⓐ, Ⓓ [Detail Question]
9. Ⓒ [Connecting Content Question]
10. Ⓑ [Understanding Organization Question]
11. Ⓓ [Understanding Function Question]

Script

| 08-02 |

M Student: Marcia, Sally told me that you wanted to have a word with me. Is there something I can help you with?

W Theater Employee: Well, Paul, I just wanted to give you an update on how progress is going with the costumes for the performance of *Romeo and Juliet* next week.

M: [4]Ah, that's great. Okay. Is everything ready?

W: Everything? No, not by a long shot. So, uh, do you want the good news or the bad news first?

M: Hmm . . . Let's go with the bad news first.

W: No problem. Well, there are actually a couple of problems that we have encountered. The first has to do with Juliet's wardrobe. As you know, she has to change clothes a few times during the performance. We've got most of her outfits prepared. However, we're having trouble with the one she's supposed to wear for the scene in which she sees Romeo for the first time.

M: Trouble? What kind of trouble?

W: Well, er . . . We had an outfit picked out for Sandra to wear, but, when we talked to the company that makes it, we found out that the dress is well above our budget.

We simply can't afford to purchase it unless we get some more money.

M: How much more money are we talking about here?

W: Er, about three hundred dollars or so.

M: Yikes. You're right. That's out of our budget. Okay. Suggestions?

W: Fortunately, I have one. Do you remember that the drama club put on a performance by Christopher Marlowe a couple of years ago?

M: Two years ago? I was only a freshman, so I can barely recall that. But I will take your word for it.

W: Anyway, as you know, Marlowe and William Shakespeare were contemporaries, so several of their plays were set in roughly the same era. Recently, I noticed that we still have the wardrobe from that performance in a storage room in this building. I believe that we should be able to find a sufficient dress for Sandra to wear. Do you mind if she wears one of the dresses from the Marlowe performance?

M: No, not at all. I doubt anyone will notice that Sandra's wearing an old dress. Besides, we don't really have any other options, do we?

W: When you put it that way, I guess not. Okay. I'll go back to the storage room and look through the dresses.

M: Good . . . Oh, wait a minute. You said that there were a few problems. I assume that Sandra's wardrobe is the major problem. What else do we need to solve?

W: Nothing too big. One of the fake swords we were planning to use broke, so we've ordered a new one. It should come in sometime next week. And a few of the other costumes that some minor characters are going to wear need to be adjusted because of the, uh, large sizes of some of our performers. I've got a seamstress coming tomorrow afternoon, so we need to make sure everyone is here to get measured properly.

M: Great. I'll make a note of that and remind everyone not to miss rehearsal tomorrow.

W: Excellent. All right, uh, that covers the bad news. I suppose it's time to give you the good news now.

Translation

M Student: Marcia 선생님, Sally가 선생님께서 저와 이야기를 나누고 싶어 하신다고 말해 주었어요. 제가 도와드릴 일이 있나요?

W Theater Employee: 음, Paul, 다음 주에 있을 로미오와 줄리엣 공연의 의상이 어떻게 진행되고 있는지 알려 주고자 했어요.

M: 아, 잘 되었군요. 좋아요. 모든 준비가 다 되었나요?

W: 모든 준비라고요? 전혀 그렇지 않아요. 그러니까, 어, 좋은 소식과 나쁜 소식 중 어떤 소식을 먼저 듣고 싶나요?

M: 흠… 나쁜 소식을 먼저 들을게요.

W: 걱정하지 말아요. 그러니까, 사실 두 가지의 문제가 있어요. 첫 번째 문제는 줄리엣의 무대 의상과 관련이 있어요. 알다시피, 그녀 역할은 공연 도중에 여러 번 의상을 갈아 입어야 해요. 그녀 의상은 대부분 준비가 끝났어요. 하지만, 그녀가 로미오를 처음으로 만나는 장면에 입어야 할 의상에 문제가 생겼어요.

M: 문제라고요? 어떤 문제인가요?

W: 그러니까, 어… Sandra가 입을 의상을 선택해 두었는데, 그 의상 제작 업체와 말을 할 때, 그 의상이 예산을 초과한다는 사실을 알게 되었어요. 돈이 더 없다면, 그 의상을 구입할 여유가 없는 것이지요.

M: 지금 이야기하고 있는 의상에 더 필요한 돈이 얼마인가요?

W: 어, 약 300달러 정도에요.

M: 이런. 선생님 말씀이 맞네요. 예산 초과군요. 좋아요. 제안하실 것은요?

W: 다행스럽게도, 한 가지 방법이 있어요. 2년 전에 연극 동아리에서 크리스토퍼 말로의 공연을 했던 것을 기억하고 있나요?

M: 2년 전이라고요? 저는 신입생이라서, 그에 대한 기억이 없어요. 하지만 선생님의 말씀을 믿을게요.

W: 어쨌든, 그러니까, 말로와 윌리엄 셰익스피어는 동시대 인물이라서, 그들의 몇몇 작품들은 배경도 대략 비슷한 시기죠. 최근, 그 공연에 사용했던 의상이 아직 이 건물의 창고에 보관되어 있다는 것을 알게 되었어요. 제 생각에 Sandra가 입을 수 있는 적절한 의상을 찾을 수 있을 것 같아요. 그녀가 말로의 공연에 사용했던 의상을 입는 것이 마음에 걸리나요?

M: 아니오, 전혀 그렇지 않아요. 제 생각에 Sandra가 기존 의상을 입고 있다는 점은 아무도 모를 거예요. 게다가, 다른 대안도 없고요, 그렇죠?

W: 그렇게 생각한다면, 대안은 없죠. 그래요. 창고에 가서 의상을 살펴보도록 할게요.

M: 좋아요… 오, 잠시만요. 선생님께서는 문제가 몇 가지 있다고 하셨어요. Sandra의 의상 문제가 주된 문제일 것 같고요. 해결해야 하는 또 다른 문제는 무엇인가요?

W: 그렇게 큰 문제는 없어요. 사용해야 할 모형 검들 중 한 자루가 부러져서, 새 검을 하나 주문했어요. 그 검은 다음 주에 도착할 거에요. 그리고 조연들이 입을 의상 중 몇 벌, 음, 몇몇 연기자들의 신체보다 더 커서 수선을 해야 돼죠. 내일 오후에 재봉사를 불렀기 때문에, 올바른 치수를 측정하기 위해서는 모든 연기자들을 이곳으로 불러야 해요.

M: 좋아요. 그 내용을 적어두었다가 모든 연기자들이 내일의 리허설에 불참하지 않도록 할게요.

W: 훌륭하군요. 좋아요, 어, 나쁜 소식은 다 다루었네요. 이제 좋은 소식을 들려주어야 할 때 같군요.

Script

| 08-03 |

M Professor: Another geological feature associated with continental drift is the rift valley. Rift valleys form in places where parts of the Earth's crust are drifting away from one another. There are some extensive rift valleys found in eastern Africa. There's also a lengthy underwater ridge in the middle of the Atlantic Ocean. Many ancient rift valleys are located all around the world. Lakes often form in rift valleys, and, interestingly, some of the world's deepest and largest lakes are found in them.

A rift valley may be dormant or active. A dormant rift valley is one where the spread has stopped. An active rift valley, as I'm sure you can figure out, is one where the spread is continuing. The spreading is a result of tectonic forces. As we learned when we talked about continental drift, our world is not a stable place. It's divided into many tectonic plates, all of which have been moving since the world began. Under these plates in the crust is the mantle. There, the forces of convection slowly push the plates around. In places where the plates are moving away from one another, such as in eastern Africa, rift valleys form. What happens is that, as the plates drift apart, magma underground pushes up a central mass of rock into the crust. This central mass of rock then falls down as its sides spread out. Over time . . . say, uh, hundreds of thousands of years . . . the spread widens, and debris from the sides fills in the newly formed rift valley. Water comes in and winds up in the deepest parts of the valley, which become freshwater lakes.

W Student: Professor Kelly, could you give an example of one of these lakes?

M: No problem. Lake Baikal in eastern Russia is, I feel, the best example. It formed in a rift valley millions of years ago. Lake Baikal is the deepest lake in the world and also holds the greatest amount of fresh water. That's, um, about twenty percent of the world's total supply. Hold on a sec . . . Ah, yes, there's a shot of it on the screen now. [11]As you can clearly see from this satellite photo, here's the rift valley in which it's located. Now, look at this shot . . . This is in eastern Africa, where the world's longest rift valley is. Uh, I mean the longest that's on the surface of the Earth. It extends almost 6,000 kilometers from north to south. Some very large lakes are here. This includes Lake Tanganyika, the world's second largest lake. And when I say largest, I am referring to the volume of water the lake holds. Other lakes may have a greater surface volume, but none holds more water than Lake Baikal and Lake Tanganyika. Anyway, this rift valley in eastern Africa spread so far that the Red Sea is believed to be a part of it. Now, up here . . . you can see Lake Superior, one of the Great Lakes found between the United States and Canada. It too is located in an ancient rift valley.

All right, uh, I mentioned underwater rift valleys a moment ago. The Mid-Atlantic Ridge, which is, obviously, in the central Atlantic Ocean, forms an extremely long system of ridges and rift valleys. Here it is . . . As you can see, it extends from Iceland here . . . all the way down almost to Antarctica. So it's the longest rift valley system on Earth despite being underwater. And, in case you're curious, the process involved in a rift valley forming underwater is similar to that involved on land. Underwater, the magma wells up, and, if it emerges above the crust, it cools and forms a new ocean floor. Over time, the spreading continues, and eventually the ocean floor in some places becomes so wide that deep undersea plains are formed. The Mid-Atlantic Ridge has many extensions that form hundreds of smaller valleys that are themselves widening over time. This area remains quite active geologically.

As you may have guessed because of the importance of magma in forming rift valleys, volcanoes are frequently associated with them. Iceland is one place where there is very much volcanic activity near rift valleys. In fact, Iceland was created by magma pushing up from below. There are many other islands that were created by volcanoes found in ocean rift valleys. And the east African rift valley system contains many dormant volcanoes and a few active ones as well.

Sometimes, rift valleys offer scientists unique ways to learn about the Earth's past. You see, some rift valleys were once underwater but are no longer. Western North America, for instance, was underwater about, oh, 140 million years ago. Scientists have discovered numerous marine fossils there, which is how we know it was once submerged. This has led some scientists to propose that parts of North America were covered by a vast inland sea. Some believe that this sea eventually was cut off from the rest of the world's oceans by the movement of the continents and, over time, dried up and became exposed land.

Translation

M Professor: 대륙판과 관련이 있는 또 다른 지질학적인 특성은 열곡입니다. 열곡은 지구의 지각이 서로 갈라지는 곳에서 형성됩니다. 아프리카 동부에 몇몇 대규모 열곡이 있습니다. 또한 대서양의 한 가운데에는 긴 해저 산맥이 있습니다. 전 세계적으로 다수의 오래된 열곡이 있습니다. 열곡에서 호수가 형성되는 경우도 많은데, 흥미롭게도, 세계에서 가장 깊고 가장 큰 호수들은 열곡에서 발견되고 있습니다.

열곡은 휴지 상태이거나 활동 상태일 수 있습니다. 휴지 상태에 있는 열곡은 확장을 하지 않는 상태입니다. 활동 상태의 열곡은, 여러분들도 알 수 있을 것이라고 생각하는데, 계속적으로 확장을 하는 곳입니다. 이러한 확장은 구조력에 의한 것입니다. 우리가 대륙 이동에 대해서 이야기했을 때 배웠던 것처럼, 우리의 세상은 고정된 장소가 아닙니다. 여러 개의 판들로 나뉘어져 있고, 이 판들은 세상이 생겼을 때부터 계속 이동해 왔습니다. 이러한 판들 아래에는 맨틀이 있습니다. 이곳에서, 대류의 힘이 판들을 밀어냅니다. 아프리카의 동부와 같이 판들이 서로 멀어지는 지역에서, 열곡이 형성됩니다. 판들이 서로 떨어지면서 지하의 마그마가 암석 덩어리를 지각으로 밀어 올립니다. 그러면 암석의 측면이 퍼져 나가면서 암석이 주저 앉게 됩니다. 시간이 흐르면서… 이를테면, 어, 수십만 년에 걸쳐서… 퍼져 나간 부분은 넓어지고, 측면으로부터 나온 잔해들이 새로이 형성된 열곡을 채웁니다. 물이 계곡의 가장 깊은 부분으로 흘러 들어가면, 이것이 담수호가 됩니다.

W Student: Kelly 교수님, 그러한 호수의 사례를 하나 들어 주실 수 있나요?

M: 물론이죠. 러시아 동쪽에 있는 바이칼 호가, 제 생각에는, 가장 좋은 사례가 될 것 같군요. 바이칼 호는 수백만 년 전 열곡에서 생성되었습니다. 바이칼 호는 세계에서 가장 수심이 깊고 가장

많은 양의 담수를 담고 있습니다. 음, 전 세계 전체 담수의 20% 정도입니다. 잠시만요… 아, 네, 이제 스크린에서 사진이 보이는군요. 이 위성 사진에서 확실히 볼 수 있듯이, 바이칼 호가 위치해 있는 열곡은 이곳입니다. 자, 이 사진을 보세요… 이 열곡은 아프리카의 동부에 있는데, 이곳은 전 세계에서 가장 긴 열곡입니다. 어, 제 말은 지구의 표면에서 가장 길다는 의미입니다. 북쪽에서 남쪽까지 거의 6,000킬로미터에 뻗어 있습니다. 매우 거대한 호수들 중 일부가 이곳에 있습니다. 여기에는 전 세계에서 두 번째로 큰 호수인 탕가니카 호수가 포함되어 있습니다. 제가 가장 크다고 말하는 것은, 호수에 담겨 있는 물의 부피를 의미합니다. 표면의 크기가 더 큰 호수들이 있을 수 있으나, 어떠한 호수도 바이칼 호나 탕가니카 호수보다 더 많은 양의 물을 담고 있지는 않습니다. 어쨌든, 아프리카 동부의 이 열곡은 너무 멀리까지 확장되어 있어서 홍해가 이 열곡의 일부라고 생각되고 있습니다. 자, 여기… 미국과 캐나다 사이에 위치한 오대호 중 하나인 수페리어 호수를 볼 수 있습니다. 이 또한 오래 전에 생성된 열곡에 위치해 있습니다.

좋습니다. 어, 제가 잠시 전에 수중에 있는 열곡에 대해서 언급했습니다. 대서양 중앙 해령은, 분명, 대서양의 가운데에 있는데, 매우 긴 해령과 열곡을 형성시켰습니다. 여기를 보세요… 여러분들이 볼 수 있는 것처럼, 이곳 아이슬란드로부터… 거의 남극 대륙까지 뻗어 있습니다. 그래서 수중에 있기는 하지만 지구상에서 가장 긴 열곡입니다. 그리고, 여러분들이 궁금해 할 것 같아서 말씀드리면, 수중 열곡의 형성 과정은 육지에서의 과정과 유사합니다. 수중에서, 마그마가 상승하고, 이것이 지각을 뚫고 나오면, 마그마가 냉각되어 새로운 대양저를 형성합니다. 시간이 흐르면서, 확장이 계속되어, 결국 몇몇 지역의 대양저가 상당히 넓어져서 심해저 평원이 형성됩니다. 대서양 중앙 해령에는 여러 확장된 지역이 있는데 이들은 시간이 흐르면서 점차 넓어진 수백 개의 작은 계곡을 형성시켰습니다. 이러한 지역은 지질학적 활동이 매우 활발한 곳입니다.

열곡 형성에 있어서 마그마가 중요하다는 사실로부터 알 수 있듯이, 화산이 열곡과 관련되어 있는 경우가 많습니다. 아이슬란드는 열곡 근처에서 화산 활동이 상당히 많은 곳 중 하나입니다. 실제로, 아이슬란드는 마그마가 아래에서 위로 올라가면서 생겨났습니다. 해양 열곡에 있는 화산에 의해 생성된 섬들도 많습니다. 그리고 아프리카 동부의 열곡에는 많은 휴화산들뿐만 아니라 활화산들도 몇몇 있습니다.

때때로, 열곡은 과학자들이 지구의 과거에 대해 알 수 있도록 몇 가지 독특한 방법을 제공해 줍니다. 그러니까, 일부 열곡은 한때 수중에 있었으나 지금은 그렇지 않습니다. 예를 들면, 북미 지역의 서부는, 어, 약 1억 4천만 년 전 수중에 있었습니다. 과학자들은 그곳에서 수많은 해양 생물의 화석을 발견했는데, 우리는 이를 통하여 이 지역이 한때 물에 잠겨 있었다는 사실을 알 수 있습니다. 이를 근거로 과학자들은 북미 지역의 일부가 거대한 내해로 덮여있었다는 이론을 제시했습니다. 몇몇 학자들은 이 바다가 대륙의 이동에 의하여 결국 다른 바다들과 분리되었고, 시간이 흐르면서, 물이 증발하여 이곳이 육지가 되었다고 생각합니다.

Actual Test 09

Reading Section p.105

Answers

1. Ⓐ [Vocabulary Question]
2. Ⓒ [Factual Question]
3. Ⓐ [Reference Question]
4. Ⓑ [Inference Question]
5. Ⓑ [Negative Factual Question]
6. Ⓑ [Vocabulary Question]
7. Ⓐ [Vocabulary Question]
8. Ⓓ [Negative Factual Question]
9. Ⓒ [Inference Question]
10. Ⓐ [Rhetorical Purpose Question]
11. Ⓒ [Vocabulary Question]
12. Ⓑ [Factual Question]
13. Ⓐ [Factual Question]
14. Ⓐ, Ⓑ, Ⓒ [Prose Summary Question]

Translation

로마의 빵과 서커스

로마는 로마 제국의 수도였기 때문에, 이곳에 살던 사람들은 상당한 영향력을 행사했다. 로마가 공화정이었던 때와 제국이었던 때 모두, 정치가들 및 황제들은 로마인들의 충성심을 인식하고 있었고 안정과 평화를 굳건히 하기 위해 대중들의 지지를 계속해서 유지해 나가려고 했다. 수년 동안, 사람들의 이 같은 충성심은 로마의 최고 정치인들에게 바쳐졌는데, 이들은 공화국의 지도자나 황제가 되었다. 그럼에도 불구하고, 시간이 흐르면서, 정치 담론에 참여하는 시민들의 수는 점차 줄어들었고, 그 과정 자체도 부패되었다. 대중의 지지를 얻기 위해, 정치가들과 황제들은 서커스나 게임 같은 사치스러운 오락적 요소들을 기획하기 시작했다. 게다가, 로마 시민들은 무상으로 식량을 제공받았는데 — 주로 곡물과 기름이었다 — 이는 시민들에게 식량을 공급하고 그들을 만족시키기 위해 수입되었다. 로마인들을 달래기 위한 이러한 시도는 "빵과 서커스"라고 알려지게 되었다.

로마의 한 가지 주목할 만한 특징은, 로마가 수많은 훌륭한 연설가, 웅변가, 그리고 시인을 배출한, 상당히 교양이 있는 사회였다는 점이다. 이들 중 가장 훌륭한 인물은, 서기 55년에 태어나 130년에 사망한 시인 쥬베날이었다. 서기 100년 무렵, 풍자적인 작품을 집필하는 동안, 쥬베날은 *panem et circenses*라는 구절을 처음으로 사용했는데, 이 구절은 "빵과 서커스"라고 번역된다. 쥬베날은 서기

1세기에 로마에서 살고 있었는데, 이 시기는 막대한 재앙을 가져온 네로와 칼리굴라와 같은 황제들이나 도미니아누스와 같이 몹시 부패한 황제가 통치하던 시대였다. 그는 또한 로마의 시민들이 시민으로서의 책임감을 잃어버렸다는 점에 주목했다. 로마가 공화정이었을 때, 로마의 최고 지도자로 누구를 결정할 것인지에 대해서 시민들은 강력한 영향력을 행사했다. 하지만, 기원전 1세기에, 줄리어스 시저와 같은 사람들이 공화국을 부패시켰고 이러한 절차를 폐지해 버렸다. 이들은 사람들의 보다 기본적인 욕구 — 배를 채우고 즐기는 것에 대한 충동에 호소하였다. 무상으로 식량과 오락거리를 제공함으로써, 줄리어스 시저와 같은 사람들이 보다 쉽게 독재자가 될 수 있었다.

제공되었던 빵은 주로 옥수수였던 곡물과 조리용 기름으로 만들어져 있었다. 대부분의 곡물은 북아프리카에서 공수해 온 것이었는데, 특히 비옥한 이집트의 평야에서 가져온 것이었다. 이러한 곡물 지대, 수송선, 그리고 로마 인근의 저장 시설을 관리하는 것은 정치적인 지배력을 유지하는데 있어서 필수적인 것이었다. 게임에 대해서 이야기하면, 콜로세움과 같은 대규모 경기장에서 열렸던 다양한 종류의 즐길 거리들이 존재했다. 검투사들 사이의 싸움이 가장 흔한 경기였다. 때때로, 수백 명의 검투사들이 서로 죽음의 결투를 벌이기도 했고, 검투사가 사자와 호랑이와 같은 야생 동물과 싸우는 경기도 있었다. 때로는 콜로세움에 물을 채워서 가상 해전을 연출할 수도 있었다. 게다가, 로마 제국이 그리스도교들을 박해했던 시기에는, 비무장 상태의 신자들이 동물들에게 던져져서, 환호하는 수천 명의 관중들 앞에서 온몸이 찢겨지기도 했다. 하지만 모든 게임들이 이처럼 잔인했던 것은 아니었다; 전차 경주도 상당히 인기 있는 형태의 경기였고, 마찬가지로 음악 공연, 마술 공연, 외래종 동물의 공연, 그리고 현대의 서커스와 유사한 곡예도 많은 인기를 얻었다.

수천 명의 사람들에게 음식을 제공하고 잔인한 경기들을 연출하기 위해서는 많은 비용이 필요했는데, 이러한 비용을 감당할 수 있는 정치인들은 거의 없었다. 줄리어서 시저와 같이 사람들의 지지를 얻은 사람들이 파산하는 경우도 종종 있었다. 칼리굴라의 경우, 자신이 종종 개최했던 화려한 공연들로 인하여 로마 제국 전체가 파산하기도 했다. 하지만 선거에서의 승리나 사람들의 지지를 확보하기 위해서는, 계속 권력을 유지하고자 하는 경우, 선택할 수 있는 다른 방법이 없었다. 이와 같은 상황은 로마 제국의 마지막 세기에 더욱 그러했는데, 이 시기 동안에는 황제들의 통치 기간이 몇 년 되지 않게 되었다. 결국, 무상으로 지급받는 식량의 양과 사람들에게 즐길 수 있는 요소들이 얼마나 아낌없이 제공되었는가는 더 이상 중요하지 않게 되었다. 야만인들의 무리가 로마의 국경에 있던 상황에서는, 전 세계의 모든 빵과 서커스라 할 지라도 제국을 지켜줄 수는 없었으며, 로마는 476년 침략 부족들에 의해 정복을 당하게 된다.

하지만, 빵과 서커스가 로마의 몰락과 함께 사라진 것은 아니었다. 심지어 오늘날에도, 전 세계의 정치인들은 자신이 통치하는 사람들의 환심을 사기 위해 노력하고 있으며, 이를 위해 국민들에게 먹거리와 즐길 거리를 계속적으로 제공하는 것보다 용이한 방법은 존재하지 않는다. 검투사의 결투는 더 이상 존재하지 않지만, 정치인들은 그 대신 무상 교육과 무상 의료의 제공뿐만 아니라 국민들을 계속해서 만족시킬 수 있는 다른 수단들을 강구하고 있다.

Listening Section

p.111

Answers

1. Ⓓ [Gist-Purpose Question]
2. Ⓑ [Detail Question]
3. Ⓒ [Understanding Organization Question]
4. Ⓑ [Making Inferences Question]
5. Ⓐ [Understanding Application Question]
6. Ⓑ [Gist-Content Question]
7. Ⓓ [Gist-Purpose Question]
8. Ⓑ [Understanding Function Question]
9. Ⓓ [Detail Question]
10. Ⓑ [Detail Question]
11. Ⓐ [Making Inferences Question]

Script

| 09-02 |

M1 Professor: Jeremy, you sure seem as if you are in a happy mood today. May I assume that you are the bearer of good news this morning?

M2 Student: ⁵I sure am, Professor Morgan. Guess what . . .

M1: You got into the program?

M2: Yes, sir, I did. I just got an email from the school today. I've been accepted to study abroad in France for my final semester before I graduate. But that's not the only good news that I have.

M1: Oh? What else is going on?

M2: The school is offering me a full scholarship for the semester. Apparently, the school was impressed with my grades, so someone there decided to reward me with an academic scholarship. Talk about a dream come true. I was kind of worried about how I'd be able to pay for my semester abroad, but now I don't need to be concerned about that at all.

M1: Congratulations, Jeremy. You should be proud of yourself. You've done an outstanding job in your time here, and this is a great reward for you. But I must say that all of us in the department are going to miss you while you're away.

M2: And I'm going to miss being here as well. But this is so exciting. I've never really traveled abroad. Okay, uh, I've been to some islands in the Caribbean, but I'm talking about going to Europe for four months. This is going to be wonderful.

M1: Well, I hate to ruin your excitement, Jeremy, but since we now know that you're not going to be here the semester before you graduate, we really ought to take care of a few things.

M2: Huh? Like what?

M1: We need to make sure that you have taken the right classes in order to graduate for one.

M2: Oh, yeah. Right. Can we do that now?

M1: Of course. Have a seat . . .

M2: I'm pretty sure that I have taken all of the classes that I need. At least, uh, I sure hope so.

M1: Let's find out, shall we . . . ? Okay . . . Everything looks good so far.

M2: That's a relief.

M1: Hmm . . . Jeremy, didn't you take Modern English Literature last spring? I thought you were going to do that.

M2: No, I couldn't take it last spring, so I'm going to take it next . . . Uh, oops.

M1: Yeah, oops. That's a required course you know.

M2: Oh my gosh. If I don't take that class, I'm not going to be able to graduate. I'm going to have to cancel my semester abroad. What a disaster.

M1: Now, now, Jeremy. Relax for a minute. I've got the perfect solution to your problem. You can just take the class while you're at school in France.

M2: Uh, take a class in English literature in French? That sounds, uh, interesting.

M1: That's not exactly the word that I'd use, but it seems that you're left with no choice. That is, uh, unless you want to stay here next semester.

M2: No way. I'll check the school's course catalog right away and make sure that the class is being offered in the spring semester. I sure hope it is. I'll be right back.

Translation

M1 Professor: *Jeremy*, 오늘 기분이 좋아 보이는군요. 오늘 아침에 뭔가 좋은 소식이라도 있는 것 같은데요?

M2 Student: 정말 그래요, *Morgan* 교수님. 맞춰보세요…

M1: 프로그램에 참여하게 되었군요?

M2: 네, 교수님, 그렇게 되었어요. 오늘 학교에서 이메일을 받았어요. 졸업하기 전 마지막 학기에 프랑스에서 공부할 수 있게 되었어요. 하지만 좋은 소식은 이것뿐만이 아니에요.

M1: 오? 또 어떤 소식인가요?

M2: 그 학교에서 저에게 한 학기에 대한 전액 장학금을 지급할 거에요. 분명, 제 성적에 좋은 인상을 받아서, 저에게 장학금을 지급하기로 결정을 했던 모양이에요. 꿈이 실현되었어요. 교환 학생으로 공부하기 위해 학비를 어떻게 마련해야 할 지 걱정을 하고 있었는데, 이제 전혀 걱정을 할 필요가 없게 되었죠.

M1: 축하해요, *Jeremy*. 자랑스러워할 만하군요. 학생이 이곳에서 훌륭히 해냈고, 이번 일이 학생에게 멋진 보상이 되겠네요. 하지만 학생이 떠나 있는 동안 우리 학과의 모든 사람들은 학생을 그리워하게 될 거에요.

M2: 저도 역시 이곳이 그리워질 것 같아요. 하지만 이번 일은 정말 멋져요. 저는 한 번도 외국에 나가본 적이 없거든요. 물론, 어, 카리브 해의 몇몇 섬에는 가본 적이 있지만, 저는 지금 4개월 동안 유럽에 나가 있는 것을 말씀드리고 있는 거에요. 정말 멋질 것 같아요.

M1: 음, 학생의 기분을 망치고 싶지는 않지만, *Jeremy*, 졸업 전 학기에 학생이 이 곳에 없을 것이기 때문에, 몇 가지 사항들을 처리해야 해요.

M2: 네, 어떤 사항들이죠?

M1: 학생이 졸업을 하기 위해 필요한 과목들을 제대로 수강했는지 확인해야 할 필요가 있어요.

M2: 아, 네. 좋아요. 지금 확인을 할까요?

M1: 물론이에요. 앉으세요…

M2: 저는 필요한 모든 과목들을 수강했다고 확신해요. 최소한, 어, 그렇게 했기를 바라요.

M1: 살펴보도록 하죠, 그럴까요…? 좋아요… 지금까지는 모든 것이 좋군요.

M2: 다행이네요.

M1: 흠… *Jeremy*, 지난 봄 학기에 현대 영문학을 수강하지 않았네요? 학생이 그 과목을 수강할 것이라고 생각했는데요.

M2: 아니오, 지난 봄 학기에 그 과목을 수강하지 않아서, 다음 학기에 수강하려고… 아, 이런.

M1: 네, 큰일이네요. 알다시피 그 과목은 필수 과목이에요.

M2: 오 이럴 수가. 그 과목을 수강하지 않으면, 저는 졸업을 할 수 없을 거에요. 교환 학생 과정을 취소해야만 하겠군요. 어떻게 이런 일이.

M1: 자, 자, *Jeremy*. 잠시 진정해요. 학생의 문제에 대한 완벽한 해결책이 있어요. 학생이 프랑스에서 학교를 다니는 동안 그 과목을 수강하면 되죠.

M2: 어, 프랑스에서 영문학 수업을 수강한다고요? 그것 참, 어, 흥미롭네요.

M1: 내가 정확히 그렇게 말한 것은 아니지만, 학생에게는 다른 선택권이 없는 것 같군요. 그러니까, 어, 학생이 다음 학기에도 이곳에 있기를 원하지 않는다면 말이에요.

M2: 그럴 리가요. 지금 즉시 그 학교의 교과 과정표를 확인해서 봄 학기에 그 과목이 있는지 알아볼게요. 꼭 있었으면 좋겠어요. 곧 돌아올게요.

Script

| 09-03 |

W Professor: Good afternoon, everyone. I'd like to continue where we left off in our last class and get right back into our discussion on the characteristics of flight in birds. In particular, I'd like to start with the concept of soaring. For this, we're going to look at the albatross family and discuss some unique characteristics of those birds, particularly when it comes to flight. Just so you know, um, the albatross has the longest wingspan of any bird on Earth. This is one of the special qualities that, uh, enable it to soar across thousands of kilometers of ocean without ever touching down on land.

Here's a little information about the albatross for you . . . There are more than two dozen species of albatrosses, the vast majority of which live in the southern latitudes. By this, I mean the areas around New Zealand, Australia, the Falkland Islands, and many small islands in the Antarctic Ocean. Other species, however, live in the northern Pacific between the Hawaiian Islands and Japan. A typical albatross finds a mate about two or three years after hatching and then keeps its mate for life. A female albatross lays one egg a year at most, and one parent remains with the egg until it hatches. Colonies comprising tens of thousands of albatrosses have been seen in New Zealand and on a few southern islands. That must be a sight to behold. Anyway, while one parent sits, the other searches for food. That parent may travel for days or even weeks before returning. Usually, the parent regurgitates food it had swallowed and gives the partially digested food to its chick. This process can be exhausting for many albatrosses, so they may often not have another chick for up to two years as they recover from this ordeal.

While searching for food, an albatross can soar hundreds, or even thousands, of kilometers. Its unique wings, bones, and lungs help it do this. Please look at page 235 in your textbooks to see some pictures of the internal structures of an albatross. Notice the wingspan in particular . . . Just so you know, the southern royal albatross has the longest wingspan at about three and a half meters. And even the smallest species of albatross has a wingspan of around, oh, 1.7 meters or so. Look at the picture in the bottom left-hand part of the page. See there . . . The wings have a tendon that locks them into place between the shoulder and the elbow. This allows the albatross to keep its wings unfurled with minimum muscular effort. The albatross has proportionally less muscle mass in its wings and shoulders than most birds that rely on flapping their wings to sustain flight. Its weight is further reduced by having bones that are almost hollow and very light. Like all birds, as we've studied, the albatross doesn't directly bring air into its lungs. Instead, the air goes into a pair of sacs, and these sacs then act like a bellows to force air into the lungs. This gives the albatross maximum efficiency when it breathes.

All of these features combine to make the albatross nature's best glider. Its wings have a large lifting surface and are used to soar on the ocean winds while the albatross stays close to the surface of the water. The albatross can glide more than eight meters forward for every third of a meter that it drops because of gravity. This glide ratio means that an albatross should eventually land in the ocean no matter how high it starts, but it doesn't do this because of its gliding styles. There are two ways in which it glides: dynamic soaring and slope soaring.

Dynamic soaring involves the albatross using the wind to lift it into the air. The albatross flies perpendicular to the direction of the wind. Uh, that means that the wind is coming at the albatross from the side. It then dives toward the water. In doing so, it picks up speed, which it then transfers into altitude with the help of the wind. Like all birds, the albatross's wing is curved, so the top has a greater surface area than the bottom. The air thus flies faster over the top of its wings to let it reach the other side at the same time as the wind at the bottom. This creates a low pressure system on top of the wing, which creates lift. As the bird reaches the bottom of its dive—around five meters above the ocean surface—it turns toward the wind. The faster wind speed gives it more lift. The albatross's downward speed can reach more than sixty kilometers per hour, and the bird can soar almost twenty meters before it must repeat this action. Since it can endlessly do this over thousands of miles, the albatross is able to remain aloft. So, um, that's the first way in which the albatross is able to soar. Are there any questions about that?

Translation

W Professor: 모두 안녕하세요. 지난 수업에서 중단했던 부분에 이어 새의 비행에 있어서의 특징에 대한 논의로 되돌아가도록 하겠습니다. 특히, 활강에 대한 개념으로 시작해 보도록 하죠. 이를 위해서, 알바트로스과의 새들을 살펴보고, 이 새들의 몇 가지 독특한 특성, 특히 비행을 할 때의 특성에 대해 논의해 보도록 하겠습니다. 여러분들이 알고 있는 것처럼, 음, 알바트로스는 지구상에서 가장 긴 날개를 가지고 있습니다. 이는, 어, 알바트로스가 땅에 착륙하지 않고 바다 위 수천 킬로미터의 거리를 활강할 수 있도록 하는 독특한 특징입니다.

여러분께 알려드릴 알바트로스에 대한 약간의 정보가 있습니다… 12종 이상의 알바트로스가 있는데, 이들의 대다수는 남위도 지역에 서식합니다. 뉴질랜드, 오스트레일리아, 포클랜드 제도, 그리고 남극해의 여러 작은 섬들 근처를 말씀드리는 것입니다. 하지만, 다른 종들은 하와이 제도와 일본 사이의 북태평양 지역에 서식하기도 합니다. 일반적으로 알바트로스는 부화한지 2년에서 3년 정도가 지나면 짝을 찾고, 자신의 짝과 평생을 함께합니다. 암컷 알바트로스는 일 년에 최대 한 개의 알을 낳고, 부화할 때까지 한 마리의 부모새가 알을 지킵니다. 수만 여 마리로 구성된 알바트로스의 군락들이 뉴질랜드와 몇몇 남쪽의 섬에서 목격되고 있습니다. 장관임에 틀림없습니다. 어쨌든, 한 부모새가 앉아 있는 동안, 다른 부모새는 먹이를 구해 옵니다. 이 부모새는 며칠에서 몇 주 동안을 돌아다니다가 돌아오기도 합니다. 통상, 이 부모새는 자신이 삼킨 먹이를 게워내어 새끼들에게 부분적으로 소화된 먹이를 줍니다. 이러한 과정으로 인하여 많은 부모새들이 지치게 되기 때문에, 2년 정도의 시간이 흘러 힘든 일로부터 기력을 회복할 때까지 또 다른 새끼를 낳지 않는 경우가 많습니다.

먹이를 찾는 동안, 알바트로스는 수백, 혹은 심지어 수천 킬로미터의 거리를 활강합니다. 알바트로스의 독특한 날개, 골격, 그리고 폐가 활강에 도움을 줍니다. 여러분들 교과서 235쪽에서 알바트로스의 내부 구조를 보여 주는 몇 장의 그림을 보십시오. 특히 날개의 폭에 주목하세요… 알 수 있듯이, 서던 로얄 알바트로스의 날개폭이 가장 큰데, 그 폭은 무려 3.5미터나 됩니다. 알바트로스의 가장 작은 종도 그 날개폭이, 오, 대략 1.7미터 정도입니다. 페이지의 왼쪽 아랫부분에 있는 그림을 보세요. 그곳을 보시면… 어깨와 팔꿈치에 해당되는 부분 사이에 날개를 고정시키고 있는 힘줄이 있습니다. 이 힘줄로 알바트로스는 최소한의 근육을 움직여서 날개를 편 채로 있을 수 있습니다. 비행하기 위해 날갯짓을 하는 대부분의 새들과 비교해 볼 때, 알바트로스는 날개와 어깨 부분에 있는 근육의 양이 보다 적습니다. 뼈의 내부는 거의 텅 비어 있어서 매우 가벼운데, 이는 알바트로스의 몸무게를 줄여 줍니다. 모든 새들과 마찬가지로, 우리가 공부해온 것처럼, 알바트로스도 공기를 폐로 직접 들이마시지는 않습니다. 대신, 공기는 기낭으로 들어가게 되는데, 기낭은 공기를 폐로 밀어 넣는 풀무와 같은 역할을 합니다. 이로써 알바트로스는 최대한 효율적으로 호흡을 하게 됩니다.

이러한 특징들이 합쳐져서 알바트로스가 자연계에서 활강을 가장 잘하는 새가 됩니다. 날개에는 커다란 양력면이 있는데, 알바트로스는 수면 가까이를 비행할 때 해풍을 타고 활강하기 위해서 이 부분을 사용합니다. 알바트로스는 8미터 이상의 거리를 활강할 수 있는데, 중력에 의해서 3미터마다 그 고도가 낮아집니다. 이러한 활공비는 알바트로스가 얼마나 높은 고도에서 비행을 시작했는지에 상관없이 결국 바다로 떨어지게 된다는 점을 의미하지만, 이들의 활강 형태 덕분에 그렇게 되지 않습니다. 활강에는 두 가지 형태가 있습니다: 역학 활공과 경사 활공이 그것입니다.

역학 활공은 알바트로스가 공중으로 날아오르기 위해 바람을 활용하는 것과 관련이 있습니다. 알바트로스는 바람이 불어오는 방향과 수직으로 비행합니다. 어, 이는 바람이 알바트로스의 옆에서 불어온다는 것을 의미합니다. 그런 다음 수면을 향해 하강합니다. 이렇게 하면서, 속도를 올리는데, 그런 다음에는 바람의 도움을 받아 하늘 높이 올라갑니다. 모든 새들과 마찬가지로, 알바트로스의 날개도 휘어져 있기 때문에, 날개의 아랫부분보다 윗부분의 면적이 더 넓습니다. 따라서 공기가 날개의 아랫부분에 도달하는 동시에 윗부분에도 도달하므로, 날개의 아랫부분보다 면적이 넓은 윗부분에서 공기의 흐름 속도가 더 빠릅니다. 이로 인하여 날개 윗부분의 압력이 낮아지게 되고, 따라서 양력이 발생합니다. 이 새가 가장 낮은 지점까지 하강하고 나면 — 해수면에서 5미터 정도인데 — 바람이 불어오는 방향으로 몸을 돌립니다. 바람이 세게 불수록 더 많은 양력을 얻게 됩니다. 알바트로스의 하강 속도는 시속 60킬로미터까지 이를 수 있으며, 이러한 행동을 반복하기 전까지 거의 20미터를 날아오를 수 있습니다. 알바트로스는 이러한 행동을 수천 마일에 걸쳐서 끊임없이 할 수 있기 때문에, 공중에 계속 머물러 있을 수 있습니다. 자, 음, 이것이 알바트로스가 활강을 하는 첫 번째 방법입니다. 이에 대해 질문이 있는 학생은 없나요?

Actual Test 10

Reading Section p.117

Answers

1. Ⓒ [Vocabulary Question]
2. Ⓒ [Reference Question]
3. Ⓓ [Inference Question]
4. Ⓐ [Vocabulary Question]
5. Ⓑ [Sentence Simplification Question]
6. Ⓒ [Negative Factual Question]
7. Ⓑ [Vocabulary Question]
8. Ⓓ [Factual Question]
9. Ⓑ [Rhetorical Purpose Question]
10. Ⓐ [Factual Question]
11. Ⓐ [Vocabulary Question]
12. Ⓒ [Reference Question]
13. Ⓑ [Factual Question]
14. Ⓐ, Ⓒ, Ⓕ [Prose Summary Question]

Translation

소련의 고전주의 건축

끝없는 아파트 단지와 현대적인 유리 및 철골 구조물들이 들어서 있는 단조로운 모스크바의 풍경 내에, 지평선 위에 솟아있는 일곱 개의 높고 인상적인 건물들이 있다. 이 건물들은, 종종 세븐 시스터즈라고 불리기도 하는데, 소련의 고전주의 건축의 시대를 보여 주는 결정적인 사례이다. 1930년대에서 1950년대까지 지속되었던 이 시기에, 세련된 여러 지하철 역을 포함하여, 소련 건축 양식의 수많은 훌륭한 작품들이 건축되었다. 소련의 고전주의 건축의 웅대함은 부분적으로 소련의 지도자였던 요제프 스탈린의 비전에 의한 것이었지만, 그가 사망한 후, 그의 꿈도 함께 사라져 버렸다. 그 후 흐루시쵸프와 브레즈네프 시대에 나타난 것은 단조롭고 생동감 없는 건물들이었는데, 이는 그 이전에 건축된 건물들과 확연한 대조를 이루었다.

1920년대 초반 소련이 건국되어 1930년대가 될 때까지, 소련의 고전주의 건축이라고 간주될 수 있는 양식은 등장하지 않았다. 이전에, 러시아 건축은 아시아와 유럽 양식이 결합된 것이었다. 하지만 소련의 고전주의 시기 동안, 유럽의 영향, 특히 신고전주의의 영향이, 보다 뚜렷해졌다. 몇몇 소련 건축가들은 아르데코 및 구성주의와 같은 동시대 양식에 영향을 받았지만, 스탈린 시대에는 기준으로부터 벗어나는 것이 바람직하지 않은 것으로 여겨졌기 때문에, 이러한 양식의 건축물이 건설되는 일은 거의 없었다. 실제로, 스탈린은 자신이 소련을 이끌었을 당시 막대한 영향력을 행사했기 때문에, 많은 건축 계획은 실행되기에 앞서서 그의 비공개적인 승인을 필요로 했다.

1939년에 끝난 전전 시기에, 소련의 수도인 모스크바에서 있던 주요한 프로젝트는 지하철 건설이었다. 완공되었을 때, 지하철은 건축 분야에서 소련이 달성한 가장 훌륭한 위업이 되었다. 건설은 1930년대 초반에 시작되었고, 1호선이 완공되어 1935년에는 즉시 개통되었다. 모든 역은 호화롭게 설계되었고, 각각의 역은 서로 달랐다. 일부 역들은 놀랄 정도로 너무나 화려했다; 프레스코 벽화, 대리석 조각, 거대한 샹들리에, 그리고 다른 장식물들이 일부 역에 장식되어 있어서, 지하철 전체가 전 세계적으로 가장 아름다운 것 중의 하나가 되었다. 제 2차 세계 대전이 발발했을 때, 새로운 노선 및 역사의 건설이 지체되기는 했지만, 중단되지는 않았다. 하지만 전쟁으로 인하여 독일을 물리치는데 최대의 노력을 기울여야 했기 때문에 다른 프로젝트들은 완성되지 못했다.

소련 시기의 하나의 원칙으로서, 아파트 건물들은 어떤 계층의 시민들이 거주하는지에 따라 지어졌다. 당원, 고위 관료, 그리고 고위 장교들은 비교적 호화로운 곳에 살았지만 일반 시민들은 거주가 가능한 곳에서 임시로 살아야 했다. 1945년 제 2차 세계 대전이 끝날 무렵, 소련의 서부 지역 대부분은 폐허가 되어 있었다. 공습으로 큰 피해를 입은 소련의 여러 도시의 수백만 명의 사람들에게 — 계층을 막론하고 — 주택 부족은 가장 큰 문제였다. 그럼에도 불구하고, 전쟁으로 집을 잃어버린 사람들을 위한 주택 건설에 초점을 맞추는 대신, 스탈린은 모스크바를 건축적으로 놀라운 곳으로 만들고자 하는 꿈을 가지고 있었기 때문에, 건축가들에게 세븐 시스터즈와 같은 건축물의 설계와 시공을 지시했다. 이 웅장한 건물들은 1947년에 세워지기 시작했는데, 그 결과 다른 프로젝트들을 위한 건설 자재가 부족해 졌다. 어떠한 저지도 받지 않은 채, 스탈린은 프로젝트를 계속해 나갔다. 완공되자, 세븐 시스터즈는 모스크바에 상당 양의 주거 공간을 더해 주었다. 하지만, 건물 내 공간의 제곱미터당 비용은, 보다 작고 호화롭지 않은 건물의 공간에 비해서 더욱 높았다.

1953년 스탈린이 사망한 후, 그의 야심 찬 여러 가지 계획들은, 제 2차 세계 대전 이후에도 여전히 존재하고 있었던 폐허와 파괴라는 현실의 뒷전으로 밀려나게 되었다. 심각한 주택 부족이 가장 큰 문제로 남아 있었기 때문에, 비슷하게 생긴 아파트 건물들로 끝없이 늘어선 구역들이 빠르게 도시의 풍경을 채워 나갔다. 흐루시쵸프와 브레즈네프 시대의 특징은 단조로움이었는데, 이는 당시에 건설된 아파트 및 기타 건물들에 반영되었다. 게다가, 대부분의 건물들은 겉만 번지르르하게 건설되었고, 각 건물을 설계한 건축가들은 실생활을 고려하지 못했다. 대부분의 건물에는 거실과 침실을 겸하는 싱글룸, 작은 부엌 한 개, 그리고 작은 욕실이 하나 있었다. 가족들은, 그 인원 수에 상관없이, 이렇게 비좁은 공간에서 살아야만 했다. 대부분의 러시아인들의 생활 환경이 적정 수준으로 향상된 것은 수십 년이 지난, 1991년 소련이 몰락한 이후였다.

Listening Section

Answers

1. Ⓐ [Gist-Purpose Question]
2. Ⓑ [Detail Question]
3. Ⓐ [Making Inferences Question]
4. Ⓓ [Understanding Function Question]
5. Ⓓ [Understanding Attitude Question]
6. Ⓐ [Gist-Content Question]
7. Ⓑ [Understanding Organization Question]
8. Ⓒ [Detail Question]
9. Ⓒ [Making Inferences Question]
10. Ⓐ [Gist-Purpose Question]
11. Ⓒ [Understanding Attitude Question]

Script

| 10-02 |

M Registrar's Office Employee: If anyone's waiting, I can help someone at this window here . . .

W Student: Uh, hello. I suppose I'm the next person in line.

M: Great. Then how may I help you this morning?

W: I'm going to transfer to another school next semester. I, uh, want to be somewhere closer to my parents since they're getting older. Anyway, I need to get a copy of my transcript so that I can send it to the school I'm going to apply to.

M: Sure thing. That's simple. May I have your name and student number, please?

W: My name is Amy Perry. That's P-E-R-R-Y. And my student number is 32-910-4583.

M: Okay . . . Hmm . . . Could I have that student number one more time, please?

W: Sure. 32 . . . 910 . . . 4583.

M: That's odd. Your name is coming up, but that's not the right student number. Do you happen to have your student ID with you? May I take a look at it, please?

W: Uh, yeah. I've got it right here in my purse . . . Here you are.

M: Okay. Thanks. Hmm . . . That's definitely you in the picture. And here's the student ID number just like you said . . . Aha, I've got it figured out.

W: What? What's the problem?

M: You're not enrolled at school this semester, are you?

W: ⁴Uh, no, I'm not. Like I said, I need to look after my parents, so I took this semester off. **I'm only on campus for a couple of days, and then I have to fly back home.**

M: All right. See, uh, when a student takes time off like you're doing, then your ID number changes. That's what caused the problem. But I've got your information on the screen now, so there's nothing to worry about.

W: Great.

M: ⁵But you need to fill out this form for me if you're going to get a copy of your transcript. It costs five dollars per transcript. We take cash, checks, and credit cards. And please be sure to write the address where you want us to send the transcript when you fill out the form.

W: Oh, uh, actually, I was hoping that you could just give me the transcript right now. I was planning to bring it by the school in person when I apply.

M: I would advise against doing that. You see, first, most schools prefer to receive transcripts directly from the school that's sending it. That way, there's no chance for the transcripts to get, uh, tampered with. So the school you're applying to might not even accept a transcript from you in the first place. Second, it takes two days to process a transcript. So you simply won't be able to walk out of here with a copy of your transcript today. Sorry about that.

W: Oh, I see. What do you recommend that I do then?

M: If I were you, I'd let us handle it. We will mail the transcript out no later than Thursday afternoon. If you want, we can use express mail, so it will get to the school by Friday. Express mail will cost a little extra, but, uh, if you're in a hurry, it's definitely the best option.

W: Er, good point. Okay. Sign me up for express mail. And let me put the address down on that form, too.

Translation

M Registrar's Office Employee: 기다리시는 분이 계시면, 이 쪽 창구로 오시면 도와드릴게요…

W Student: 어, 안녕하세요. 제가 다음 차례인 것 같은데요.

M: 좋아요. 그렇다면 무엇을 도와드릴까요?

W: 저는 다음 학기에 다른 학교로 전학을 가려고 해요. 저는, 어, 부모님께서 점점 연로해 지셔서 부모님 댁에서 가까운 학교에 다니려고요. 어쨌든, 제가 지원하려는 학교에 발송할 성적증명서 사본이 필요해요.

M: 알겠어요. 간단한 일이에요. 이름과 학번을 알려 주시겠어요?

W: 제 이름은 *Amy Perry*예요. P-E-R-R-Y. 그리고 제 학번은 32-910-4583이고요.

M: 알겠어요… 홈… 학번을 다시 한 번 이야기해 주시겠어요?

W: 네. 32… 910… 4583.

M: 이상하군요. 학생의 이름은 검색이 되는데, 학번은 일치하지가 않는군요. 지금 학생증을 소지하고 있나요? 제가 잠시 볼 수 있을까요?

W: 어, 네. 지갑에 학생증이 있어요… 여기요.

M: 좋아요. 고마워요. 흠… 학생의 사진이 분명하군요. 그리고 학생이 말한 학번도 여기에 적혀 있고… 아하, 무슨 일인지 알겠어요.

W: 무엇인가요? 무엇이 문제인가요?

M: 이번 학기에 등록을 하지 않았죠, 그렇죠?

W: 음, 네, 등록하지 않았어요. 말씀 드린 것처럼, 부모님을 보살펴 드려야 해서, 이번 학기에는 등록을 하지 않았죠. 학교에는 이틀 정도만 있을 것이고, 그런 다음에는 집으로 돌아가야만 해요.

M: 좋아요. 그러니까, 어, 학생의 경우처럼 휴학을 하게 되면, 학번이 바뀌죠. 그래서 이러한 문제가 발생한 거예요. 하지만 학생의 정보를 화면으로 확인했으니, 걱정할 것은 없어요.

W: 잘 됐군요.

M: 하지만 성적증명서를 발급받으려면 이 양식을 작성해야 해요. 비용은 성적증명서 한 부에 5달러고요. 현금, 현금 카드, 그리고 신용 카드로도 납부가 가능해요. 그리고 양식을 작성할 때, 성적증명서를 발송할 주소를 확실히 적어 주세요.

W: 오, 어, 사실, 선생님께서 성적증명서를 지금 바로 저에게 주시기를 바랐는데요. 제가 지원할 때 학교에 직접 제출할 생각이었거든요.

M: 그렇게 하지 않는 것이 좋다고 하고 싶군요. 그러니까, 우선, 대부분의 학교들은 다른 학교에서 송부한 성적증명서를 직접 받아 보는 것을 선호해요. 그렇게 함으로써, 성적증명서가, 어, 변조될 여지가 없어지죠. 그래서 학생이 지원하고자 하는 학교에서 학생이 직접 제출하는 성적증명서는 받지 않을 수도 있어요. 둘째로, 성적증명서 발급에는 이틀의 시간이 필요해요. 따라서 성적증명서 사본을 오늘 발급받아 갈 수는 없어요. 미안하게 생각해요.

W: 오, 알았어요. 그렇다면 제가 어떻게 하는 것이 좋을까요?

M: 제가 학생이라면, 우리가 처리하도록 일을 맡기겠어요. 늦어도 목요일 오후에는 성적증명서를 발송할 거예요. 학생이 원한다면, 속달 우편을 이용할 수도 있는데, 속달 우편을 이용하면 금요일에 학교로 성적증명서가 도착할 거예요. 속달 우편을 이용하는 것은 비용이 조금 더 들지만, 어, 급한 경우라면, 분명 가장 좋은 선택이 될 거예요.

W: 어, 좋은 지적이네요. 좋아요. 속달 우편으로 신청할게요. 그리고 양식에 주소 역시 기입하도록 할게요.

Script

| 10-03 |

W Professor: In the United States, people frequently resort to the courts to attain justice. There are two types of legal trials. There are trials by jury and bench trials. A trial by jury is one in which a group of citizens decides the outcome of a legal case. A bench trial is one in which a judge determines the outcome. The right to a trial by jury is explicitly mentioned in the Constitution, but not all states permit jury trials for all cases. For example, for divorces or child custody cases, not all states have jury trials. But before we get into that, let's cover the two different types of legal trials.

 I want to begin with jury trials. First, a jury trial can be held for both a civil and a criminal case. In a civil case, a trial occurs when the two parties involved cannot reach an out-of-court settlement. In a criminal case, a trial typically occurs when the accused does not confess or when the accused does not agree to a plea bargain. A plea bargain is when the accused admits to being guilty in return for a reduced sentence. In both types of trials—jury and bench—the onus is on one party to prove that the other did something wrong. In a civil case, the onus is on, uh, on the plaintiff—the party that's suing—to prove that the defendant did something wrong. In a criminal case, the prosecutor, who represents the government, must prove that the accused, the defendant, committed a crime.

Who decides the innocence or guilt of the defendant in a jury trial? In most cases, the jury consists of twelve impartial members of the community. These jurors are supposed to have no connection with the people involved in the case. The two parties present their evidence. The jury hears the evidence and then makes a decision. This system comes from English common law. That's actually true of most of the traditions in American law. For example, centuries ago in England, a jury of twelve men would hear and decide on disputes between locals. This evolved into the jury system we use today. Brian, you have a question?

M Student: [11]Yes, ma'am, I do. Why is the number of jurors twelve?

W: Hmm . . . I can't give you a definitive answer on that. I believe, however, that it has something to do with superstition. For instance, thirteen was considered an unlucky number whereas twelve was not. But that's the best answer I can give you for now. Anyway, as I said, this system comes from England, and most countries with an English heritage, including the U.S., have adopted some form of this jury system. Traditionally, twelve men who had some status in the community served on juries. At first, they were landowners, but, as time passed, the requirements changed. Nowadays, any taxpaying citizen can sit on a jury.

Despite being used for hundreds of years, the jury system has some drawbacks. The first is the impartiality of the jury. Namely, are the members of the jury neutral? Or do they have some strong feelings about the case? Or, in some instances, might jury members have personal connections to those involved? Well, today, lawyers on both sides have the right to question potential jurors and to reject them for a number of reasons. In doing this, the lawyers hope to weed out those potential jurors who may not be impartial. But this isn't a perfect system. Jurors can sometimes hide their biases and manage to get seated for some trials.

A second problem is that defense attorneys always try to stack the jury with people whom they believe will be more favorable to their clients. So they try to select people of the same race and economic background under the belief that they may sympathize with their clients. Remember that in most criminal cases, all twelve jurors must agree on the verdict. It's simply got to be unanimous. And, in many civil cases, at least a two-thirds majority is required.

A third problem with juries is called jury nullification. This has been a problem ever since jury trials were first used. Here's what happens. The two sides present their evidence. The evidence clearly shows that the defendant is either innocent or guilty. However, the jury decides the opposite of what the evidence proves. The jurors simply ignore the evidence. The classic modern example of jury nullification is the O.J. Simpson verdict from 1995. The famous former football star was accused of murdering two people, including his ex-wife. The evidence appeared solid, and Simpson seemed guilty. But the jury returned with a not-guilty verdict after deliberating for a short amount of time. It appeared as though the jury had ignored the evidence to find Simpson not guilty.

So this brings up another issue: Are jurors qualified to judge evidence? It would appear that the answer is . . . not always. But that's the system we have. Now, let's examine bench trials and see how they differ from jury trials.

▶ Translation

W Professor: 미국에서, 사람들은 정의를 구하기 위해 재판에 의존하는 경우가 많습니다. 법률 재판에는 두 가지 종류가 있습니다. 배심 재판과 재판관 재판이 존재하는 것이죠. 배심 재판은 시민들이 법정 사건의 결과를 결정하는 재판입니다. 재판관 재판은 한 명의 판사가 그 결과를 결정하는 재판입니다. 배심 재판을 받을 권리는 헌법에 명백히 언급되어 있지만, 모든 주에서 모든 사건에 대해 배심 재판을 인정하고 있는 것은 아닙니다. 예를 들어, 이혼이나 자녀 양육권 관련 소송의 경우, 모든 주에서 배심 재판을 하지는 않습니다. 하지만 이 문제에 대해 논하기 전에, 두 가지 서로 다른 종류의 법률 재판에 대해서 알아보도록 하겠습니다.

배심 재판으로 이야기를 시작해 보도록 하죠. 우선, 배심 재판은 민사 사건과 형사 사건의 경우 모두 진행될 수 있습니다. 민사 사건의 경우, 양측 당사자들이 법정 외 화해에 이르지 못할 때 재판이 이루어집니다. 형사 사건의 경우, 피고가 자백을 하지 않거나 유죄 답변 교섭에 동의하지 않는 경우 재판이 열리게 됩니다. 유죄 답변 교섭이란 피고가 유죄를 시인하는 대가로 감형을 받는 것입니다. 두 종류의 재판에서 — 배심 재판과 재판관 재판에서 — 상대편이 잘못을 했다는 점을 입증할 책임은 그 반대편에 있습니다. 민사 사건의 경우, 입증 책임은, 어, 피고가 잘못된 행동을 했다는 사실을 증명해야 하는 원고에게 — 고소를 한 쪽에 — 있습니다. 형사 사건의 경우, 정부를 대표하는 검사가 고소를 당한 사람, 즉 피고가 범죄를 저질렀다는 사실을 입증해야 합니다.

자, 배심 재판에서 피고가 무죄인지 유죄인지를 결정하는 사람은 누구일까요? 대부분의 소송에서, 배심원은 해당 지역의 12명의 공정한 사람들로 구성됩니다. 이 배심원들은 사건의 관련자들과 아무런 관계가 없어야 합니다. 양측이 증거를 제시합니다. 배심원들은 증언을 듣고 결정을 내립니다. 이러한 제도는 영국의 관습법에서 유래된 것입니다. 실제로 미국법의 대부분이 그렇습니다. 예를 들면, 수세기 전 영국에서는, 12명의 배심원이 양측의 진술을 듣고 논쟁을 해결해 주었습니다. 이로부터 오늘날의 배심원 제도가 생겼습니다. *Brian*, 질문이 있나요?

M Student: 네, 교수님, 그렇습니다. 배심원의 인원이 12명인 이유는 무엇인가요?

W: 흠… 그것에 대해서는 확실한 대답을 드릴 수가 없군요. 하지만, 제 생각에는, 미신과 관련이 있는 것 같습니다. 예를 들어, 13이라는 숫자는 불운하다고 생각되었지만 12라는 숫자는 그렇지

않았죠. 지금으로서는 이것이 제가 해드릴 수 있는 가장 좋은 답변이군요. 어쨌든, 말씀드린 것처럼, 이 제도는 영국에서 유래되었고, 미국을 포함한 영국의 유산을 물려받은 대부분의 국가에서 배심원 제도를 채택하고 있습니다. 전통적으로, 해당 지역에서 일정 지위에 있는 12명의 사람들이 배심원의 역할을 수행했습니다. 처음에는, 지주들이었지만, 시간이 흐르면서, 조건이 바뀌었습니다. 오늘날에는, 세금을 납부하는 시민이라면 누구나 배심원이 될 수 있습니다.

수백 년 동안 사용되어 왔음에도 불구하고, 배심원 제도에는 몇 가지 문제점이 있습니다. 첫째는 배심원단의 공정성입니다. 즉, 배심원들은 중립적일까요? 혹은 그들이 사건에 대해서 격한 감정을 느끼고 있지는 않을까요? 또는, 일부 경우, 배심원들이 소송 관련자와 어떤 관계가 있지는 않을까요? 그래서, 오늘날, 양측의 변호사들에게는 배심원 후보자들에게 질문을 해서 여러 가지 이유로 그들을 받아들이지 않을 권리가 있습니다. 이렇게 함으로써, 변호사들은 공정하지 않을지도 모르는 배심원들을 배제시키고자 합니다. 하지만 이것이 완벽한 제도는 아닙니다. 배심원들이 때때로 자신의 편견을 숨기고 재판에 참여할 수도 있습니다.

두 번째 문제는 피고측 변호인이 항상 자신의 의뢰인에게 보다 호의적일 것 같은 사람들을 배심원으로 선정하려고 한다는 점입니다. 그래서 인종이나 경제적 배경이 같은 사람들을 배심원으로 선정하려고 하는데, 이들이 자신의 의뢰인을 동정할 것이라고 생각하기 때문입니다. 대부분의 형사 사건의 경우, 12명의 배심원들이 모두 평결에 동의해야 한다는 점을 기억하세요. 만장일치에 도달해야 하는 것이죠. 그리고, 많은 민사 사건의 경우, 최소한 2/3의 동의가 필요합니다.

배심원 제도의 세 번째 문제는 배심원 불복 제도입니다. 이는 배심 재판이 처음 사용되었을 때부터 문제가 되었습니다. 어떤 일이 일어나는지 알려 드리죠. 양측에서 증거를 제출합니다. 증거를 통해 피고가 무죄인지 유죄인지를 명확하게 알 수 있습니다. 하지만, 배심원단은 증거가 입증하는 바와 반대인 결정을 내립니다. 배심원들이 증거를 기각하는 것입니다. 배심원 불복 제도의 전형적인 최근 사례는 1995년에 있었던 O. J. 심슨에 대한 평결입니다. 유명한 전직 미식축구 스타가 자신의 전처를 포함하여 두 명을 살해한 혐의로 기소되었습니다. 증거는 확실해 보였고, 심슨은 유죄인 것 같았습니다. 하지만 배심원단은 짧은 시간 동안의 심의 과정을 거친 뒤, 무죄 평결을 내렸습니다. 마치 배심원단이 심슨에게 죄가 없다는 평결을 내리기 위해서 증거를 무시한 것처럼 보였습니다.

그래서 이는 또 다른 문제를 야기시킵니다: 배심원들에게 증거를 판단할 자격이 있는 걸까요? 이에 대한 대답은… 항상 그런 것은 아니라는 점입니다. 하지만 그것이 우리가 가지고 있는 제도입니다. 자, 이제 재판관 재판에 대해 알아보고 이것이 배심 재판과 어떻게 다른지에 대해서 알아보도록 합시다.

Compact Actual iBT Reading & Listening

1

Compact Actual iBT Reading & Listening has been designed to be used both in the classroom and by test takers working on an individual basis. Each compact test consists of one Reading passage, one Listening conversation, and one Listening lecture. All three of them are the standard length of actual TOEFL® iBT passages, conversations, and lectures. In addition, they all have the same number of questions and the same types of questions that are found on the actual test. By using this book, test takers will be more prepared for the test when they actually take it.

<Compact Actual iBT Reading & Listening Book 1> Components

- Main Book
- Answers, Listening Scripts, and Translations
- Free MP3 Downloads
- For More Student and Teacher Support Materials, Free Downloads at http://www.darakwon.co.kr